Give Children the Vote

Also available from Bloomsbury

Give Children the Vote

On Democratizing Democracy

John Wall

BLOOMSBURY ACADEMIC
LONDON • NEW YORK • OXFORD • NEW DELHI • SYDNEY

BLOOMSBURY ACADEMIC
Bloomsbury Publishing Plc
50 Bedford Square, London, WC1B 3DP, UK
1385 Broadway, New York, NY 10018, USA
29 Earlsfort Terrace, Dublin 2, Ireland

BLOOMSBURY, BLOOMSBURY ACADEMIC and the Diana logo are trademarks
of Bloomsbury Publishing Plc

First published in Great Britain, 2022

Cover design by Jade Barnett
Cover image © YAY Media AS / Alamy Stock Photo

A catalogue record for this book is available from the British Library.

Library of Congress Cataloging-in-Publication Data
Names: Wall, John, author.
Title: Give children the vote : on democratizing democracy / John Wall.
Description: London ; New York : Bloomsbury Academic, 2022. |
Includes bibliographical references and index.
Identifiers: LCCN 2021023543 (print) | LCCN 2021023544 (ebook) |
ISBN 9781350196285 (hardback) | ISBN 9781350196261 (paperback) |
ISBN 9781350196292 (pdf) | ISBN 9781350196308 (epub)
Subjects: LCSH: Voting age. | Youth–Political activity. |
Election law. Classification: LCC JF841 .W36 2022 (print) |
LCC JF841 (ebook) | DDC 324.6/2083–dc23
LC record available at https://lccn.loc.gov/2021023543
LC ebook record available at https://lccn.loc.gov/2021023544

ISBN: HB: 978-1-3501-9628-5
PB: 978-1-3501-9626-1
ePDF: 978-1-3501-9629-2
eBook: 978-1-3501-9630-8

Typeset by Newgen KnowledgeWorks Pvt. Ltd., Chennai, India

To find out more about our authors and books visit www.bloomsbury.com
and sign up for our newsletters.

Contents

Figures

Acknowledgments

The ideas in this book originated with my involvement in the Department of Childhood Studies at Rutgers University Camden, the Childhood Studies and Religion Group of the American Academy of Religion, and the Child Studies Department at Linköping University. I am grateful for early discussions with Don Browning, Marcia Bunge, Bruno Vanobbergen, Anandini Dar, Trygve Wyller, William Schweiker, Anna Mae Duane, Pamela Couture, Barbara Pitkin, Wendy Love Anderson, Jonathan Josefsson, Anna Sparrman, Bengt Sandin, Wendy Russell, Michael Freeman, Nigel Thomas, Shelly Newstead, Wendy Russell, Annemie Dillen, Barbara Bennett Woodhouse, Jana Mohr Lone, the students in my annual graduate course in Children's Rights, and others.

I have been fortunate over the years to learn from many inspiring interlocuters and activists. These include members of the Children's Voting Colloquium, especially its cofounder (with myself) Robin Chen, as well as Kristiina Vares-Wartiovaara, Markus Wartiovaara, Kalle Öhman, Joseph Rathinam, Claudio López-Guerra, Michael Cummings, Neena Modi, Katherine Walton, Ralph Hall, David Runciman, Cheryl Milne, Luigi Campiglio, Lavinia Mello Rella, Miles Corak, Adam Fletcher, Brian Conner, Alex Koroknay-Palicz, Robert Ludbrook, Nicholas Munn, Mary Birdsell, Lily Stelling, Jester Jersey, Neil Bhateja, and others. I appreciate the invaluable input of my graduate students Elisabeth Yang, Sebastian Barajas, Ines Meier, and Diana Garcia. I have also learned much in my time as director of the Childism Institute, including from Hanne Warming, Tanu Biswas, Sarada Balagopalan, Lauren Silver, Kate Cairns, Dan Cook, Erica Burman, Karin Murris, Nathan Walker, Fikile Nxumalo, Anne Graham, Antonia Canosa, Justyna Deszcz-Tryhubczak, and others. I am grateful for the support of my Rutgers University Camden colleagues Stuart Charmé, Charlie Jarrett, Melissa Yates, Nicole Karapanagiotis, Eric Chwang, Craig

Agule, Margaret Betz, Michael Palis, Daniel Hart, Beth Rabinowitz, Lynne Vallone, Kriste Lindenmeyer, and Howard Marchitello.

As always, I am especially thankful for the love and support of Mili Lozada and my parents, Tony and Geraldine Wall. I dedicate this book to my daughters, Isabel and Simona Wall.

Introduction

So long as I do not firmly and irrevocably possess the right to vote I do not possess myself. I cannot make up my mind—it is made up for me. I cannot live as a democratic citizen, observing the laws I have helped to enact—I can only submit to the edict of others.

Martin Luther King Jr.

In September 2019, I participated in a Fridays for Future climate rally in my home town of Philadelphia in the United States. It was a powerful and moving event. Thousands of demonstrators filled up the square and streets around City Hall cheering and holding up homemade signs, listening to impassioned speakers, and then marching for a few blocks past commuters, onlookers, and clapping passers-by. But as I stood and chanted with the crowd, it eventually dawned on me that I was far older than most of the other protesters around me. There were a few infants and young children with their parents, plus a few other adult stragglers. But the vast majority of sign-waving, hugging, and shouting demonstrators were between about eight and eighteen years old. As were virtually all of the speakers. It became clear that the rally was organized by, and meant to give voice to the urgent concerns of, primarily children and youth.

This was an expression of young people's political power. Inspired by fifteen-year-old Greta Thunberg's school strikes outside the Swedish parliament, Fridays for Future rallies had been taking place for months in thousands of cities around the world and involving millions of child and youth strikers. Perhaps never before had there been such a global outpouring of grassroots solidarity. And never before had the climate emergency gained such global attention. The climate movement has turned into one of history's most powerful social actions. Minors are showing that serious action is needed if their lives are to approximate the quality of life of their elders. It is they and not adults who face its most serious immediate and long-term consequences. And it is they, more than adults, who are joining forces to bring about real change.

I should not have been surprised. I had been studying child and youth engagement in politics for over a decade. Since before some of these protesters had even been born. But it turned out, I have to admit, that while adult support is needed, it is not necessarily the point. Indeed, it is more the other way around. Adults have so far done a poor job addressing the greatest crisis humanity has ever confronted. They have remained largely paralyzed in the face of a globally existential threat. And it is mainly adult greed, ideology, and blindness that created the crisis in the first place. I have a lot to learn from these creative, impassioned, and thoughtful young people.

If you look, you can find child-led political activism everywhere. Many adults assume that children are not yet political persons. But this would be surprising to the five-year-old Black Lives Matter protesters marching against racism in the UK. Or the six-year-old child parliamentarians demanding government-funded sewer systems in India. Or the eight-year-olds throwing stones at Israeli tanks in Palestine. Or the ten-year-old labor union organizers fighting for working rights in Bolivia. Or the fourteen-year-old organizers suing the courts for child suffrage in Germany. Or the sixteen-year-old protestors demanding civilian government in Sudan. Though little seen or heard, children and youth participate in the important issues of politics in every corner of the world.

This book is a culmination of years of reflection on one particular avenue of children's political engagement: their right to vote. When I mention this work, most people find it shocking, even dangerous. Perhaps children's voting is ok to consider as a lofty academic exercise. Perhaps there are a few children agitating for it. But as a serious proposal? I'm sorry to say that, yes, indeed, I am now convinced that all age limits on the right to vote should be eliminated. They are both unjust and counterproductive. Denying children the right to vote is very much like denying them the right to free speech. It is simply not the kind of right that ought to be limited by any particular age. Like the protesters at Philadelphia City Hall, I mean it for real. Restricting the franchise to adults now seems to me profoundly wrong and undemocratic.

I stayed at the rally and learned a great deal. I saw in the flesh and blood children's political vitality. If I had been writing about lowering the voting age to eighteen only sixty years ago, it would have seemed just as preposterous then. Or women's suffrage half a century before that. Or universal male suffrage half a century earlier still. Voting rights change over time. They tend to become more rather than less inclusive. They make up the core of democratic life and stand for something deeply meaningful and precious. But that does not mean they cannot be subject to critique once again. It does not mean that what we are used to at the moment is the final answer. On the contrary, democracy means remaining open to questioning who should hold power.

Democracy is an ideal. It aims to hold those in power accountable to all, instead of just a few. The word itself is from the Greek *demokratia*, meaning "rule by the people." The democratic ideal always falls short in reality. Today, it is under attack from a rising authoritarian populism. Not to mention global neoliberalism. Or the increasing power of nondemocratic states like China. But the democratic ideal has remained a vital beacon for political life in much of the world over many centuries. It makes it possible to imagine that political power belongs not just to those who govern but also to those who are governed. As Winston Churchill famously said, "democracy is the worst form of government except all those other forms that have been tried from time to time." It holds out the greatest promise among the known alternatives for achieving a measure of political justice.

Democracy is also, however, a struggle. Over history, it has grown and changed as diverse groups have battled for inclusion. Early democratic societies in ancient Mesopotamia, India, Greece, and Rome only enfranchised tiny minorities of the population, largely wealthy male elders. The first parliaments in late medieval England shared the franchise just among the aristocratic elite. The US and French Revolutions only provided suffrage to about the 6 percent of their populations who were landowning white men. Non-landowners, the poor, racial and ethnic minorities, women, and younger adults gained full democratic rights over the course of no more than the last century and a half. The struggle for suffrage is a fight against raw power and long-ingrained historical norms.

This struggle to realize the democratic ideal has been about many things, but first and foremost it is about people's right to vote. Voting is the cornerstone of democratic citizenship. It can take many different forms, whether direct, representative, parliamentary, presidential, or what have you. Voting has its problems and leads to corruptions and distortions. It is not always as effective as other democratic processes such as protest, dialogue, or using the free press. It may lack meaning without educated citizens, strong legal institutions, relative economic equality, and a culture of respect, tolerance, openness, and inclusivity. But no one who has the right to vote willingly gives it up. The ability to cast a ballot is the historically proven method for deciding which particular members of a community are best empowered to make decisions on behalf of the whole. It is the historically proven method for building a foundation for equal justice. As such, it is a necessary, if not by itself sufficient, condition for real democratic life.

But this struggle for enfranchisement has so far excluded a third of all people living in democracies: namely children and youth under the age of eighteen. There are as many children in the world—using the UN definition of "children" as anyone under age eighteen—as there are either women or men. Each is a third of the current world's population. In some countries, as throughout much of history, minors constitute as much as half the population. The world's largest democracy, India, is 41 percent under age eighteen. Even though children's lives are just as deeply impacted by democratic politics as are adults', and even though children clearly have their own political voices and interests, every democracy that has ever existed in the world has systematically and more or less unquestioningly denied them any right to vote.

The argument in this book is that this exclusion of children from suffrage is fundamentally mistaken. It undermines the very purpose of democracies and therefore makes democracies undemocratic. There is something profoundly wrong with democratic governments that deny the franchise to a full third of their people. Children currently lack voting rights not, as generally thought, because of something deficient in children; they lack voting rights, I claim, because of something deficient in democracies. It is not good for anyone, child or adult, to live in an unrepresentative political system. It poisons political life to tolerate such enormous imbalances of power in the population. It leaves the democratic experiment incomplete.

If the ideal is that governments be held accountable to the people, then this ideal needs to be imagined and reached in a new way. It is equally unjust to deny suffrage to children as it was to deny it to the poor, minorities, and women. Democracy can and should evolve to become more just and inclusive. Voting needs to be conceived of differently. It needs once again to be reimagined boldly, even radically. Otherwise, democracy cannot survive the strains of inequality, authoritarianism, globalization, and the rising climate catastrophe.

Over its history, democracy has been enriched from a diversity of points of view. There have been critiques according to class, race, and gender, each of which has provided new ways to understand what democracy is all about in the first place. Over time, as we will see, democracy has been structured and enacted in many very different ways. It is one thing for democracy to be a prerogative of gentlemen, another to give equal power to the poor, another to overcome racism and colonialism, another to welcome the voices of women, and so on. This book argues that it is time to look at democracy through the new perspective of age. It is time to reexamine voting through a new lens, not just of feminism or anti-racism, but now of what can be called childism, or the transformation of assumptions in light of the lived experiences of children. It is time to recognize that history's longstanding patriarchalism is not just about gender but also about age, that the traditional *pater* or father is not only male, wealthy, and typically white but also adult.

A movement for children's suffrage has been emerging slowly in the past few decades, as we will see. It remains fragmented and largely under the public radar. But since the 1970s, children, academics, and young people's advocates have increasingly argued that children should be able to vote. The 1990s saw an explosion of child and youth political participation around the world in children's councils, youth labor unions, and the first children's parliaments. Around twenty countries have now lowered their national voting ages to sixteen, along with many localities and cities. And fully universal child suffrage is now actively sought, as I describe in the next chapter, by grassroots child- and adult-led organizations such as KRÄTZÄ and the Foundation for the Rights of Future Generations in Germany; the National Youth Rights Association (NYRA), the Freechild Institute, Represent MA Children 2020, and the Children's Voting Colloquium in the United States; Amnesty International UK and the Children's Rights International Network (CRIN) based in the UK, and the Children's Voice Association in Finland, to name but a few.

These movements are raising important questions about contemporary democracies: Why are young people still excluded from the vote? Is it right for democracies to directly empower only adults? Why are democracies struggling? Is age a different kind of division among citizens than class, race, or gender? What does it mean to possess voting competence? Does children's non-enfranchisement help or hurt them? Does it help or hurt adults and societies? And how would children's right to vote transform basic theories and practices of democracy itself?

These are the kinds of questions this book attempts to answer. I am convinced that careful and systematic consideration leaves only one answer: that the democratic ideal requires that age exclusions are eliminated. Age-biased democracies are both unjust and dysfunctional. They violate inherent human rights and are instrumentally counterproductive. Children should have the right to vote because this is the only way to hold governments truly accountable to the people.

The case made in this book for children's suffrage rests on two main pillars: that most children are competent, knowledgeable, and independent enough to vote; and that children's voting would significantly benefit children, adults, and societies. The first claim is about basic democratic justice. It is discriminatory and a double standard to bar children from the right to hold governments accountable to their interests through the ballot. The second is about social outcomes. Just as with the removal of past voter exclusions such as by class, race, and gender, the elimination of exclusion by age will improve societies and politics in systemic ways for all. Giving children the vote is the single best way to improve the lives of both children and democracies.

Democratic ideals have transformed through struggle over time, and new work is needed to reimagine what democracy means and how it should be practiced. My view is not simply that children should now be treated just like adults. It is, rather, that voting needs to change in such a way as to be fully responsive to everyone. Casting a ballot ought to be understood and practiced in new ways that include not only adults but also children as children. Democracy changes over time and it needs to change once again to overcome this last major historical distortion.

The groundwork for these new ways of understanding democracy lies in two main ideas. One, already mentioned, is childism. As I and others define it, childism is like feminism but for children. It means the effort to transform social norms and structures in response to the diverse and intersectional lived experiences of children. Why this lens is needed will become clear as the discussion proceeds. What is most important is the willingness to deconstruct democracy's current adultist foundations and reconstruct them in new ways that fully and equally include people of all ages.

The other underlying idea, which is explained in greater depth in Chapter 6, is a related political theory of reconstructionism. Existing theories of democracy—such as liberalism, neoliberalism, and deconstructionism—all understand the basic purpose of democracy in a way that ends up, in one way or another, marginalizing children. A new theory is needed of democratic reconstructionism that can understand democracy as responding to the people's differences of lived experience. Democracy on this view strives always to expand the political space. Both of these theoretical underpinnings lie in the background of the argument of this book.

In terms of actual practice, I argue for what I call a proxy-claim right to vote. A proxy-claim vote means that everyone is provided a *proxy* vote at birth, to be exercised by a parent or guardian, which anyone can then *claim* to exercise on their own behalf at any time of their choosing. This proposal eliminates age as a basis for voting discrimination and so makes suffrage truly universal. My view is that such an arrangement is more democratic than either simply removing age restrictions, giving all children proxy votes, or lowering the voting age to one or another particular number. It is more democratic because it accounts for the political experiences of children in particular as children.

The proxy side of the proxy-claim vote ensures that every single citizen has equal rights to political representation. A proxy vote would be held not only by infants and young children but also by adults who, for whatever reason, are unable to exercise their vote on their own behalf. Many adults find themselves in this situation, whether through dementia, severe cognitive disability, mental illness, temporary hospitalization, or in cases like felony convictions where their vote is removed by the state. Approximately the same number of adults would likely end up with proxy votes as would children. The proxy vote is for any person of any age who is unable to exercise their voting right for themselves.

The claim side of the proxy-claim vote ensures that no one is barred from voting on their own behalf should they wish to do so. The simple desire to vote, and not some predetermined age or type of capacity, is the proper democratic threshold for exercising one's franchise for oneself. Children and youth with an interest in voting would be able to claim their voting right whenever they liked, as would any adult with a voting proxy. There could, in addition, potentially exist an automatic claim vote that is granted at a culturally appropriate age such as twelve or fourteen. Or, in principle, any such automatic claim vote could be unnecessary. The important point is that anyone with the desire to vote, regardless of age or any other nonrelevant factor, has thereby demonstrated sufficient democratic competence to claim the right to vote on their own behalf.

This is an admittedly radical proposal and there are many possible objections to it, or indeed to any other version of children's rights to vote. Here are just some of them: Children are not competent. Their brains are not fully developed. They will do themselves and others harm. They will make poor choices such as ending compulsory schooling, outlawing bedtimes, or eliminating internet controls. Their right to vote will rob them of their childhoods. It will give them undue power over adults. It will undermine parents' and teachers' rights and authority. It will destroy families as the bedrock of societies. It will lead to further inappropriate rights such as to sex, marriage, major health decisions, emancipation from parents, and full-time work. It will enable children also to run for political office. And, as I hear surprisingly often, it would be unfair that parents with large numbers of children would get more proxy votes than other adults.

I respond to these and other counterarguments at length in the pages that follow. For now, it can simply be noted how easily such objections spring to mind. Most people today, adult or child, find it intuitive and obvious that, of course, children should not have the right to vote. But in the past, it seemed just as intuitive and obvious that women should not be permitted to vote either. Or racial and ethnic minorities, the poor, non-landowners, or anyone outside the aristocracy. Our assumptions about children's enfranchisement grow out of voting's long historical development. They are baked into how democracies have evolved over time. Indeed, they are baked into larger assumptions about age. But, as with every other previously excluded group, historical assumptions are not necessarily well founded. They may not stand up to careful scrutiny. Nor are they necessarily set in stone. Denying the vote to such a significant group as a third of all humanity should at least be defensible by very good and sound reasons.

A close examination of the pros and cons of the issue shows that children's voting is both necessary and good. It is vital to making contemporary societies truly democratic. It is the only way to pressure political leaders to respond to the lived experiences of all instead of just some of the people. It is the only way to make the franchise fully just and effective. And it is the needed antidote to democracies' rising authoritarian tendencies and global weaknesses. It is not the answer to everything. Democracies depend on a great deal more than just voting. But children's suffrage must be part of the solution. Things need realigning, and this is our best hope for doing so. No politics is perfect. But if societies want to be fully democratic, they have to overcome their engrained adultist biases and embrace the whole human community. Democracies are in need of democratization.

Voting over History

We demand our right to vote because we think that everyone has a right to take part in decisions. Everyone concerned by decisions must have the chance to influence them. People under 18 years still lack this opportunity.

KinderRÄchTsZÄnker (KRÄTZÄ), a child activist group

Xiuhtezcatl Martinez is an environmental activist who has been making speeches and leading climate justice organizations since he was six years old. He spoke at the United Nations on several occasions as a child, including to the General Assembly in English, Spanish, and his indigenous Aztec language of Nahuatl. At the age of sixteen, Martinez and his worldwide organization Earth Guardians led a group of twenty-one youth plaintiffs in 2015, in *Juliana v. United States*, to sue the US government for denying children's rights to a sustainable future environment. (In 2020, I joined an amicus brief arguing for a rehearing of this case after the Ninth Circuit dismissed it because of the plaintiffs' lack of legal standing.) This lawsuit inspired Greta Thunberg and other youth climate activists aged 8–17 to file a similar legal complaint in 2019 to the United Nations against Argentina, Brazil, France, Germany, and Turkey for failing to protect children's rights to consideration of their best interests in climate decisions. Martinez is also a hip-hop artist who at fourteen released his first album featuring environmental protest songs.

While Martinez demonstrates a clear capacity for democratic participation, he would not have had the right to vote at any point in democratic history, nor in any democratic country today. What is the reason for this exclusion? Why would democracies systematically bar the franchise to impassioned citizens who have so much to offer? A look into democracy's past helps excavate why voting has been restricted in the many ways that it has. And why the assumption today is that voting rights are a realm only for adults. Democratic beliefs are built on many historical layers. They have been subjected to feminist and other kinds of critique over time. This chapter develops a careful childist critique from the point of view of the young.

In fact, the history of voting rights is one of continual experimentation and transformation. It is a much more complex and contested story than people often think. It is easy and convenient for those already enjoying the franchise—at the moment, adults—to assume that voting has more or less always meant the same thing. The safe view is that the identical concept of voting has simply been extended to more and more people over time. This approach has always been used to maintain the status quo.

But nothing could be further from the truth. Democracy has transformed radically over the centuries, not just in who can participate in it but also, and more fundamentally, in how it is understood. It has involved a long series of painful but creative experiments. It does not mean the same thing, for example, when suffrage only belongs to the wealthy few as when it also extends to landowners, or to the poor, or to ethnic minorities, or to women. To undertake such momentous shifts in democratic consciousness, both the powerful and the disenfranchised have had to question their own deep assumptions about politics and human relations. And they needed to learn to think about and exercise democracy in unfamiliar new ways, ways that welcomed the stranger into power.

The usual way that scholars think about these historical shifts is through the lens of adulthood. The chief question that gets asked is how certain kinds of adults were eventually included. But when looked at through the lens of childhood, this changing history looks quite different. It was not a foregone conclusion that children should be denied rights to vote. Rather, changes over time gradually formed an association of voting with maturity, to the point where voting is now almost synonymous with politically competent adulthood. Why this is the case, and why therefore the Martinezes of the world are presumed not fit for voting, remains an untold story.

If the very meaning of democratic voting rights has transformed over time, today's presumed adult-only franchise is also in principle open to change. It is not set in stone but constructed upon particular historical foundations that could be reconstructed again. The only universal in democratic history is the effort to provide voting rights to more than just the powerful few. Predemocratic aristocracies had voting rights, but only for aristocrats themselves. Democracies expanded the franchise to the people. Even though democracies have often combined with aristocratic, monarchic, oligarchic, and other forms of government, what makes a democracy a democracy is the enfranchisement of nonruling groups. But there are many different ways to understand what this means and who it should include.

It is disputed exactly when and where the world's first democracies arose. Some would argue that prehistoric hunter-gathers could be called "democratic" insofar as small tribes of only a few dozen people probably made some of their decisions collectively.[1] The ancient world frequently contained aristocratic governing systems in which various levels of the higher classes got to vote on kings' or tribal leaders' policies. But aristocracies are not generally considered democratic, since those getting the right to vote already belong to the ruling class to begin with, simply by birth.

Some claim that ancient democracies can be found around the time of Gilgamesh in some city-states in late second millennium BCE Mesopotamia. Most scholars view their councils of free men, however, as more aristocratic than democratic. What thin evidence exists does not point to an enfranchisement of common people. Others see democracies in a number of sixth- to fourth-century BCE Indian *sanghas* or kingdoms. Here, some free men do seem likely to have voted in local village assemblies. It is disputed, however, given the paucity of evidence, whether suffrage truly extended beyond the ruling castes here too.[2]

The clearest example of an ancient democracy can be found in 594 BCE in the city-state of Athens, from where, indeed, we get the root word *demokratia*.[3] This distinctive political system encompassed the town of Athens and its surrounding countryside and lasted about 250 years, spawning similar experiments across other Greek city-states around the same time. Athens's democracy arose as a radical experiment to overcome years of violent rivalry between local aristocratic clans. The chief magistrate, Solon, managed to convince tribal elders to come together under a common *ecclesia* or assembly. The assembly was open to all free men, that is, all nonslave adult male citizens over twenty years of age. It met up to four times a month to vote on legislation, decide military strategy, and elect magistrates and officials. And it typically involved around six thousand voters gathering on a hill called the Pnyx to hear candidates' speeches from a large rock platform before voting with a simple show of hands or with stones or broken pottery.

What changed here should not be exaggerated. The free adult male citizens who became enfranchised had in fact largely enjoyed rights to vote on the policies of their tribal elders in the previous aristocratic system. In effect, much the same group of aristocratic men shifted the way they voted from within their clans to across the city-state. Indeed, it is likely that fewer rather than more people actually voted in this new system. The six thousand who typically showed up to elections would have constituted only about 20 percent of eligible voters and no more than 3 percent of the total Athenian population. Many free men would not have been able to afford to take time off to travel and spend all day in the city. And many of lesser status would have considered themselves insufficiently high-class to do so anyway.

Another ancient example is the Roman Republic, which lasted five hundred years between 509 and 27 BCE, immediately preceding the onset of the Roman Empire. The Roman Republic modeled itself on Athens. It held annual elections for (eventually) forty-four public officers with responsibilities over the city of Rome and its rural surroundings. Different public officers were elected by each of three assemblies representing, respectively, the military elite, Rome's thirty-five tribes, and the plebians or commoners. This third assembly, the Plebeian Council, was largely made up of rural farmers and provided greater power to ordinary commoners than in ancient Athens. Indeed, the Plebian Council gradually took on more important roles over the course of the republic's history. However, in practice, the entire system was dominated throughout by a small number of aristocratic families that held all the higher offices and chose all the candidates who could run for them. And, like in Athens, the actual number of voters constituted less than 3 percent of the total population.

These ancient examples are clearly quite different from how we understand democracy today. A democracy of the elite male 3 percent is hardly recognizable any more as a democracy at all.

However, ancient Athens and Rome did enact a key shift in perspective. The real shift is not, in fact, in who or how many gained the right to vote. Rather, the fundamental transformation lay in how voting was organized. Voting changed from a tribal to a geographic act. It shifted from the election of clan leaders to the election of leaders of a city. To put it broadly, it was a shift from political time to political space. Roughly the same elite adult men now exercised power, not (just) within their temporal ancestry, but (also) within their spatial region. Rather than voting within a tribal lineage, they now voted across a geographical area. Their status as voters had less to do with family temporality, the lineage from the past that they were born into, and more with geographic spatiality, the city-state region they shared with others regardless of lineage. This struggle between political time and political space will pervade future democratic experiments as well.

What does this ancient history mean for children? These origins of democracy would prove fateful. If democracy means a victory of political space over political time—the geographic city over family lineage—then any group associated with temporality has less democratic value. This includes groups like women, children, and servants, all of whom came to be associated with the temporal lifecycles of families rather than the spatial geographies of open public discourse. It includes non-wealthy, minority, and noncitizen adult men as well, since they can more easily be assumed to lack a stake in the larger political space.

Democracy comes to be defined as the very opposite of anything to do with the reproduction of families over time. And so, of course, this means most of all children, who are the most visibly temporal and family-dependent of all. Indeed, children are easily seen as time-bound in their very essence, insofar as they can appear to exist in a separate time of preadult development. Children can be seen as doubly bound by time: as members only of the reproductive cycles of families and as developing into citizens only in the future. Even though neither is actually the case (or so I will argue), the ancient origins of democracy set up the young to be marginalized especially profoundly.

If one looks around the world at the next thousand years, it is difficult to find political systems that take even these modest steps into democracy. As in the ancient world, there continued to exist voting, but only within aristocracies: in Persia during the five-hundred-year Parthian Empire of 247 BCE to 224 CE; in England during the Witenagemot councils of the 600s CE; in Iceland at Althing assembly field meetings; in king's councils in Spain starting in 873 CE; in the great Incan Empire's fifteenth- and sixteenth-century Council of the Realm; among the Iroquois Confederation's Grand Council from 1451 to 1600 in North America; and so on. Each of these instances involved real powers of voting, but only by members of the ruling aristocratic classes.

New democratic experiments emerged with the rise of a new medieval class in Europe known as freemen (or burgesses). Freemen were wealthy traders who started to demand a share in power alongside their local aristocratic lords. They were paying large sums in government taxes and wanted a say in how those taxes were to be spent. And this demand grew as local cities and villages were starting to coalesce into larger political kingdoms where taxes were being spent on more and more remote projects such as far-flung wars and trade.[4]

The earliest instance of medieval democracy was the extension of voting rights to freemen in the English parliament of 1265. Previous English parliaments dating back to the Norman conquest in 1066 ("parliament" deriving from the French *parler*, to speak) had involved voting only by nobility and clergy. But in 1215, the unpopular King John was forced to sign the Magna Carta granting the barons in parliament significant powers over judicial procedures and taxes. As the power struggle deepened into civil war under John's equally unpopular son Henry III, the head of parliament, Simon de Montfort, decided to seek broader popular support by expanding parliamentary representation. In 1265, he invited each county and borough across England to elect two local freemen to serve alongside the aristocratic barons as voting parliamentary members. This arrangement soon evolved in 1295 into the so-called Model Parliament, consisting of forty-nine lords and 292 regionally elected freemen, the latter made up of two burgesses from each borough, two knights from each county, and two locally elected citizens from each major city.[5]

The conceptual shift here is subtle but profound. Suffrage was still only granted to a small number of already powerful and wealthy men. (It remained rather vague who exactly could vote until 1430, when voters were required to earn the considerable sum of forty shillings in annual rental income.) But now voters consisted in a combination of aristocrats and freemen: those born with titles and those earning wealth for themselves. As in ancient Greece and Rome, temporal power was supplemented with a degree of spatial or regional power. Freemen got to run for office and vote for one another, not according to birth but according to the city and borough in which they lived. The main medieval innovation was that the democratic space became pluralized. Voters did not all vote in the same place, but in separate regions for local representatives. Elected representatives then came together in a national parliament to speak for their own regions' interests. And a corollary of this shift is that each region needed to be represented more or less equally.

What does this evolution mean for children? In part, the old idea persists that suffrage can only belong to those engaged in the larger political space. Along with women and the poor, children were not tax-paying earners and therefore not in need of parliamentary representation. Their interests lie in the cycles of family life as opposed to the affairs of their region. What is more, children can easily be understood as lacking a stake in interregional conflicts. Unlike wealthy freemen and aristocrats, children (along with women and the poor) do not have to be given a vote because they cannot demand power by threatening war. Democracy need pay little attention to the vulnerable and the powerless whose lives and concerns do not require parliamentary mediation.

The eighteenth-century Enlightenment changed things again, but in a way that only deepened the problem for children. Some political philosophers view this era as the origin of properly modern democratic life, seeing it as the start of a fully fledged embrace of a common public sphere.[6] But the change here is again more conceptual than numerical and more complex than it first appears. It is less about creating a public space per se than about configuring it in a new way. What really happens is that another shift takes place in how a small number of elite and wealthy men exercise political power. The key shift here is that voting comes to be based on a different kind of spatiality: whether one owns significant land.

Landownership became the basis for voting rights because it meant that one had a vested interest in the larger commonwealth. The basis of political power was felt not to lie in wealth or title, but rather in owning property that can be impacted by political decisions. Of course, landowners tended also to be wealthy aristocrats and freemen. But the point was that having "property" means one has a political stake that is "proper" or owned by oneself. The idea developed across Europe and North America that landownership gives you a personal stake in the larger affairs of the state. While such voters are still a very small percentage of any population, landowners have a direct financial and social interest in broader policy decisions. Everyone else only has a stake, or so it was thought, in the immediate well-being of their families.

The clearest example of this shift can be found in the US Constitution of 1789. The United States had previously operated under the above English system of rule by wealthy freemen. This system had secured parliament as the supreme legislative authority, even above the king, in the English Bill of Rights 1689 (as well as dividing the House of Commons from the House of Lords in 1707, "commons" referring not to commoners but to representatives of "communes" or communities). The new US Constitution, while not defining who holds the franchise explicitly, removed all special aristocratic voting privileges. In practice, it meant that anyone owning land, aristocratic or not, now gained the right to vote. Most historians believe that the enfranchised population remained about the same in terms of size, at around 6 percent of the total population.[7] Indeed, the percentage of democratic voters had actually been higher in previous decades, because wealth had previously been more widely distributed. The 1789 Constitution did not create a democracy, but rather shifted it from rule of aristocrats and freemen to rule of landowners.

Another example is the 1789 French Revolution. In the first article of its Declaration of the Rights of Man and of the Citizen, the French revolutionaries stated: "Men are born and remain free and equal in rights. Social distinctions can be founded only on the common good." In practice, the new French parliament made a distinction between "active" and "passive" citizens, only the former having rights to vote and run for office. Voters included any adult male over twenty-five who paid a certain level of taxes, effectively meaning they had to be landowners here as well, since only land was taxed. Those with the right to vote in France at the time would have constituted up to 15 percent of the population, even less after restrictions were imposed in 1792. Indeed, a chief reason the French Revolution was so short-lived is that the urban petite bourgeois, women, and peasants who had helped overthrow the king started demanding the right to vote as well. Eventually, peasants backed a return to monarchical power since they saw it as fairer to them than the new democracy.[8]

Why, though, landowners? What is the connection between owning property and having rights to vote? Here it is useful to remember that the chief intellectual resource of the American revolutionaries was the Enlightenment philosopher John Locke. Locke famously defined democratic people's principal rights as those to life, liberty, and property (the origin of the rights to life, liberty, and the pursuit of happiness in the US Declaration of Independence).[9] It is the third of these rights, property, that is key for suffrage. By "property," Locke broadly meant any type of belongings owed by an individual as a result of their own labor. It includes such things as wealth, land, buildings, and possessions, as well as, at the time, women, children, and slaves. All of these could only belong to "free men" (not to be confused with previous "freemen") because only free men could own their own property. Everyone else is the property of them.

But while just about all men owned wives, children, slaves, or businesses, it was land in particular that was necessary for voting. This is because only land was thought to endow its owner with a vested interest in the commonwealth, the *common* property of the whole state or nation. Only landowners have what the Pennsylvania legislature called "a sufficient evident common interest with and attachment to the community."[10] Owning land gives you a direct stake in the advancement of the larger geographical whole. Some states did subsequently provide suffrage also to white men who paid a certain level of taxes, without owning actual land itself. But the principal transformation of the Enlightenment era was that voting became a right for anyone owning land and hence a vested interest in the commonwealth.

For children, however, another layer of soil is piled over their potential for enfranchisement. Women, slaves, minorities, and the poor have been able over time to escape their status as men's property. But the same cannot be said for children and youth. Both socially and legally, minors are still today the legal and social property of their parents. They are "our" children depending on adults for legal representation, economic survival, health and welfare choices, and political recognition. For the same reason, children remain the sole group still largely barred from owning land. Insofar as voting continues to be associated in the recesses of democratic consciousness with a proper stake in the landed commonwealth, it will continue to be assumed inappropriate for minors in their status as the property not of themselves but of adults.

It is again a question of time and space. If children belong to the natural rhythms of family life and personal development, they can hardly have a vested interest, it is thought, in the common space of public life. Women and minorities were eventually able to establish themselves as not only property owners but also their own property, not that of white men. But it is still considered entirely uncontroversial to see children as the property of their parents. They still live under a patriarchal system in which the *pater* owns them as one of his (and now her) private possessions. In a democracy, this means that children are easily assumed not to have a vested interest in the public space of the commonwealth, only private interests as the temporal and temporary property of others.

You might be surprised that we still haven't got to the story about suffrage for men overall. It is often assumed that, prior to women's suffrage, men had the vote for a long time. But in reality this is true only for a very small percentage of men with great wealth. For most of democratic history, there was no question of suffrage for non-landowners, racial and ethnic minorities, colonized subjects, the middle classes, or the poor.

The very first time a democracy extended voting rights to all adult men, regardless of wealth or landownership, was in the Second French Republic starting in 1848. This is only about a century and a half ago. And it was only in the decades to come that other democracies followed suit. Even then, different groups of men often continued to be left out.

The Second French Republic arose out of a socialist uprising of factory workers against the monarchy that was later joined by the bourgeoisie and rural peasants. The revolutionaries used demonstrations, barricades, and street violence to demand equal representation in parliament. Ultimately, France created a new constitution granting suffrage to all male citizens twenty-five and older. Voters elected a single assembly of 750 members as well as an executive president. This meant, considering the demographics of the time, that voting rights now belonged to approximately 25 percent of the French population. The qualification to vote was no longer whether one owned land. It was whether one was an adult male of sufficient age. Suffrage was thereby extended to the growing urban bourgeoisie, the new factory-working proletariat, freed former slaves, large numbers of rural peasants, and the urban poor.

What permitted this new imagination of democratic life? There is in effect another transformation in the meaning of democratic space. Voting no longer depended on owning a literal plot of land. It depended instead on owning a stake in a metaphorical public sphere. Men became the public representatives of a supposedly private family. Voting came to reflect an emerging industrialized ethos marked by the separation of private and public spaces. The private sphere of family and school was associated with women and children; the public sphere of work and politics, with men. The chief democratic division involved a combination of age and gender. Of course, most women and children did in fact work in the public sphere. And most men lived in private families. But in a metaphorical sense, democratic life came to be understood as a common space for adult men to represent their public interests.

This broadening of the electorate gradually spread around the world, albeit with various qualifications. Switzerland developed an adult male vote in 1848, but not for Jews until 1866. Denmark granted the vote in 1849 for "men over 30 of good reputation." South Africa permitted a universal white male vote in 1910, extending suffrage to nonwhites only after apartheid in 1994. The UK gradually loosened property qualifications over the late nineteenth century, but did not extend voting rights to all men twenty-one and over until 1918 (alongside women thirty and over). Mexico and Russia achieved universal adult male suffrage in 1917, Canada in 1920 (along with women, but excluding

Chinese and Aboriginal Canadians), and Japan in 1925 (also along with women).

The most common exception to universal adult male suffrage had to do with ethnicity or race. Nowhere was this more evident than in the United States, where the enslavement of African Americans remained legal until after the Civil War in 1865. While the United States extended the vote to all white males over twenty-one in 1856 (though it had existed in some individual states as early as 1800), it did not enfranchise all men regardless of race until 1870. Even after that, many states found new legal means for barring African American men from voting through poll taxes and Jim Crow laws all the way up to the Voting Rights Act of 1965 (and one could argue later still). The idea of some men as the property of others, whether literally or metaphorically, proved difficult to dispel.

The conceptual shift here is significant, though. Universal men's voting changed the grounds of democracy. The franchise was no longer based on land but on labor. Voters came to be understood as having a vested interest in governance, not because they owned property, but because they worked in the public sphere outside the home. The industrial revolution had moved large numbers of Western populations out of farms and into factories, increasingly separating work from both the home and the land. While the whole family had previously worked together in farms and household businesses, now men came to be associated (however falsely) with the distinct labor of working in the public sphere. Men were considered independent breadwinners, with women and children economically and so politically dependent upon them. While the vast majority of women and children also worked, and indeed some men did not, democracy came to be associated with a public space of adult male labor and production in opposition to a private time of domesticity and reproduction. Democratic space now becomes entirely metaphorical.

And so children find themselves excluded from the franchise for yet another reason. Not only are they considered lacking a political stake and the property of adults, but now they are consigned in the political imagination to the sheltered, apolitical, private sphere of the home. Along with women, children came to be understood to live among the romantic rhythms of personal growth and nurturance. They are bounded by a natural and private temporality. But unlike women, minorities, and the colonized, who have largely managed to escape this gilded cage, children are still today typically assumed best confined to the private sphere alone. They alone need to be protected from harsh realities of the competitive labor of the public sphere.

Women's suffrage introduced an equally radical transformation in the democratic ideal, but again one deepening the exclusion of children. The lines between public and private spaces had to be deconstructed. Instead of being defined around gender, the democratic space now came to be defined as one that expresses the collective reason of individual adult competence. Women are just as competent as men to vote. Whether one labors outside the home or not is irrelevant. Whether one belongs to some metaphorical public sphere is beside the point. In effect, property ownership became internalized. Individuals came to be understood as their own property, not that of others, insofar as they own internal rational capacities. Women gained the vote primarily on the grounds that all adults have the competence to exercise ownership over themselves and hence also over the political decisions that affect them.

The women's suffrage movement first tasted nationwide success in New Zealand in 1893. This was followed by Australia in 1902, Finland in 1906, Canada in 1917, and Poland in 1918. The United States provided national voting to women twenty-one and older in 1920, extending the franchise from the 28 percent of the population who were men to the further 29 percent who were women, or 57 percent altogether.[11] The UK enfranchised women thirty and older (with certain property restrictions) in 1918, and twenty-one and older in 1928. Women continued to gain voting rights throughout the century to come: for example, in Turkey in 1930, South Africa in 1930 (for white women only), Japan in 1947, Niger in 1948, India in 1950, Iran in 1963, Jordan in 1974, Nigeria in 1978, and most recently in Qatar in 1999, the United Arab Emirates in 2006, and Saudi Arabia in 2015.

Women's suffrage was the result of long and hard-fought historical struggle. Women were not simply admitted into a male political space. Rather, the democratic space itself had to be transformed. Taking the examples of the UK and the United States, this struggle went through three main stages: from initial efforts to extend suffrage to women on the same grounds as men; to subsequent efforts to do so based on women's moral and maternal differences; to finally successful efforts based on an entirely new idea of suffrage based on individual adult competence. This struggle fundamentally changed the idea of voting into what still holds today, namely the expression of adulthood competence in contrast with childhood incompetence.

The earliest arguments for women's suffrage, such as at the 1848 Seneca Convention in the United States, focused on women's rights to political equality with men. Seneca Falls' "Declaration of Sentiments," drafted by Elizabeth Cady Stanton, claimed that women's exclusion from the elective franchise violated the country's founding principle that "all men and women are created equal." When the 1870 Fifteenth Amendment granted suffrage to African American men, Susan B. Anthony objected that "there is, and can be, but one safe principle of government—equal rights for all." Meanwhile in the UK, the philosopher and politician John Stuart Mill proposed an ultimately unsuccessful amendment to the 1867 Reform Bill that would have enfranchised women by replacing the word "man" with "person," on the grounds that "a hard and fast line between women's occupations and men's ... belongs to a gone-by state of society."[12]

What now seems like a common-sense equal rights argument faced at the time significant and successful opposition. People viewed women's and men's abilities as fundamentally different by nature. Women have "capacities appropriate to private life and the domestic sphere rather than the public world of politics." UK representatives in the House of Commons argued that "between the sexes it was abundantly evident that Nature had drawn clear lines of distinction," men excelling in "practical force, stability of character, and intellect," women in "mildness, softness of character, and amiability." Joined to this was the notion that women are already sufficiently represented by the vote of their husbands anyway.[13]

After these failures, women's suffragists developed a second line of argument, namely that women should be enfranchised precisely *because* of their gender differences. Women voting would elevate the moral tone of politics by introducing maternal and compassionate virtues. As explained in Ohio's 1873 Constitutional Convention, "when our mothers, wives, and sisters vote with us, we will have purer legislation, and better execution of the laws, fewer tippling shops, gambling halls, and brothels." The National American Woman Suffrage Association (NAWSA), founded in 1890, "stressed ... the more palatable essentialist theme that feminine qualities would be a welcome addition to the polity." Likewise, in the UK, Millicent Garrett Fawcett asserted that "this difference between men and women, instead of being a reason against their enfranchisement, seems to me the strongest possible reason in favour of it; we want the home and the domestic side of things to count for more in politics." Women's experiences as mothers and wives would contribute to purer and more moral legislation.[14]

However, this argument also failed. The principal objection was that political enfranchisement would, on the contrary, degrade the very virtues that women uniquely possess. As one California legislator observed in 1879, "I believe that women occupy in many respects a higher position than men, and I, for one, do not wish to drag them down from that exalted sphere." It was also claimed that women's suffrage would infuse politics with an unwanted female seductive power over men, as well as household-like quarreling. Both men and women at the time insisted that women did not wish to leave the private sphere anyway, even that doing so would threaten their sanity. In the UK there were fears for the very British Empire, since "sentiment and not reason might guide the deliberations of the world." The argument that women are different from men can be used to keep women in their place.[15]

Women's suffrage only finally came about when a third and largely innovative understanding of the franchise was developed. Suffragists started to claim that voting rights should belong to anyone possessing individual adult competence. Women had proven their capabilities in the public space by taking over men's jobs in factories during the First World War and by forming powerful labor unions in the workplace. In the United States, NAWSA and similar organizations became increasingly militant: organizing locally, canvassing, picketing the White House, getting arrested, going on hunger strikes, and committing acts of civil disobedience. As Florence Kelley declared, "no one needs all the powers of fullest citizenship more urgently than the wage-earning woman." In the UK, the Women's Social and Political Union (WSPU) began in 1909 to engage in increasingly politicized acts such as civil disobedience, marches, court battles, and imprisonment by the hundreds, under the new banner, "Deeds, not words!" These movements proclaimed that suffrage was necessary to halt women's economic, social, and domestic exploitation. They insisted that, however similar or different men and women might be, women are politically competent adults deserving the right to vote on their own behalf.[16]

This complex struggle produced a new conception of democracy, for women and men both. It redrew governance by male economic interest into governance by adult political competence. Women fighting publicly for suffrage had proven once and for all that women have the competence for suffrage itself. Anyone with the skills for political life should be enfranchised. Group-related characteristics such as gender, race, and class should no longer create democratic boundaries, since they are irrelevant to democratic capacities. Rather, voting should be afforded to all adults based on their independent competence for political discourse.

As can be imagined, however, defining the franchise around adulthood leaves children even more profoundly excluded. Not only were children left as the sole major disenfranchised group. But enfranchisement itself came to be defined precisely in terms of no longer being a child. The democratic space now came to be identified precisely with the kinds of competencies imagined to belong only to adults. It is carved out for the first time in terms solely of age. Children are excluded from the vote because they are associated not only with family time but now also with individual time, the individual time of growing into adulthood. The definition of who can and cannot vote is made entirely in terms of reaching a certain age. Children are sequestered into the apolitical time of not only the private family but also individual development.

The historically most recent group to gain widespread rights to vote is young adults under twenty-one. With a few rare and short-lasting exceptions, this group did not possess any rights to vote until the second half of the twentieth century. (Exceptions include South Africa briefly lowering the age to sixteen in 1890 for white men, and Turkey lowering the age for men to eighteen between 1924 and 1934.) The first country to lower the voting age permanently from twenty-one to eighteen was Czechoslovakia in 1946, followed by Poland in 1952, South Africa in 1958 (for whites only), the UK, Canada, and Germany in 1970, and the Netherlands and the United States in 1971. Today, the vast majority of countries in the world, 159 to be precise, have a national voting ages of eighteen, leaving twelve democracies with voting ages of twenty or twenty-one.

This almost worldwide lowering of the voting age to eighteen in the past few decades has been justified along more or less the same lines as the extension of voting rights to women. That is, the chief argument is that eighteen-year-olds have equivalent voting competencies to older adults. People below the age of twenty-one already perform civic responsibilities akin to voting, such as working, paying taxes, getting married, and serving in the military. In the United States, the draft for the Vietnam War played a large role in legislators reducing the voting age to eighteen in 1971 in order to legitimize sending those same youth to war.

The overall effect of this lowering of the voting age was less to redefine voting than to move its goalposts. Most societies now associate eighteen rather than twenty-one with fully competent adulthood. As a result, most democracies consider eighteen the appropriate age of enfranchisement. If anything changed at this point, it was a further solidification of the idea that voting is tied to a particular age of maturity. Indeed, the link between suffrage and adulthood is only further cemented. The measure of competence is not working ability, public participation, or even proof of political capacity. It is simply the number of years that have elapsed so far in your life. It is time itself. Individuals must pass through a specific predemocratic time of eighteen years before they are considered ready for democratic space.

This history of democratic voting rights so far is summarized in Figure 1. Notice how voting has accelerated over time, so that the percentage of the people with suffrage in democracies first grew slowly then gained steam over the past 150 years, particularly as all men and then all women joined the franchise. There are, of course, less genuinely democratic democracies even for adults, as well as countries like China, North Korea, and Iran that are hardly democratic at all. But within functioning democracies themselves, the overall rate of inclusion has risen rapidly over time. Will

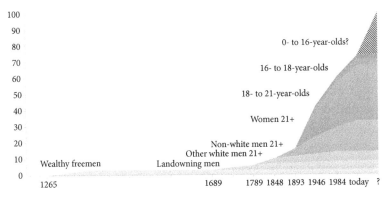

Figure 1 Voting rights over history: Percentages within democracies.

the proportion of voters now level off or continue to expand? Will the democratic experiment end or continue to change? Is it possible for the very meaning of democracy to grow still further?

In terms of suffrage for anyone under eighteen, there has in fact emerged a small but growing movement in recent decades to enfranchise either all or some children. This movement takes place generally outside public consciousness and is less a coordinated campaign than a variety of disparate actions. Like in the early stages of other suffrage movements, it combines existing conceptions of the vote with creative new thinking. We return to these developments in detail in later chapters, especially in terms of the ideas they are generating, but it is worth briefly sketching their recent history here.

Most well known is the global effort to lower the voting age to sixteen or seventeen. This has already been accomplished, as of now, in twenty-eight countries, as well as many more local regions and cities. Twelve countries have a voting age of sixteen (starting with Nicaragua in 1984 and Brazil in 1988, followed by the Isle of Man, Austria, Guernsey, Jersey, Ecuador, Malta, Cuba, Argentina, Scotland, and most recently Wales in 2020). Seven more have conditional votes at sixteen: Croatia, Bosnia and Herzegovina, Serbia, and Slovenia if you are employed; Hungary and Indonesia (actually any age in Indonesia) if you are married. And four countries now have a national voting age of seventeen (East Timor, Greece, Indonesia (lower if married), and North Korea). And the voting age is sixteen in many further localities around the world, such as all local elections in Germany and four cities in Maryland in the United States.

There are also numerous youth and adult organizations fighting to lower the voting age to sixteen elsewhere. In the United States, the youth-led National Youth Rights Association (NYRA) was behind the abovementioned cities lowering the vote to sixteen and—in coordination with a diversity of other organizations like Fair Vote, as well as politicians like Ayanna Pressley and Speaker of the House Nancy Pelosi—has actively campaigned to do so across many other cities, states, and nationally. In New Zealand, a youth group called Make It 16 has sued the High Court to reduce the voting age on antidiscrimination grounds. Votes at sixteen is part of the official platform of the UK Labour Party. The European Union has now endorsed, but not enacted, lowering the voting age to sixteen across Europe. These are just a few examples of local and national activities taking place worldwide.[17]

Below sixteen, the longest-standing effort has been for proxy voting, or what is sometimes called "family voting" or "Demeny voting." The idea is that parents or guardians should be able to exercise an extra proxy vote on behalf of one or more of their children, so that their children can also be represented in democratic considerations. As far as I know, there was only one actual instance of proxy voting in history: Between the First and Second World Wars, the French protectorates of Tunisia and Morocco gave each father of four children or more a second vote. But the idea of proxy voting actually goes back to at least 1848, when some legislators argued, at the enfranchisement of all men in the Second French Republic, for also giving men extra votes to be used on behalf of their wives and children. This, they felt (though their argument did not win the day), would properly enshrine the principle of the political equality of all. In 1871 the French parliament again considered, but ultimately rejected, a bill for fathers to have as many votes as they had family dependents (wives, unmarried adult daughters, and children). And in 1923 and again in 1943, France considered providing fathers a proxy vote for children along with its granting full suffrage for women.[18]

Other countries have entertained the idea of child proxy voting more recently. The German government's cross-party Children's Commission developed such a concept in 1993 and introduced bills into the German parliament in 2003 and 2008. These bills were supported across diverse political parties and, while ultimately tabled, would have given parents a proxy vote for children up to such a time as parents thought their children ready to exercise their vote for themselves. This, of course, would also in theory have provided some children under sixteen with a vote for themselves. However, the bill did not come to a vote largely because it was felt to violate constitutional definitions of voting as personal, secret, and free. Similarly, in 2002, the French party Forum des

Républicains Sociaux gained the support of 123 members of parliament to introduce family voting, though not enough to win passage. Since 2008, the Italian organization National Association of Large Families has worked to provide proxy voting for parents to all children in Italy and across Europe. In 2011, Hungary proposed but did not pass an act to give mothers, regardless of the number of their children, one extra vote. In 2018, the US political columnist Ross Douthat proposed proxy voting for parents in a *New York Times* op-ed, as have several other commentators and scholars in recent years, as we will see.[19]

A different kind of movement for children's voting lies in the worldwide growth since the 1990s of children's parliaments. There are currently around thirty countries that have children's parliamentary structures that roughly parallel those of adults. The first were created in schools, villages, and neighborhoods in India and remain often quite powerful. Other countries with influential children's parliaments include Norway, Finland, Germany, Slovenia, Sri Lanka, Bolivia, Ecuador, Brazil, Nigeria, Zimbabwe, Congo, Burkina Faso, Liberia, New Zealand, and Scotland. Since 2000, there has been a UNESCO-sponsored Children's United Parliament of the World.[20]

Children's parliaments vary in their actual political effectiveness, some being quite educational or tokenistic in nature, others geared toward real policy change. They generally operate from the neighborhood level up to higher district and national levels, with children electing representatives at each stage for themselves. Often there is a "house" for children around five to eleven and a "senate" for youth twelve to seventeen. Active children's parliaments have succeeded in changing environmental policies, labor laws, disabled access, nondiscrimination rights, local services, education funding, and much else. In India, they have brought new services to communities such as working sewage systems, clean water, and streetlights. Some Indian children's parliaments are seen as models of a new and less corruptible grassroots "neighborocracy" for adult parliaments too. The children's parliament of Bolivia has successfully forced adults to enact laws around child abuse, discrimination against disabled children, unequal educational resources for indigenous children, and, most famously, lowering the national working age from fourteen to ten. The children's parliament of the city of Barra Mansa, Brazil, controls parts of the city budget having to do with schools and recreation.[21]

Children's parliaments are a clear demonstration that children as young as five are entirely capable, given the opportunity, of participating effectively in suffrage. Even quite young children turn out to have serious concerns about public life and the passion and ability to make a difference in the political realm. At the same time, children's parliaments remain segregated from adult parliaments. They are a separate and only somewhat equal system. This makes them both empowering and marginalizing at once. They are a massive step forward. But other groups like women and minorities would hardly tolerate a separate parliamentary system of this kind.

Finally, and most directly of all, a number of child- and adult-led advocacy groups from around the world are now fighting for children's equal suffrage to adults.

Some argue that this right is already enshrined in international law. The United Nations' 1948 Universal Declaration of Human Rights (UDHR) declares in Article 21 that "the will of the people shall be the basis of the authority of government; this will shall be expressed in periodic and genuine elections which shall be by universal and equal suffrage." Although all original forty-eight UDHR signatory countries then had voting ages of twenty-one, technically there is no exclusion here for any particular age. Likewise, the 1989 UN Convention on the Rights of the Child (CRC) declares in Article 12 each child's "right to express [their] views freely in all matters affecting the child." Since political matters very much do affect each child, it could be argued that children should therefore have the right to express their views through the ballot. And CRC Article 13 declares even more forcefully that "the child shall have the right to freedom of expression," which is to be restricted "only" as necessary "for respect of the rights or reputations of others" and for national security, public order, or public health and morals.[22] If these truly are the *only* legitimate restrictions, then freedom of expression should again include the right to vote, as children's voting would not damage others' reputations or public order.

Most important, however, is voting rights advocacy by children themselves. An early leading organization is KRÄTZÄ (KinderRÄchTsZÄnker, or Children's Rights Fighters), founded in Germany by and for children and youth in 1992. KRÄTZÄ began a campaign in 1994 for universal children's suffrage. Members organized and demonstrated to pressure representatives for the vote, and they sued for the vote in the Federal Constitutional Court. KRÄTZÄ argues that "as long as not everyone can have a say, it is not really democracy." Another German child-led group, Foundation for the Rights of Future Generations (FRFG), created in 1997, asserts that "a right to vote irrespective of age is urgently required"; "young people and children who wish to exercise their right to vote [should] be able to do so from a point in time of their choice." Likewise, We Want the Vote, an organization of Germans aged nine to seventeen, has led a public and legislative campaign since 2011 for "everyone to be able to vote as soon as they want and can do it—regardless of their age."[23]

In the United States, NYRA, a youth-led organization formed in 1998, has campaigned since 2005 not only to lower the voting age to sixteen, as mentioned above, but ultimately to eliminate the voting age altogether. As it argues, "young people have the right to be represented and be active participants in political life. We should not be barred from voting, running for office, making political contributions, or any other means of civic engagement."[24]

Alongside such child-led organizations are advocacy groups led by adults. A prominent example is Amnesty International UK, which pursues an active campaign for universal children's suffrage and asks pointedly in a recent position paper: "Why are children denied a right [to vote] guaranteed to them in the UDHR, and rights guaranteed to them in the CRC?" The nationwide New Zealand organization of activists and lawyers called Youth Law has argued for children's voting rights based on the CRC since the late 1990s. The Finnish organization

Children's Voice Association, created in 2016, has worked with children's parliaments, adult politicians, and other groups in Finland, Estonia, and elsewhere to advance the idea that "we want our societies to be 100 percent democratic so that every citizen's opinion could be heard and valued—independent of age!" And the UK-based Children's Rights International Network (CRIN), a global research, policy, and advocacy organization for children's rights, claims that "individuals of all ages should be allowed to vote as and when they choose to do so and are able to register for voting." The reason, CRIN says, is that "not having the right to vote excludes [children] from the democratic process and is a major reason why their rights continue to be unfulfilled."[25]

There are several such adult-led groups in the United States too. A college student organization at Brown University called the Association for Children's Suffrage, created in 1997, calls for "a simple universal criteria for voting: citizenship and sufficient interest to register and then vote on election day." The Freechild Institute, founded in 2001, "advocates and works towards ... full youth suffrage or eliminating the voting age in every election in every municipality, city, state, province and country around the world." Represent MA [Massachusetts] Children 2020 and Represent PA [Pennsylvania] Children 2020 were created in 2018 and 2019 respectively (the latter by myself) to organize and campaign for "direct, accountable representation regardless of age." And a global coalition was formed in early 2020 by myself and child voting activist Robin Chen called the Children's Voting Colloquium. This group of adults and children from around the world meets monthly online to debate the issue and coordinate a campaign of universal child suffrage around the world, including through academic publications, political coordination, and public pressure.[26]

Whether by proxy, separate parliaments, or directly, a groundswell has emerged in recent years to give children equal voting representation in government. This nascent movement is taking place alongside more visible children's political movements that are engaged in issues of climate change, gun control, transgender rights, Black Lives Matter anti-racism, and much else. Children are beginning to force themselves more directly into the democratic space. They are rejecting their confinement by history to the private sphere of predemocratic time. Children and youth have always been impacted by democratic decisions. They have always been involved in democratic processes. But now they are demanding an equal right actually to exercise democratic power through the vote.

What does this history of suffrage tell us overall?

The most important conclusion is that the right to vote does not have one fixed meaning. Rather, how it is understood and practiced has transformed, often radically, over the centuries of democratic history. When voting is not placed in historical context, it is easily misunderstood as a simple expansion of the same right to more and more people. Since today voting is associated with adulthood, this means it is easy to assume it has always been based on adult competence. But from a historical perspective, the reality is quite different. Each group to gain suffrage has gained it for different reasons. The very meaning of democratic voting has transformed in many significant ways over time. And it has the potential to change again in the future.

The other important conclusion is that children's continued lack of suffrage in our own time rests on a number of deep but questionable historical assumptions. Whether these assumptions can be maintained or not is the subject of the rest of this book. But it is important first of all to understand what they are and why they are so ingrained in democratic consciousness. They are not simply built into children's biological natures. They are in great part historical constructions.

First, children still tend to be associated with ancestral time rather than democratic space. I have argued that one of the defining features of democracy vis-à-vis aristocracy is the former's invention of political geography, the idea that politics defines a particular space. Ancient and medieval democracies began as efforts to limit the power of aristocratic family lineages by creating spatial democratic regions. The definitive change enacted by democracy was not to grant power to more people; it took hundreds of years for voting rights to belong to more than just a small handful of wealthy landowning men. The real change was to base power not in temporal ancestry but in spatial geography.

However, while other groups have found diverse ways to overcome their associations with family time, children remain today largely confined within it. They are thought to need a time of growth and maturation within the home before they can fully enter the shared democratic space. They are viewed as future citizens in the making rather than existing citizens in the here and now. They are considered eventual inheritors of a better world rather than present participants in political life on their own behalf. The continued association of children with political time is perhaps the deepest reason they remain uniquely excluded from political space.

Second, children remain alone among major human groups to still be widely understood as others' property. They are generally thought of as the property of parents (and, to some extent, societies) rather than, like adults, the property of themselves. Ever since the Enlightenment, voters have had to be property owners in some sense. They have to be thought to have a stake in democratic affairs. For various reasons, the poor, slaves, and women have gradually escaped being considered the property of wealthy white men and been able to claim the political space as property of their own. But children are still considered the moral, social, and legal property of their parents, and hence not the property of themselves. Any stake they might have in democratic decisions is thought to belong not to themselves but to their parents and societies. They are assumed to exist as investments of adults rather than as politically vested persons in their own right.

Third, children also remain alone among major human groups to still find themselves confined chiefly within the private sphere. Unlike adults, who of course also belong to the private sphere, they are not thought of as full members of the public sphere as well. Starting in the mid-nineteenth century, democracy came to be understood as a public space in which men share control over social, economic, and legal rights. Women gradually managed to overcome their systemic exclusion from public space. But young people continue to be widely associated with a supposed romantic prepolitical innocence in which they need to be protected from public life's harsh realities rather than included in helping to shape them.

Finally, children are alone among major human groups in being assumed by default to lack individual voting competence. Starting in the early twentieth century, the public space of democracy came to be defined chiefly in terms of adulthood. It was reshaped into a space governed by supposedly independent and individual rationality. Women and then young adults gained suffrage primarily on the grounds that voting should be open to any mature person. The democratic space transformed from a public sphere of male workers to an adult sphere of competent individuals. As a consequence, voting came to be imagined, indeed primarily defined, as a space precisely of non-childhood. The main reason you deserve the right to vote is that you are no longer a developing and dependent child but rather a mature and independent adult. Only then can you be presumed capable, regardless of any demonstrated abilities, of exercising political power responsibly.

These historical ideas of democratic space, property, publicness, and competence are deeply entrenched in our present democratic psyche. They are the foundations upon which contemporary voting rights are built. And they are the underlying reasons why suffrage continues to be thought impossible for children.

At the same time, these ideas also show that imaginations and practices of democracy can and do change, often radically. The democratic ideal has regularly transformed in previously unimagined ways. Those with democratic power, which today means adults, have every incentive not to look into the matter too closely. But in reality, democracy is always capable of greater democratization. It is always pressing for more equal justice. The excluded have the wind of change at their backs. It is part of the internal logic of democracy to expand the political space over time.

2

Competence

I dwell deep in the heart of everyone; memory, knowledge, and reasoning come from me.

Krishna, *The Bhagavad-Gita*

The children's parliament of Patti, India, meets weekly in a circle on the dirt ground under the tall magnolia and papyrus trees at the edge of the small town. The dozen or so youth representatives, ranging in age from five to seventeen, are highly active in their community. At parliament meetings every Sunday (see Figure 2), they discuss what to do about climate change, people burning plastic, and a project to plant more trees. They debate solutions to school affordability for children who fail to attend, disabilities access to public buildings, domestic violence and alcoholism, high rates of maternal suicide, child labor exploitation in local businesses, sustainable agriculture, poor families' health-care access, and much else. The child parliamentarians are passionate and hopeful. They develop many campaigns on these and other issues. They meet regularly with local adult politicians to demand responses to their concerns.[1]

Such activities are repeated in one form or another around the world. Even very young children are politically engaged, whether in the thirty or so countries currently with children's parliaments, in national children's rights assemblies, in thousands of children's city councils, or in less formal expressions of free speech, protests, demonstrations, community forums, political organizations, or just around the kitchen table. Children and youth have their own political voices. It is part of being a person in any society.

Figure 2 Meeting of a children's parliament, Patti, India, 2016. Still from the documentary *Power to the Children*. Courtesy Anna Kersting, director.

Despite children's political engagement and activism, most people do not believe that children are competent to vote. Their perceived lack of competence is the main reason young people continue to be denied suffrage. The history sketched in the previous chapter suggests why. Starting about a century ago, with the onset of voting for all adults, democracies began to define themselves as expressions of independent capacities. Any adult, male or female, brown or white, rich or poor, should be able to vote because any adult can be presumed to possess the mature competence to do so. Suffrage should not be denied on any other ground of intelligence, education, gender, ethnicity, property, land, wealth, or title. It simply belongs, with some exceptions, to anyone reaching their society's established definition of adulthood.

But this idea is deeply flawed. Indeed, as this chapter shows, it is entirely undemocratic. Voting competence and adulthood are not at all the same thing. Voting competence is difficult to define. But if there must be a democratic competence criterion for suffrage, it should be much different and broader than currently understood. It cannot legitimately be mapped onto any specific age, whether 25, 18, 16, 12, or even 6. The right to vote is more like rights to freedom of expression and assembly than it is like other more appropriately age-limited rights such as to driving and marriage. The competence required to vote should match the democratic ideal, not historical prejudice.

The competence to vote is best defined in a democracy, I argue, not by age or maturity but by a person's desire to vote. Wishing to vote includes all the capacities needed for being granted the franchise. It is in fact the only competence currently demanded of adults. Democratic competence should be defined in terms of whatever holds representatives the most accountable to the views and experiences of the people. This means that voters should have the competence to cast ballots, examine their own and others' views, and make political choices. And absolutely nothing more. These requirements do not arise at any specific age. They are not tied to age at all. Rather, they are exactly measured by the simple desire to vote.

There are various reasons people think that children and youth are electorally incompetent. No one will deny that children have competencies of other kinds: a great ability to learn, mathematical dexterity, the complex use of language, self-expression through music and art, compassion for suffering, even great wisdom. But, the argument goes, it takes time and training to develop the specific capacities required for the enormous responsibility of participating in the democratic franchise. Such skills must develop just like abilities for moral maturity, higher academic study, and critical understandings of society, not to mention driving, marriage, work, and much else. There is a reason why some rights are provided only upon reaching maturity, so the argument goes. Voting is this kind of right because, like other rights, it rests on developed abilities and has serious consequences for oneself and one's world.

This objection to children voting is supported by various kinds of argument. One is to point to children's mental development. Each person is born without political competencies of any kind and so must gradually learn to think in increasingly complex ways about political relations and systems. According to the philosopher David Archard, "we do not know what a child would choose if possessed of adult rational powers of choice because what makes a child a child is just her lack of such powers (her ignorance, inconstant wants, inconsistent beliefs and limited powers of ratiocination)." Children need time to develop the "powers of ratiocination" needed to work through difficult societal choices like when to go to war, how to improve the economy, and what systems best provide health care.[2]

A democracy, on this view, should be able to rely on minimally rational voters. Voting, after all, affects others besides oneself. Voters should be capable of "elaborating, reflecting on, and revising ideas about justice." They have the right to know that they are involved in a morally rational debate with others. Even Immanuel Kant long ago insisted that democratic citizens have to be able to act with autonomy, independence, and fairness. These are skills that take time and education to form.[3]

Another way to object is by using neuroscience. The claim here is that children's brains have not yet developed the necessary biological hardwiring for complex political choices. Children's and adolescents' prefrontal cortexes are still undergoing the myelination and synaptic pruning that allows for multidimensional information processing. Young people even up to the age of twenty-five are more susceptible than adults to short-term impulse and peer pressure. Some even argue that the voting age should be raised rather than lowered. Of course, neuroscience cannot explain everything that is involved in political competence. And clearly there are great variations among individuals. But, that said, the human brain is relatively fixed by evolution to need a lengthy period of growth into full cognitive maturity. Only after many years can one think through the difficult responsibilities of exercising political power.[4]

And yet another way to object to children's voting competence is to say that children lack not just cognitive or neurological but, as well, interpersonal skills. Young people, on this view, do not yet possess the competence to engage in productive political dialogue. They lack mature abilities to debate and negotiate public interests with others. According to Jürgen Habermas, children and adolescents lack the "communicative competence" for intersubjective "reciprocal perspective taking." They are too egocentric to put themselves properly in other people's shoes. Another way to say this is that children have yet to develop sufficient political "civility." Voting depends on mature competences to listen and respond to disagreements sympathetically and productively.[5]

The idea that children and youth lack the competence to vote can be stated in various ways, but these all come down to the idea that children's political skills are not yet sufficiently developed. (Sometimes competence is also linked to political knowledge, but we take up that question separately in the next chapter.) Young people, so the argument goes, are not mature enough to speak up on their own behalf and lack the capacities to engage with others responsibly. Being politically incompetent, they would undermine rather than enhance democratic justice. Voting needs to be based on reasonable levels of political thought and deliberation.

This idea of children's voting incompetence is today's default view. Before examining whether children really are politically incompetent, it is first important to ask whether competence itself is the right basis for deciding who gets voting rights in the first place. As we saw, many different justifications for voting exclusion have been used over history, from status to landownership, and race to gender. Lack of adult competence arose as a basis only in the past century. But is it the right measure?

One reason for doubt is that voting competence is nowhere in fact required of adults themselves. No laws subject adults to any kind of voting capacities at all. At most there are sometimes very broad laws excluding persons like the severely mentally ill. Sometimes moral competencies are exclusionary, as in the disenfranchisement of felons. And yet, as we all know, adults possess a tremendously wide variety of political thinking skills. They frequently fail to vote in sensible ways. Some adults with the right to vote have severe cognitive disabilities or outright dementia. Some have very low IQs. Many if not most adult voters around the world are illiterate. Many have little formal education.

And many simply have narcissistic personalities, little to no concern for others, or are just plain thoughtless about political life.

But none of these political incapacities are thought to disbar adults. As the legal scholar Robert Ludbrook puts it in an argument for children's voting, "it is absurd to suggest that every person who votes exercises a rational and informed judgement having carefully scrutinised and weighed up the policies of all the candidates for election."[6] Yet all adults are presumed, nevertheless, competent to vote. Just about any adult citizen has the right to vote regardless of how stupid, naïve, self-centered, or indifferent they may be. Competence is not in reality a requirement for voting in any meaningful sense.

In the United States, the only voting competence legally required of adults is the ability to express a voting preference. More than twenty-three million US adult citizens—close to 10 percent of the adult population—have significantly limited mental functioning abilities, whether from dementia, cognitive impairment, traumatic brain injury, severe mental illness, or major intellectual disabilities. Yet every single one of them has the right to vote. This is roughly the same as the entire US population of zero- to twelve-year-olds. A guide for assisting elderly and cognitively impaired adults in voting, prepared by the American Bar Association, states that, "if a person can indicate a desire to vote, he or she can also indicate a choice among available ballot selections." And it clarifies: "Capacity to vote is much like the capacity to ride a bicycle, which can be determined accurately only by allowing the individual to mount a bike and start pedaling. If capacity is lacking, the task just won't be completed." It is even legal to fill in such a person's ballot on their behalf, so long as it is according to their stated wishes. If they say they want to vote for Abraham Lincoln for president, the helper is instructed to enter Abraham Lincoln as a write-in candidate.[7]

If a degree of competence *is* necessary for voting, then it at least ought to be applied equally to everyone. Taking competence seriously means using it fairly. The current age restrictions impose a classic double standard. Adults are presumed competent to vote unless proven otherwise, children exactly the opposite. As Bob Franklin argued in an extensive defense of children's voting in 1986, "the presence or absence of rationality does not justify the exclusion of children from political rights but the exclusion, if anyone, of the irrational." It would be extremely surprising if everyone aged seventeen years 364 days and younger lacked voting cognition, and everyone aged eighteen years and older somehow possessed it. Rather, if a significant measure of voting skill is really to be the standard, many children and youth certainly should have the right to vote and many adults certainly should not.[8]

The truth is that political competencies vary greatly by individual. Whatever bar is set for voting, it will not correlate with any particular number of years in existence. Political thinking capacities are not related to age in any consistent way. According to the political philosopher Lachlan Umbers, "whatever property children possess in virtue of which they are to be said to be incompetent [to vote], some non-trivial group of adults is likely to possess that same property." Or as historian David Runciman notes, "you could be frankly demented and still get to vote, which is as it should be." No measure of political competence is going to align with a specific age cut-off. Competence and age are simply not the same thing.[9]

Another problem with the competence argument is that voting competence cannot be accurately enough defined. It takes different kinds of competence to do different kinds of things: playing the piano, performing mathematics, making medical decisions, getting married, entering into contracts, running a business, and so on. What kind of competence is required to decide whether to vote for Donald Trump or Joe Biden? It is not as clear-cut as, for example, playing the piano (and even here, children are often much more skilled than adults). In Australia, the Commonwealth Electoral Act simply states that a person can only be disenfranchised if they are "incapable of understanding the nature and significance of enrolment and voting." This kind of definition is far from specific enough to warrant any particular voting age.[10]

In reality, voting competencies are complex but broad. You need to be able to examine your own social values and interests. You have to compare political options, listen to ideas from others, and balance possible consequences. You should ideally be able to interpret mass media, see through lies and distortions, and be attuned to gender, class, and other systemic biases. But these kinds of voting skills are difficult to define precisely because they are the same skills anyone needs simply to live in society. They are skills at contributing to collective well-being and justice. These competencies are not a direct function of cognitive or neurological age. Rather, they are multifaceted, situational, and highly individual.

The complex nature of voting skills makes them more rather than less widely shared. This is because everyone, including children, is already a member of a larger society. Eight-year-old Havana Chapman-Edwards walked out of her elementary school in Virginia, United States, to join protests against gun violence. Children of various ages launched a #DarwenGetsHangry in Blackburn, UK, to raise awareness about how the young are impacted by food poverty. Nine-year-old Eliza Cummings testified before the Colorado State Legislature on behalf of a bill to give parents the right to attend school activities without workplace punishment. Sixteen-year-old Sandy Ibrahim campaigned in Wales for mental health policies to support people who do not speak English as their first language.[11] They did not do these things because they'd suddenly surpassed some magical age of competence development. They did them because they live in the world.

Young people think about politics, listen to the views of others, imagine social consequences, engage with mass media, and deal with issues of gender, race, and class. Simply being alive integrates you into a dizzying array of public and political networks. Children could not, even if they wanted to, live in a separate private sphere. They have been exercising political competence their entire lives. Voting skills are difficult to define because they are the same skills it takes merely to exist in relation to others in complex communities. Like any meaningful relationship, they do not kick in at some predetermined age of maturity.

And then there is the problem of who should have the right to define this rather broad voting competence in the first place. Usually it will be those already in power. In the past, wealthy men argued it should only be men with significant wealth. Landowners argued that you need to possess the vested public interest of owning land. White men argued that you should be of a certain gender and race. And so on. Now it is adults who argue that voting should only be permitted for adults. Any such restriction needs to be viewed with a degree of healthy skepticism. It usually turns out to be rather self-serving. Why should the world deny voting to Xiuhtezcatl Martinez and Greta Thunberg simply because they are not yet eighteen? It does not seem they lack democratic competence at all. On the contrary, they have it in spades. They have much more of it than most adults. If anything is lacking, it is a democratic enough definition of voting competence itself.

Finally, competence is a flawed measure because imposing any predetermined measure of voting competence may be itself inherently undemocratic. Democracies ought to provide a universal vote by default, and then justify any exception with clear and strong reasons. The burden of proof should belong to those arguing for exclusions, not those arguing for inclusions. As the philosopher Eric Wiland puts it, "citizens should have the right to vote, unless there is a good reason to disenfranchise them." Or, in the words of Stefan Olsson, "the question whether children should have the right to vote or not depends on how well this exception can be justified." In a democracy, children ought to be assumed competent to vote unless it can be proven beyond a reasonable doubt that they are not.[12]

The purpose of democratic voting is to bring to the table the maximum possible diversity of pressures on politicians. When societies limit the vote according to nonrelevant capacities, this reduces the people's range and diversity of political influence. Consider the Jim Crow laws of the southern United States in the 1880s–1960s. These laws disenfranchised most African Americans by conditioning the right to vote on poll taxes and literacy and comprehension tests. In this case, voting was limited according to wealth and abilities that, because they obscured the effects of historical slavery, were systematically racist. If voting capacities are applied too specifically, they distort democracy as a whole. Limitations should be imposed only for very good reasons that do not eliminate the people's capacities to pressure politicians for themselves.

It is not even necessarily the case that a reasoned and fair democracy depends on reasonable and fair voters. The ultimate goal is not for all thinking persons to make their views known. The ultimate goal is for political representatives to make the most inclusive and beneficial decisions for all. The current assumption is that representatives will think and reason well if they are chosen by voters with mature thinking and reasoning capacities. But the case of children shows especially clearly why, even if adults can be assumed more reasonable (which they cannot), this is a false equivalence. A reasoned democracy is not one expressing certain ideas of reason, but, rather, one inclusive of reason's great human diversity.

By limiting voting only to adults, democracies pressure representatives to prioritize adult over child concerns. Representatives are incentivized to respond to those who can vote them out of office. Even if, just for the sake of argument, all minors were incapable of political rationality, it does not necessarily follow that denying them the vote will lead to more rational political decisions. It could turn out to be the case, as I will argue shortly, that the most rational overall democratic outcomes depend instead on representatives being forced to listen to everyone.

There are many reasons, then, to be skeptical of the idea that voting should be based on adult competence. No kind of competence is in fact required of adults. The competencies needed to vote cannot be sharply defined. And declaring a whole group incompetent is undemocratic unless supported by very strong reasons. None of this is to suggest that there are *no* competencies needed for voting. It is only to say that, when you actually examine it, the competence to vote is far different than any supposed age of maturity.

What, then, does democratic voting competence actually consist in?

This question can only be answered properly by working backward from the democratic ideal. The competencies needed to vote should be defined by whatever outcome voting is supposed to achieve. As history shows, the defining purpose of voting in democracies has always been to guarantee rule by the people. The argument has been that aristocratic, monarchic, oligarchic, and other nondemocratic systems might purport to do the good of the people, but in fact they fail. And they fail because the people themselves are not provided a formal mechanism to hold political leaders accountable to their real diversity of experiences.

Over history, the answer to what competence means has in fact changed radically. In ancient Greece and Rome, it was thought that politicians will make the best decisions for everyone if they are elected by the best and wisest citizens. This idea is only one small step beyond aristocracy. During the Enlightenment, it was believed that only landowners are competent to vote since only they have a vested interest in political affairs. This was the belief at the founding of the United States and the French Republic. Eventually the idea developed that true voting competence consists in adult maleness, since men are capable of taking responsibility for affairs beyond the private realm. And finally, around a century ago, the notion developed that representatives would only act democratically if voted in and out of office by all citizens who are independent adults. Each of these changes has certainly made elected representatives increasingly accountable to the will of the people. But each is historically specific and far from fully and equally responsive to the people.

But consider what skills are actually involved in voting, for example, in the relatively complex 2017 election of Germany's national parliamentary Bundestag. The 709 representative seats were contested by thirty-eight parties, seven of which actually won representation. Angela Merkel's center-right CDU/CSU coalition lost 65 seats but still retained the highest number at 246. The center-left SDP lost 40 seats but came in second with 153. The greatest shift was the far-right neofascist AfD gaining seats for the first time, with 94, which was more than the libertarian FDP with 80, the democratic socialist Left with 69, and the Greens with 67. Overall, the Bundestag shifted sharply to the right, seemingly in response to fears about migration and globalization.

At the very simplest level, the most basic competence that German voters had to exercise was the ability actually to cast a ballot. One cannot put pressure on representatives without being physically and cognitively capable of employing the available voting mechanisms. These mechanisms can be various. In Germany, a voter must show identification at their precinct or vote by mail. In the United States, one has to register ahead of time. In other places like Estonia, the vote is conducted electronically using one's digital identification. In countries with high rates of illiteracy, such as in the world's largest democracy, India, each name on the ballot is accompanied by an identifying party symbol.

This competence to cast a ballot might seem obvious, but it is important when it comes to questions around childhood. We need to recognize what casting a ballot truly requires, as opposed to what it is often imagined to require. For example, it does not depend on being literate. Like the US Jim Crow laws, literacy tests are undemocratic because they disenfranchise many who do in fact possess the thinking skills to vote. Nor does pressuring representatives necessarily demand spatial mobility, physical independence, or manual dexterity—skills lacked, for example, by many disabled and elderly adults. If, for the sake of argument, a toddler possessed all the other needed skills and knowledge to vote, the fact that they cannot walk alone to a voting booth or read a ballot should not in itself be disqualifying. Rather, the voting mechanism itself should be changed to meet every capable voter's needs. The most basic requirement is simply that a voter possess the ability to make their voting choice known.

Second, voting competence also involves the capacity to examine your own and others' political views. To be able to pressure representatives, you need to be able to reflect to some degree on what you yourself think. And you have to have some degree of ability to reflect on how your own ideas differ from those of others. This does not mean you have to be able to understand the ideas of everyone else in one's society, which is both impossible and undemocratic. You simply need to be able to enter into political dialogue of some kind, both internally and externally. Otherwise, you cannot know what you are holding politicians accountable for. You cannot understand that you are actually making a choice.

Are these capacities exclusive to adults? Clearly not. Even if adults can think more broadly and long-term (which is debatable), such abilities are not directly relevant. The real purpose of democracies is for people to contribute a diversity of views to the larger political conversation. No one can entirely understand the views and experiences of everyone else or anticipate all the consequences for them or others. Democracies combine multiple perspectives so that long-term choices are shaped by as many perspectives as possible. The idea of "mature" voting is in reality paradoxical. Voting exists precisely because no view is inherently more valuable than any other. All experiences should be taken into account.

Most children and youth can and do reflect on their own and others' views. Many like the children of Patti's parliament or climate activists do so in profound and effective ways. Adults comprehend only so much about their own views, let alone those of others. People's beliefs are based to a large extent on received ideas from their upbringings, histories, and cultures. Two hundred years ago, most voting Americans were rabid racists and sexists, since this was the largely accepted thinking among voting white men at the time. All of us hold views that we cannot entirely explain or justify. Our views arise out of our environments, cultures, and relationships. They are never purely independent. Why some Germans voted to the left while others voted to the right is partly based on individuals thinking through the issues, for sure; but it was also, to a very significant degree, based on family background, culture, class, gender, habit, and many other less-than-fully examined or examinable factors.

Children and youth are no different from adults in this regard. Their political views are a combination of individual reflections and contextual assumptions. There is no good measure of this kind of voting competence. Since it is a broad competence, it should be defined broadly. The idea is not for sufficiently rational people to produce a thereby rational outcome. Rather, it is for the people as a whole to exert pressure on politicians to respond to their lives. Children as young as five in children's parliaments have already demonstrated great abilities to examine their political interests and respond to the views of others. It is more rational to include their voices in democratic deliberations than not.

It is also worth pointing out that we cannot know what children's voting competencies really are when they have never had the chance to vote in actuality. Any empirical study of children's voting skills could at present only measure the voting competence of children who have never had any reason to develop it in the first place. And who have been told from birth that they don't have it. Children are necessarily going to appear today less competent on paper than they really are. "Children learn by doing. They learn about decision-making by making decisions. They can learn about politics and the electoral system by being able to express their views and preferences through the ballot box."[13] If a study had been conducted of women's voting competences around 1900, women would almost certainly have appeared less competent to vote than men, not because they actually were but because they had had no reason to develop this competence to begin with. Not only are children generally competent to vote, but they are more competent than they presently might appear.

Beyond the abilities to cast a ballot and reflect on political perspectives, there is one final competence needed to hold representatives accountable, which is the ability to make voting choices among the available alternatives. Voters have to pick which of the many candidates or options best represent their ideas. As the political philosopher Nicholas Munn puts it, "someone is politically capable who understands the nature and effect of voting, and has the ability to make a choice."[14] Included in this ability is some capacity to decide which platform or set of policies you believe is more just or right. Some believe that voters should vote solely in their own self-interest, others that they should take a larger view. In either case, the basic competence needed is the ability to think through which of the available options one ultimately prefers.

Take again the choice faced in Germany. Among the seven major parties, voters had to decide whether to throw their support behind the far-left, center-left, center-right, or far-right alternatives. On the left was a choice among green environmental, social democratic, and centrist parties, while on the right it was among centrist, neoliberal, and anti-immigrant parties. This is of course an oversimplification. Political choices do not come down to simple left–right comparisons. At a minimum, however, voters have to be able to distinguish among these kinds of available option and make their preferences known accordingly.

It is important in a democracy for voters to make such choices on their own terms. No democracy requires voters to provide any justification for their decision. Indeed, voting typically takes place in secret, to ensure that voters' private views prevail. Voters have the right to vote for any of the given options they like, sometimes even to write in options of their own, for any reason they like. It is not even required that voters vote in their own self-interest; indeed, arguably many do not. Voters can and do use irrelevant factors like gender, race, ethnicity, and class in making their choices. The only competence required here is the ability to translate your views into one or other of the given alternatives. So long as the people are thought to have voted based on their own experiences, then successfully elected representatives will feel pressure to accomplish what their voters claim to have desired. Politicians will have gained a mandate from the people.

It is difficult to imagine why most children and youth should be thought uniformly lacking in this competence to apply their views to specific voting choices. One can easily think of many children who know exactly who they would vote for if given the chance. If you march for Black Lives Matter, you are already thinking in more complex political ways than just which candidate to vote for. If you spearhead campaigns to save the environment, you are thinking on a higher political level than many adults. It is not brain surgery to recognize that left-wing parties tend to want stronger government programs and right-wing parties fewer. Or that Greens think the highest priority is the environment, the far right that it is ethnic identity. These are fairly straightforward choices among a limited set of options.

There are of course young people not competent to make such distinctions. But then there are clearly adults not competent to do so either. No one's conception of the alternatives is perfect. But few have no conception whatsoever. Whatever skills should be required on this score, they should be broad rather than narrow ones. Vague conceptions of incapacity should form no legal restraint. It is better to include many types of political input if a democracy is to respond to the widest possible range of the people's actual concerns.

If there must be a competence bar for voting, then, it need only include these basic abilities: to cast a ballot, to reflect on one's own and others' views, and to translate one's views into a choice among the available alternatives. Some people may be better or worse at these skills than others. But the right to vote should depend only on meeting the minimum threshold. Certainly, the bar is not impartiality or long-term vision. The impartial is a way of perhaps describing democracy's aim, but not its precondition. Longer-term thinking is certainly helpful. But the only precondition that can legitimately be imposed is that a person be able to pick a candidate or platform they think best represents their ideas.

The wager of democracy is that while the people often make poor choices, they make less poor choices than if only a small number of people decided all by themselves. This wager is more likely to pay off the more people are included in who can make political decisions. As a result, the inclusion of young people, even if they have spent fewer years in the world than adults, would actually produce more just and rational results than the inclusion only of supposedly rational adults. The skills needed to vote may not be present at birth, but neither do they suddenly appear at some particular age of maturity. Political competence is present in different people in different ways and depending on different contexts. Voting competence should be broadly defined so as to hold politicians maximally responsible to the people.

Are there other competencies besides these that would make it prudent, nevertheless, for societies to set a minimum voting age? My answer is no. The competencies already outlined are not only necessary for suffrage but also sufficient. There are other cognitive abilities that may be thought relevant to voting but that in reality would be undemocratic or counterproductive to require. One already mentioned is literacy. A child who cannot read should no more be banned from voting for this reason than an illiterate adult. A bar of literacy would be both unjust and narrowing. Here are some others.

Voting competence is not equivalent to the competence for making major medical decisions. The vast literature on medical competence is interesting for our purposes. It generally ties competent thinking skills to the degree of personal medical risk. If you are fighting cancer or a terminal illness, your thinking skills need to be high. Your decision could save or end your own life. You should be able to think very carefully about what you choose. This is why major medical decisions call for serious help from the expert opinion of specialized doctors. But if you have a cold or a scraped knee, your thinking skills have more latitude. It is not particularly difficult to make a good choice. And a wrong decision involves far fewer consequences.

Voting is not like major or even minor medical decisions. It does not put you at any kind of personal risk at all. Yes, the collective vote of a society results in exceptionally major consequences. You could end up going to war or enriching the 1 percent. But one person's vote neither affects that person in particular nor affects anyone else directly. As one writer puts it: "An eight year old behind the wheel of a car, for example, can kill people. An eight year old in the voting booth can, at worst, get a paper cut."[15] Voting does not have a direct impact on the voter's life, but instead an indirect one. It decides which out of a small choice of representatives will go on actually to make policy decisions for all, including oneself. Because it is indirect, as well as anonymous, voting only influences people's lives in the aggregate. Politicians will not make one choice for me and another for someone else. Rather, they make the same choices for everyone based, in theory at least, on everyone's views.

It can hardly be argued, then, that a child voting risks anything like the potential harm of making a poor medical decision. Nor could the same be said of adults. Even less can it be argued that voting is equivalent to imposing medical decisions on others. Voting is diluted among the many. It is not the individual's particular voting choice that affects their life. It is the collective choice of the society around them. What does impact the individual directly is whether or not they have the right to vote in the first place. Only having the right to vote makes representatives directly accountable to you. Even if children, like adults, made terrible political choices, simply having the right to vote itself would improve, not hurt, their lives.

Voting competence is also not equivalent to economic skills like holding a job, paying taxes, or being financially independent. Political and economic skills are not the same thing. This distinction was already made when voting was historically decoupled from property ownership and work. Of course, many children do in fact perform economic activities like working and making money, sometimes as young as five years old. So it is just factually incorrect to say that these are skills children could not have. But more importantly, economic competencies are not relevant to voting in the first place. The reason young people are often denied rights to work and pay taxes is not that they lack the skills to do so. It is because they do have those skills but should be protected from having to use them. Any six-year-old could easily stock shelves at Walmart. Labor rights are denied because many societies believe that children's time is better spent on other things like education and play. The competence to vote is a competence not for economic independence but for political influence.

To take just one more example, voting competence is different also than the competence to marry or have sex. Rights to marriage and sex are typically set at certain ages of maturity (though these differ by country and region) because, for similar reasons as for work, marriage and sex could cause children significant harm. They could subject children to exploitation, trauma, and physical and psychological abuse. They can result in offspring that children may not be in a position to raise. The point of protecting children from sex and marriage is to guard them against clear and present dangers.

The right to vote carries no such risks. It does not need to be accompanied by protections against exploitation or damage. Unlike marriage and sex, voting is not something from which children need to be safeguarded until such as an age as they are mature enough to handle it for themselves. Rather, voting is a right to have an influence in political life. It simply involves expressing oneself at the ballot box. The only alternative is to be excluded from voting, which really does constitute a clear and present harm. It makes one a second-class citizen and robs one of a basic source of human dignity and influence. If children need protection when it comes to voting, it is protection against *not* being to vote. All voters need protections against voter discrimination, fraud, and misinformation. But they do not need to be protected against the act of voting itself. Unlike marriage and sex, the act of voting does not place the voter in harm's way.

From these examples, it is evident that the usual objections to children voting based on their incompetence do not hold up.

First, it is inaccurate to equate voting competence with adult cognitive development. Adults have highly variable political capacities. The cognitive skills needed to vote are not the same as for such things as medical decision-making and marriage. This is because voting does not put the voter or anyone else at immediate risk. It does not require the voter to be protected from harm. On the contrary, the real harm involved comes with lacking the vote.

What is actually required in order to vote are the abilities to examine diverse views and make political choices. These are the skills necessary for holding representatives accountable to one's interests. In order for democracies to include the people broadly, nothing more should be required. Any additional bar to voting is discriminatory. Any mythical standard of adult impartiality is both impossible and undemocratic. As sixteen-year-old Vita Wallace puts it, "democratic society has its risks, but we must gamble on the reasonableness of all our citizens, because it is less dangerous than gambling on the reasonableness of a few."[16]

Nor is voting dependent on some supposedly adult capacity for controlling impulses. Voting does not happen all of a sudden. It is the result of thinking about the options over time. "Modern election campaigns and media coverage expose persons to a wide range of perspectives, and afford substantial time for deliberation. We are not called upon to make voting decisions impulsively."[17] Besides, adults are not required to check their impulses at the ballot box. They have the right to vote however impulsively they wish. Democracy is not about nonemotional deliberators making purely rational choices. It is about giving voice to the true diversity of a people's always limited and partial perspectives.

Even very young children can be cognitively developed enough to vote responsibly. Most five-year-olds likely have greater voting capacities than adults with severe mental illness or dementia who cannot understand their own thoughts. Responsible voting simply means being able to make one's actual views known in terms of a limited political choice. We do not know how many children and youth have this competence because it is not a competence that can be sharply defined. But the idea that it is absent in all children is obviously false.

Similarly, voting competence cannot be established by age of neurological maturity. Brain development is just one part of the voting person, alongside experiences, relationships, circumstances, culture, class, religion, conscience, and much else. Neuroscience does not offer a cut-and-dried voting competence measure. A nine-year-old who fought as a child soldier in Colombia is likely to grasp the meaning of war better than an adult who has never set eyes on a battlefield. Neuroscience does not yield definitive universal stages of political development. Indeed, it shows that the brain changes not just over childhood but over the entire lifespan. As we age, our neurological capacities can go into serious decline. But just because an average 89-year-old is relatively less cognitively skilled than they used to be does not mean that all people that age should be excluded from voting. Neuroscience does not give us a road map of political competence.

If neuroscience is relevant at all, it shows that most children do in fact possess sufficient capacities to vote, so long as those capacities are defined democratically. Even young infants have cognitive capacities for morality and empathy.[18] The fact that adolescents are on average more likely to engage in risky behavior than adults is totally beside the point. Many adults engage in risky behavior but are not thereby stripped of their voting rights. Many children and teens are unusually cautious. Besides, personal risk-taking is not the same thing as political risk-taking. Greta Thunberg at age fifteen is more politically competent by a mile than most of the adults on the planet. The proper cut-off for suffrage is not adult brain functioning. It is whether an individual can make reflective political choices. Most children and youth can. There is no specific age of neurological development at which this capacity comes into being.

Finally, the right to vote cannot properly be tied to any particular age of communicative competence. The idea of communicative competence was developed in detail by the political philosopher Jürgen Habermas based on the moral psychological theories of Lawrence Kohlberg. Kohlberg used empirical studies to argue that children and youth pass through six stages of moral development: obedience, self-interestedness, conformity, social order maintaining, social contracting, and universalization. Many criticisms have been made of this model, both of the specific stages and of the whole idea of moral stages as such. But for our purposes it is sufficient to point out what Kohlberg's own data clearly shows: that very few adults actually reach the final stages of impartiality, and that both children and adults jump back and forth between different so-called stages in different situations. These stages are at best extremely rough approximations, at worst false equivalences between communicative competencies and specific ages of maturity.[19]

The actual communicative competence required for voting is very different. It cannot be based on some idealized view of adulthood. It is not the ability to enter into social contracts or think universalistically. Rather, it is the simple ability to engage with one's own and others' political experiences. The degree to which this skill must be exercised is impossible to calculate and beside the point. Does it require abilities for thoughtful political conversation? For discourse with a certain number of other people? For debate with people with whom you disagree? For winning others over? For considering the lives of those systemically marginalized? None of these competencies are black-and-white. None can be defined with sufficient precision to bar groups from voting rights. And none is especially lacking in children.

If age of maturity is the wrong measure of who has the competence for suffrage, then what is the right one?

A truly democratic right to vote requires nothing more and nothing less than each individual's desire to vote. Possessing this desire is sufficient evidence of the basic needed competence. Wanting to vote unites all three competencies actually needed for suffrage: casting a ballot, examining one's own and others' views, and applying one's understanding to political choices. The simple desire to vote is the most democratic measure of the competence to make one's own voting choices. It is the strongest way to hold representatives accountable to the people they are supposed to represent. Nothing more should be required for the right to vote.

In a detailed examination of voting competence, the political theorist Claudio López-Guerra argues that children and youth generally possess what he calls the "franchise capacity." This he defines as "the ability to experience the benefits of enfranchisement and the harms of disenfranchisement." Children experience the benefits of enfranchisement insofar as they recognize that voting is in their interest. They experience the harms of disenfranchisement insofar as they see that not being able to vote puts them at a disadvantage in society or harms their dignity. Most children do or could in fact possess "the moral and rational faculty to value the position of being a voter."[20] As a result, most children deserve the right to vote and are harmed by having it denied. If you understand the benefits of voting, you ought to be able to participate in it.

My proposal is much the same. You could only have a desire to vote if you understood that your views are different from those of others and that there are electoral mechanisms for making your views known. Desiring the vote means valuing the vote. What matters is that a voter understands the wish to have an influence in political life. The aim, after all, is to affect the decisions of representatives. A voter only needs to believe that their vote is important to them. If they believe that, then they already possess all the necessary competencies to vote. The democratic ideal of rule by the people is best achieved if, barring well-founded exceptions, all of the people who want to vote have the right actually to do so.

Possessing a desire to vote means, first of all, that you can imagine yourself casting an actual ballot. This seemingly obvious point is important when it comes to children. Imagine a seven-year-old in Germany. Perhaps they cannot walk to school alone, make doctors' appointments, or hold a job. But none of these prevents them from potentially wanting to take part in the democratic processes around them. Just as it does not prevent them from marching against racism or campaigning for gay rights. Perhaps that seven-year-old is particularly interested in political issues. Perhaps they engage in active debate at the dinner table. Perhaps they follow the news on social media. Some seven-year-olds may of course have no interest in politics or voting at all. Neither do many 37- and 67-year-olds. But as long as an individual has the desire to vote, this means that they have the basic competence required to actually cast a ballot.

The desire to vote furthermore implies that you are able to reflect on your own and others' political views. A six-year-old concerned about the climate emergency is someone who both has political views of their own and realizes that those views are not shared by everyone. They would only want to vote if they could see that people's politics are different, that not everyone agrees with them already, that there is something at stake in whose perspective prevails. It does not matter where a voter's views come from. It does not matter, for example, if a child's views are exactly the same as those of their parents, or grow out of their community, class, or culture. Wishing to vote still indicates a capacity to reflect on alternative viewpoints. The mere desire to take part in the voting process already involves the capacity to have political views of one's own and to weigh them against those of others.

Finally, the desire to vote also implies that you are capable of making discrete political choices. A five-year-old child parliamentarian in India is able to understand how their views on the local sewer system align with those of their political leaders. Such a child has the competence to make real choices among political candidates and parties. They see that one candidate is more likely to invest in better local infrastructure than another. That one cares more than another about providing disability access to public buildings. That one party will invest in climate action while the other will stall. Having a desire to vote already implies that you believe certain representatives will respond to your experiences and beliefs better than others. It means hoping to influence political life in particular directions.

If a person desires to vote, they already possess all the competencies that should be needed for the right to vote. You could not desire the vote if you could not reflect on different political perspectives and wish to influence the given political space. To require any further competence is irrelevant, discriminatory, and undemocratic. And it is counterproductive, as it fails to force representatives to attend to the full range of the people's concerns. Desiring the vote is the most accurate and democratic measure for who the right to vote should belong to.

It is clear, then, that children and youth are, on the whole, entirely competent to vote. The current standard of adult-only voting is based on historical assumptions about political competence that are both ill-defined and profoundly undemocratic. Whatever competence is needed to vote should be based on the democratic ideal. That is, it should be defined by whatever places the greatest pressure on representatives to represent the interests of the people. By this standard, voting competence is nothing more and nothing less than the capacity to express one's views in political choices. This capacity cannot be measured in terms of any specific age. Indeed, it has as little to do with age as it does with gender, class, and race. The competence to vote is most accurately measured by the simple desire to vote.

3

Knowledge

*It is a narrow mind which cannot look at a subject from various points
of view.*

George Eliot, *Middlemarch*

The Peruvian National Movement of Organized Working Children and
Adolescents (MNNATSOP) is a youth labor organization representing
approximately 10,000 working Peruvians aged six to seventeen. Many
children and youth in Peru, just like across the world, work in family
businesses, indigenous farms, household industries, street vending, and
other capacities. They are sometimes unpaid or working in hazardous
conditions. But on the whole, they provide vital economic support to
their families, learn traditional skills, and earn money to pay their fees
to attend school.

MNNATSOP is one of the world's oldest child labor organizations,
dating back to 1976, the entire time run exclusively by children and
youth. Their goal is to advocate for fair wages and nonexploitative
working conditions. While some think child labor should be abolished,
many child laborers themselves seek a balance between dignified work
and schooling. As twelve-year-old union representative Anabella puts
it, working children deserve to "participate, give your opinion [and]
express yourself without fear."[1] They deserve to have their voices heard
by policy-makers. And they have made many strides for working
children in their almost half a century of existence.

Sometimes the young are thought to be inherently ignorant about
politics. But as these Peruvian children illustrate, this is not a natural
fact but a social construction. Ignorance about politics is not inherent in

children's conditions. The idea reflects a historical concept of childhood originating largely in European modernity. In reality, children are capable of knowing a great deal about politics. Many children understand political life deeply and complexly. Many have engaged in campaigns across history for women's suffrage, racial justice, school desegregation, gun laws, and much else. And many today are climate, anti-racist, and working rights activists who understand the political landscape just as well as adults. The question for suffrage is not whether children have any knowledge about politics. It is whether children have enough.

This question of voting knowledge is slightly different from the question above of competence. It is not about voting skills or abilities. Rather, it is about the education, understanding, and experience needed to vote in a sufficiently informed way. Peruvian working children might be capable of making voting choices, but do they adequately understand their country's political system, others' perspectives on the issues, and the longer-term consequences of their preferred policies for society? Democracies have an interest in voters possessing enough knowledge and experience to vote in thoughtful and intelligent ways.

Children in particular may be said to stand at a disadvantage in this regard. By definition, they have not lived as long as adults in the world. They may possess less political experience or insight into policies' wider ramifications. What is more, they have likely received less formal political education than once they have grown up. They might not yet have learned about the different branches of government, their country's political history, taxes and economics, and key political debates and platforms. From this perspective, even if one were to accept that children can be politically competent, it could still be argued that the electorate should have a mature degree of political knowledge so that voting is performed in a minimally informed way.

My view is that this objection to children's voting does not hold up either. There are two basic reasons. First, children do, in fact, or certainly can, comprehend the formal mechanisms of democratic governance.

Most adults know only a certain amount about their political systems, and most children are able to understand as much just as well. And second, formal knowledge of government processes is not the most important kind of knowledge needed for suffrage anyway. The more fundamental knowledge required for voting is informal knowledge of one's own and others' lived political experiences. Formal knowledge is but a means to the larger end of empowering the people's informal grassroots perspectives. Children know a great deal about their own and others' political experiences and should have the chance to help pressure representatives to take the people's full diversity of these experiences into consideration.

Indeed, children's knowledge is not only not a basis to exclude them but, on the contrary, one of the most important reasons for their

Figure 3 Climate emergency rally, Washington DC, November 2019. Credit: Jim West/Alamy Live News.

enfranchisement (Figure 3). Everyone in a political sphere comes from a distinct social position. At the moment, democracies systematically silence the vast wealth of knowledge, perspectives, and experiences of the young. Poverty law is formulated without input from what is generally the poorest age group in societies. Education policy is not accountable to those actually being educated. Climate regulation lacks pressure from those facing its direst short- and long-term consequences. Health initiatives fail to respond to those in their most formative years of growth. Without enfranchising children and youth, democracies make less, not more, informed policies.

Many people imagine that democracies exist to bring together knowledgeable people to develop knowledgeable policies. Perhaps they imagine this because the opposite seems frightening. No one wants to live under laws that might have been created in ill-informed or thoughtless ways. This is a major reason given for barring suffrage to children, the mentally ill, and even noncitizens. Voters ought at least to possess a basic comprehension of their political systems, the viewpoints and interests in dispute, and the likely larger consequences of decisions. Otherwise, it is thought, democracies cannot be expected to act responsibly and effectively.

This usual view asserts itself at the slightest suggestion of change. The UK Electoral Commission recently opposed lowering the voting age to sixteen because of adolescents' supposed lack of "the development of sufficient social awareness." Scholars have argued that children should not vote because they do not possess "knowledge of the political system, and understanding of the nature and significance of issues that are the subject of public and political debate." Indeed, "an eight-year-old child can hardly be enlightened enough to participate equally with adults in deciding on laws to be enforced by the government of the state." Voting is a significant responsibility demanding a well-educated electorate. Most political theorists and ordinary citizens assume that children and youth would dilute rather than enhance the democratic knowledge pool.[2]

But this view is deeply undemocratic, and for a number of reasons.

In the first place, just as with competence, it is important to notice that there is no voting knowledge requirement for adults. Democracies do not demand that adults know anything at all. Adults can still vote if they are illiterate, have never done any research, care little about politics, believe in crazy conspiracy theories, or are just plain stupid. Adults can vote if they have never received an education. Adults can vote if they are severely cognitively impaired or think their prime minister is Elvis Presley. In fact, "you don't even need to know what an election is about to vote in it."[3] The simple reality is that democracies do not establish knowledge requirements for voting in any form.

Why is this? When tests of knowledge have been imposed, such as in the Jim Crow US South, they have always proven democratically unjust. Any knowledge bars for suffrage will reflect the hidden or overt biases of those establishing them. They are inherently discriminatory because they prejudge what democratic knowledge is in the first place. One of the most important functions of voting is to establish what knowledge legislators need to know. Any prior limits on knowledge circumvents the whole process.

Some theorists have argued that democracies, even for adults, should be "epistocratic," meaning that "citizens should have to possess sufficient moral and epistemic competence in order to have the right to vote."[4] This view finds that contemporary democracies often make deeply uninformed choices and that voters often know little about what they are doing. But the solution of more rigorous knowledge standards is a step backward. It assumes that a standard of epistemic competence can be established that leads to better-informed policies. Who would make such a determination? What kind of knowledge would be required? And most importantly, how would politicians be made accountable to those citizens supposedly falling below the epistemological threshold?

On this first point, then, excluding children from voting imposes another kind of double standard. Once you turn eighteen, you are forever liberated from having to know anything. Before eighteen, you are forever ruled out because of the knowledge you are presumed to lack. The reality is that children know a great deal. Youth gun activists understand better than most the impacts of gun legislation on mental health. Queer youth well grasp the complexities of the sexual identity politics they have to deal with every day. Younger people often better understand the realities and stakes of the climate crisis, the most important political issue of our time. What knowledge exactly are these young people supposed to lack? If democracies insisted on higher knowledge levels than these, there would be very few adults left who could vote. But in fact democracies make no such knowledge requirements. Or, if knowledge is so important, children and adults should at least be held to same standards.

One could argue instead that the age of sixteen or eighteen is not an exact cut-off but the best available approximation. Even if it wrongly excludes some knowledgeable children, and wrongly includes some ignorant adults, it still produces more informed outcomes overall. Some kind of age cut-off will produce better results on average.

But this too is unpersuasive. Imagine a hypothetical scenario in which people over seventy-five turned out, on average, due to dementia and general slowing of mental facilities, to fall below a particular threshold of political knowledge. More than 50 percent cannot remember who the prime minister is, name all branches of government, and explain the phrase "black lives matter." Would it be fair in this situation, once sufficient proof had been established, to disenfranchise everyone over seventy-five? Just because the political understanding of this age group is insufficient on average? Clearly not. It would obviously not be just to those in this age group who happen to know enough. But more importantly, it would be counterproductive for the body politic. Suddenly politicians would have less reason to care what the elderly need and want. They would also make poorer choices because of the lack of older persons' electoral input. Would the overall knowledgeability of the electorate nevertheless be higher? No. Because an entire segment of the population would now be excluded from the conversation.

The same is the case, but in actual reality, for children. It is unjust to exclude politically knowledgeable children from voting just because children on average are thought to be less politically knowledgeable than adults. A highly knowledgeable ten-year-old who wanted to vote should not be disenfranchised simply because other ten-year-olds are not. This is especially unfair because we do not know how knowledgeable the average ten-year-old would be if children could in fact exercise a vote. There is no way to measure average ten-year-old's voting knowledge since no ten-year-old has ever had the slightest reason to develop it.

More importantly, by excluding children from voting, democracies exclude as well whatever knowledge children have to contribute. Barring an entire group from the franchise actually weakens, rather than strengthens, the sum of democratic knowledge. It leaves out vital perspectives on education, health care, climate change, and virtually every issue on which policymakers need to be informed. Banning children from suffrage simply because they might not have enough knowledge ends up diluting and distorting the democratic knowledge pool. It unnecessarily eliminates vital knowledge input.

A related difficulty with the knowledge argument is that it assumes that adults can be presumed sufficiently knowledgeable in the first place. However, study after study has shown quite the opposite. Most adults lack even the most basic political understanding, let alone detailed conceptions of policies and laws.

Take the United States as an example. A 2017 survey found that only 26 percent of US adults could name the three branches of its government. This is perhaps the most basic formal knowledge one could ask for, and three-quarters of US adults lack it. Another survey showed that only 36 percent would pass the minimal test required of immigrants to become citizens. Only 21 percent can name either of their two state senators, and only 25 percent know their length of term in office. Far fewer adults likely know who is their elected state comptroller or railroad commissioner or even what they do. One sophisticated statistical analysis found that "25 percent of the American electorate vote directly against their own opinions ... [making them] extremely ill suited to make an informed political choice." That is almost the same number of adults in the United States as there are US children in total.[5]

And it is not just Americans. A quick look around the world offers no shortage of disappointing material. At the time of this writing, four of the seven current elected leaders of the world's largest democracies are Narendra Modi, Donald Trump, Jair Bolsonaro, and Rodrigo Duterte—leaders not known for their great minds or highly informed policies. The UK voted in 2016 for a Brexit from the European Union with very little understanding of its consequences and against the vocal opposition of virtually all experts. In 1933, 43.9 percent of German voters handed control of their country to the raging maniac Adolf Hitler. All last six presidents of Peru have been indicted or jailed for corruption. The list goes on and on. And we have not even started on the lower levels of government, where voters know even less and representatives might be even dumber. Clearly, adults worldwide often make profoundly uninformed voting choices.

Democracies put up with ignorance and stupidity because the alternative would be worse. The moment someone imposes voting knowledge requirements, democracies become less democratic. They slide back toward aristocratic tyranny. It is at the very least unjust that knowledge requirements should be imposed on children alone when they are so evidently lax when it comes to adults. The latitude granted to adults should be granted to children as well. The genius of democracy is that deliberately refusing to impose knowledge requirements on the whole leads to more knowledgeable decisions. The nightmare of autocracy is that preselecting the knowledge that is allowed to count leads to policy ignorance and suffering.

Another problem with voting knowledge requirements is that, just as with competence skills, they cannot be sharply defined. Political life is complex and multifaceted. It is as complex and multifaceted as human societies overall. Political knowledge is built upon many decades and centuries of political experience and struggle. It touches every aspect of human relations. It is about values, cultures, relationships, power, personal convictions, and much else that cannot be pinned down in a simple formula. And, just as importantly, democratic knowledge is about change: embracing new ideas and experiences that had previously not been considered. Equal pay for women was historically dismissed by men (and women) as a bad idea until relatively recently.

It is difficult to define even basic formal requirements. How much should a voter know, for example, about the specific powers of their prime minister or president, both the main ones and the more obscure or even secret ones? How much should one know about the responsibilities and possibilities of national and local legislators? To what extent ought voters understand candidates' political platforms? Does this include their views on international fishing rights? On statehood for Puerto Rico? On top of all this, what level of knowledge should be required about existing policy and law? About the ins and outs of labor law, education policy, military regulation, decisions of the justice system, and so on *ad infinitum*. Nobody can know everything. Politicians themselves can only know a fraction. How much, then, is the necessary minimum to be an informed voter?

But this is only the beginning. How much should a voter know as well about larger political forces like macroeconomics, national banking, health-care systems, and global markets? About the legal details of labor policy, deficit spending, and tax law? How much about different parties' views on family policy, abortion law, queer rights, religious freedoms, and farming protections? What basic minimum should be known about climate treaties, contributions to the World Health Organization, foreign policy on North Korea, and nuclear weapons agreements? Governments engage with laws, policies, analyses, and interpretations of just about every aspect of human existence. Even the most informed voters cannot hope to understand more than one or two tips of the iceberg.

And, most important of all, how much can any one voter know about the informal side of politics: the opinions of other citizens, the impacts on different groups of various policies, the historical currents driving rural and urban differences, local political attitudes, diverse experiences of gender and race, and so on and so on? Informal voting knowledge is so vast and deep that no one person could even know how much they are unaware of. Others' experiences of political life are by definition to a large extent unknowable. It is simply not possible to see politics fully through another's eyes. It is impossible even to see it clearly through one's own.

There is, then, no clear or precise way to define the knowledge that should be required for suffrage. To say that children lack the knowledge to vote is to make the false assumption that this knowledge can be accurately delineated. If everyone can be counted on to have enough knowledge by the age of eighteen, and if everyone under eighteen more than likely does not, then the definition would have to be very specific indeed.

But it is evident that the knowledge needed to vote cannot be pinned down with anything close to this level of exactitude. It is not clear that it can be pinned down at all. Or that in a democracy it should. On the whole, it is discriminatory to insist on a specific voting knowledge, especially if defined by one or another particular age. It would be much more democratic to admit that voting knowledge, whatever it may be, has little to do with how many years a person happens to have resided on the planet.

Indeed, the knowledge required for voting is ultimately impossible to define because elections themselves are about defining what counts as political knowledge in the first place. Voting exists to generate better understandings of the people's experiences and concerns. Voting is less a mechanism for expressing knowledge than it is one for generating it. It is how the political space itself is shaped. Different people view different things as important to understand. Libertarians focus on free markets, leftists on social inequalities, rightists on historical cultures, greens on the environment. Each perspective defines what counts as political knowledge differently. Political knowledge is not a prerequisite for joining the debate but the subject of the debate itself.

Were there in fact a basic kind of knowledge needed to vote, what would it be? Going back to first principles, it would consist in whatever is required to hold the political system accountable to the people. And what is truly required for the people's rule is not formal knowledge of democratic procedures but informal knowledge of grassroots experiences.

This knowledge involves three things. First, you have to understand yourself as a political being, as someone who occupies a democratic space. I live in Philadelphia, a large city in a large country shared by hundreds of millions of people. A newborn here does not know this. It takes time to understand that one lives in a broader political environment, that there are elected leaders at various levels responsible for shared decisions, and that the laws and policies they develop impact all the people. Everyone is part of a public policy arena that both impacts their lives and owes them political consideration.

Probably there are few adults who lack this elemental political knowledge. But probably also there are few children and youth who lack it as well. Knowledge of oneself as a political being does not arise in everyone at the same age or indeed at any single discrete age at all. Even if it did, this age would be much lower than sixteen or eighteen. Six-year-old labor organizers in Peru clearly understand themselves to exist within a broad political environment. This shows that most six-year-olds anywhere could in principle do the same. Knowledge of oneself as a political being in not a matter of age but arrives in different individuals at different times and in different ways.

Second, political knowledge involves understanding that people live in political relation to one another. One might wonder about adults in this regard. But, to be generous, let us say that even the most politically selfish and uncurious of adults at least probably realize that they are being selfish and uncurious, which implies knowledge of others of a sort. Broadly speaking, voters should understand that their political choices impact others and not just themselves. This is part of living democratically. Others' lives are impossible to understand fully. No one has more than a partial view of others' experiences. But to some extent, at least, voting assumes some knowledge of how one's political choices might affect other people in one's environment.

It would be difficult to argue that political knowledge of others is absent in most children. It is possible that time and experience in the world could broaden this kind of understanding. But it is also possible that growing older might make one's understanding more narrow and rigid. As the psychologist Alison Gopnik writes,

> We used to think that babies and young children were irrational, egocentric, and amoral. ... In fact, psychologists and neuroscientists have discovered that babies not only learn more, but imagine more, care more, and experience more than we would ever have thought possible.[6]

The mind of an infant or young child is not just a lesser version of the mind of an adult. Rather, it is a highly complex organ that in one way or another allows one to engage with and care about others in the world.

Many children have great concern for the poor and the sick and a high level of understanding of queer and transgender people, ethnic minorities, and of course other young people. Some adults fail to recognize their own sexism or xenophobia and may have less understanding than children of issues involving social media, climate change, and again young people. Older people are not necessarily more aware of the political interests of others. They might, for example, have forgotten what it is like to be a child. They might be intolerant of different races and alternative genders. Indeed, the sheer capacity of young people to better understand young people themselves should alone qualify them as sufficiently politically knowledgeable about others.

All that can be said for certain is that there is no clear measuring stick for political knowledge of human relations. Children do not suddenly one day start possessing understanding of others like they might possess a new car. Nor does this knowledge grow in clearly marked phases over the lifecycle. Rather, knowledge of others is based on a vast multitude of types of experience in the world. Children and youth experience the world in just as many ways as do adults. If they have been in the world for less time, this does not discount the value of the time they have had. If time were the measure, then seventy-year-olds should have twice the votes of 35-year-olds. The fact is that everyone's political knowledge of others is different. There is no clear division between people who understand others and people who do not.

And third, political knowledge involves understanding that political life is open to different interpretations. Even the same political experiences can be understood in diverse ways. Different people bring to the table not only different life experiences but also different ways of thinking about and assessing them. A coal miner can see that while for them coal mining is a livelihood, for others it is a threat to the environment. A corporate CEO can understand that what is hard-earned wealth in their eyes looks like undertaxed excess to others. Every voter ought to know that their own and others' actions and beliefs may be looked at from a variety of different perspectives. Lived experience is in part socially constructed. Voters ought to understand that different people's lives are not only different but also differently interpreted.

It is again difficult to pinpoint, however, exactly how much knowledge of alternative interpretations should be required to have the right to vote. Such knowledge is particularly difficult to define. One's own interpretive lenses get in the way of understanding the interpretive lenses of others. A rabid nationalist may simply not be able to grasp a globalist's orientation to the world. And vice versa. No one can escape their own frames of reference fully. No one ever fully understands the worldviews of others. All of us interpret our political environments from distinct and limited angles of vision.

Nevertheless, it seems again clear that this kind of knowledge does not suddenly arrive with one or another age of maturity. Even very young children know that others' political perspectives are different from their own. Black Lives Matter protestors of any age know that they are opposing the views of others that are racist. Children living in poverty can most likely see that others with great wealth may not understand their experiences. By interpreting the world yourself, you realize that others interpret it differently. Such knowledge would be difficult to pin down to one or another age, as it lacks a clear threshold definition. No one is really in a position to decide what it should be as everyone is limited in this regard as well.

And, of course, barring the interpretations of children from the political realm impoverishes the interpretations of adults. It makes adults more likely to subject children's experiences to oversimplification. Adults will tend to assume that all children are living similar lives. And they will not be confronted with the different angles of vision that young people bring. Adult-only democracies are flying a third blind. They deny themselves vast stores of knowledge about political experiences and ideas.

It would be difficult to argue that more is required for suffrage than these three kinds of knowledge, all of which can be found in most children. An individual needs to know that they are a political being living in relation to others with diverse interpretations of the shared political space. It is this grassroots knowledge that is the engine of an informed democracy. It is all that can be demanded for a person to contribute to holding politicians accountable to the people. Any additional knowledge requirements would have to be imposed only for strong and exceptional reasons. And they would have to help make democratic knowledge more rather than less responsive to the people's diversity of lived experiences. In no case do knowledge requirements legitimately bar the young.

Not only do children and youth possess sufficient political knowledge to vote, but their political knowledge is necessary for a functioning democracy. Democracies would be significantly better informed if the experiences and interpretations of a third of their members were equally represented.

Consider just one example of the kind of knowledge children would bring. The public elementary school down the road from my office, Cooper's Poynt Family School, serves children in one of the poorest cities in the state of New Jersey. Seventy-three percent of the students, aged five to fourteen years, come from low-income families, and 55 percent are Hispanic, 42 percent African American. Only 11 percent of its students are at a proficient grade level in English language arts, and only 9 percent in math (compared to 53 and 43 percent, respectively, statewide). A mere 49 percent will eventually graduate from high school, and less than 1 percent as "college ready" (compared to 93 and 43 percent statewide). These young people are agentic, resilient, and empowered. They turn up to school eager to learn. But they are growing up against the headwinds of deep poverty and racial segregation that severely limit their educational opportunities.

Most US adults have only a glancing understanding of what it is like to attend a school like Cooper's Poynt. Politicians in particular are generally quite well-off. The average voter can easily forget that they share a political space with children who are denied many of the most basic economic and educational resources. And there is nothing to stop them reducing such children's lives to facile interpretation. But with a vote, each child at Cooper's Poynt would have the chance to make their own experiences better known on the political stage. They could make it clearer what it means to grow up in this particular environment and why their school is failing. They won't thereby solve all the profound issues affecting them. But they would be able to offer their own interpretations of what might be done to make improvements. At the very least, politicians' calculations would have to take their distinct experiences more centrally into account.

Enfranchising children like the students at Cooper's Poynt would add to rather than subtract from democratic knowledge. Much that children experience and understand about politics is the same as for adults. Just as it is for men and women, majorities and minorities, the rich and the poor. But distinct social groups also bring to political life knowledge that is different. They introduce information that other social groups cannot necessarily access or can easily ignore. As Richard Farson said long ago, "adults neither share a child's conceptions or values, nor do they assess the problems of the world in the same way."[7] A child's interpretation of an education system is not going to be identical to that of an adult. Nor is a child's interpretation of poverty, discrimination, racism, community policing, juvenile justice, or health care. Children bring to public issues their own distinct experiences and points of view.

It is generally thought that adults can represent children's perspectives in politics better than children can themselves. But in reality, no group can put themselves fully in the shoes of others. Men cannot properly represent women, nor the rich the poor. Why? Because however smart and informed a person may be, they cannot possess the same fund of lived experiences that makes up the political life of another person. Each of our lives is unfathomably complex and multifaceted. We have distinct events that shape us, unique personalities, diverse identities, particular cultures, discrete social environments, and different historical contexts. Growing up under identical circumstances but thirty years later is still very different. Living through a pandemic as a child is different from living through a pandemic as an adult. And experiences are endlessly diverse as well within each group. None of us can in fact fully understand even ourselves. As a consequence, adults cannot hope to represent the experiences of children adequately because children, like adults, are distinct and diverse human beings.

Democracies make ill-informed choices if they bar entire groups from even coming to the table. When the poor, minorities, and women gained the vote, it broadened democracies' understandings of the people and so enabled them to make much improved policies. The women's vote, for example, helped to usher in public support for families and the elderly, more equitable workplaces, greater investments in health and education, stronger policies against violence and discrimination, and a great deal else. These advances drew on new areas of human experience that had previously been considered irrelevant to the political sphere. And the benefits accrued not only to women but also to the entire electorate. The inclusion of previously disenfranchised groups adds new knowledge that better informs the political imaginations of all.

Children's political knowledge is needed not only to improve policy but also to make democracies democratic. Children and youth are just as impacted by democratic decisions as are adults. Yet, without the vote, their knowledge remains optional rather than required for democratic consideration. It influences political life only at the pleasure of adults. Were children enfranchised, politicians would be forced to account for their grassroots experiences as much as for those of adults. That is, they would be forced to account for them democratically. Children like those at Cooper's Poynt would gain a small measure of power to add their voices despite being marginalized by poverty, race, age, and other factors. Representatives will do a better job of representing their constituents if they are directly accountable to them. They would, to some degree, have to consider the experiences of the people as a whole.

Democracies should seek out as wide and diverse a field of knowledge as possible. No voter understands everything, even about their own experiences. The beauty of democracy is that it does not require anyone to know everything. It is not rule by the *aristos* or "the best." Rather, it is structured to respond to the people's wealth of differences. No person or group can be expected to possess all the knowledge needed to exercise political power responsibly. The political space is unfathomably diverse. Rather, those who hold power must be made as beholden as possible to the full plurality of the people. If children lack knowledge, this is not because they are children but because it is the human condition. Democracies are built on a foundation of ignorance. That is, they rest on the idea that no one knows everything. Their life source is the many differences that together constitute the human community.

Children's voting is therefore not just an optional nicety but a democratic necessity. Representatives can do their jobs only if they are equally pressured by children's contributions. They need the distinct data that children's knowledge brings. Only by being accountable to everyone's ideas can politicians match policies to the actual range of constituents' interests. As one argument for child suffrage puts it, "voting is a method to distribute power. It is a way to guarantee that the people who really are deciding on the laws, the elected officials, do not forget to consider all interests equally."[8] If children could vote, politicians would have not only more information to use but also more reasons to use it democratically. They would no longer be incentivized to ignore the children at Cooper's Poynt, those afraid of being gunned down in school, those concerned about their climate futures, or those traumatized by racism. Their responsibilities would better match up with the people they are responsible to. Instead of being forced to favor adults in order to keep their jobs, they would be freed to give equal consideration to everyone.

And it is the same for voting adults. If adults wish to vote in informed ways, they need to consider the full range of political perspectives and not just some. As it stands, adult voting choices are biased toward the interests of adults. It is only other adults who formally influence debates. But imagine if adults had to consider how children might vote as well. It would impel them to understand what children are truly experiencing across society. It would transform climate, poverty, and education concerns and bring them from the periphery to the center of political life. And it would change every other political discussion as well. Adults really do care about children, but current democratic incentive structures force them to give greater consideration to adults than to children. Adult voters would finally be able to give all perspectives equal weight and know that they are not part of a system of children's subordination.

Current assumptions about democracy have led us to misunderstand the nature of democratic knowledge. The knowledge needed to vote has come to be interpreted in a way that unfairly marginalizes children and youth. The idea that voters should be experts in formal government systems is a throwback to the Enlightenment rule by educated men.

It presumes there is some definable threshold of public knowhow. It presumes that political space is only for the formally trained.

But the true knowledge needed for democratic voting is very different. It consists in understanding one's own and others' lived political experiences. It lies in difference, diversity, and the ordinary struggles of life. This grassroots rather than elite political knowledge is what democracies are specifically designed to respond to. It makes up the information for which representatives should actually be held accountable. Yes, there is formal knowledge of how governments work in practice. But this is only the mechanism for drawing together the much more important informal knowledge of what the people actually experience and think.

Democracies do not conform knowledge to politics, but instead politics to knowledge. A true democracy does not define the knowledge that counts ahead of time but generates it through multisided dialogue. There is no legitimate bar of knowledge other than what is needed to participate in the democratic conversation. Any knowledge is valuable that empowers democracy to respond to the fullness of the people. This is why democratic knowledge cannot be clearly measured or defined. The knowledge needed to vote is knowledge of one's own and others' lived experiences of the political space. The democratic commonwealth is the common wealth of knowledge.

Children's political knowledge is therefore one of the most important reasons they should be given the right to vote. Democracies need to hear from the widest possible diversity of participants. Politicians need to be pressured by the full range of the people whose lives they impact. And voters need to feel accountable to all the others in their political environment and not just certain groups. Only when all can vote can democratic life hope to become democratically informed.

4

Power

The measure of a man is what he does with power.

Plato

The landmark 1969 Supreme Court case *Tinker v. Des Moines* guaranteed all children in US public schools full protection of their rights to freedom of speech. It affirmed that students have the same First Amendment free speech rights as adults both outside and inside school settings. Just as for adults, children's free speech can be curtailed by schools only if it causes significant harm or disruption to themselves or others.

But in today's digital age, many US public schools are monitoring their students' free speech online. In some cases, they are disciplining or expelling students as a result. Some school districts hire surveillance companies to intervene when a student's social media account outside school time mentions terms like "protest" or "walkout." Others monitor online posts for what they consider suspicious behavior and have expelled students for such things as "holding too much money" or making dance poses resembling "gang-related messages." These policies are often applied disproportionately to minorities. In one particularly ironic example, a school suspended two African American students for reposting a video on social media of a white classmate using a racial slur.[1]

Children's free speech illustrates another important question about voting (Figure 4). This is the question of power. Should adults as a group have special power over children as a group when it comes influencing societies? Should adults as a whole have greater freedoms of speech and assembly? Is there a difference between the exercise of influence in areas like family, school, and work, where greater adult rights may sometimes be justified, and the broadly systemic exercise of influence in politics? Is voting a special kind of free speech right that only adults should have the power to use?

One could argue that even if children have the competence and knowledge to vote, they should still not wield its enormous power. And especially not over adults. Although any particular voter in a democracy has only a tiny fraction of power, voters as groups can exercise significant influence over each other. Women gaining the vote gave power to women's concerns insofar as they belonged to women as

Figure 4 Swedish environmental activist Greta Thunberg speaks at the Climate Action Summit at the 74th General Debate at the UN General Assembly, September 2019. Photo by Jemal Countess/UPI. Credit: UPI/ Alamy Live News.

a distinct political bloc. In the case of children, would it be right and fair for children as a group to exercise this same power over adults?

There are two main objections to children holding voting power.

Some say that children's suffrage would give them *too much* power over adults. Young people do not have as much experience in the world as their elders and generally do not bear the same responsibilities. Therefore, while young people may have the perspective to express their own interests, they do not have the right to rule as a group over the interests of adults. Children might make demands of adults that adults should not have to accept.

Others see an opposed problem. They see children's voting as actually giving them *less* power over adults. This is because children's suffrage could expose them to the power of adult manipulation. It could reduce young people's real political influence by making them instruments of the adults around them. It could decrease rather than increase their political agency. Minors as a group may lack the life experience to resist undue influence from parents, teachers, business leaders, media influencers, cultural figures, and politicians. Voting would decrease rather than increase children's collective influence in democratic life.

Both objections can be maintained at the same time. It is possible for children to wield too much power over adults as a collective group, and too little as individuals. They could simultaneously have too much influence while being overly manipulated. An even scarier proposition.

This chapter explains why such concerns are misguided. Children deserve equal voting power to everyone else. Indeed, the main point of suffrage would be to grant children equal political influence. It would give young people as a group the right to make their voices heard as much as adults on climate change, poverty, racism, education, and any other issue that impacts their world. Children's suffrage would provide only one very specific right, the right to hold politicians accountable to their experiences. Young people are much less powerful than adults in most areas of life. The real problem of children voting is not that they might gain too much power but that they might not gain enough to give their collective experiences equal weight. Democracies need to become more childist or child-responsive, not less. They need to empower children to subject them to structural transformation. The best solution to children being unduly influenced by adults is not to deny them the vote but to make it firmly established.

Children's voting would give them exactly the right amount of political power: the power of one vote for one person. This should be a central principle of any democracy. That so many are excluded should be cause to question existing power structures. Children's suffrage would ensure that, at least in principle, representatives are held equally accountable to all the people they are supposed to represent. In this way, young people as a whole would gain a chance to advance their otherwise far too easily marginalized concerns.

There might seem to be something basically unfair about the idea of the ten-year-old down the street contributing as much to major decisions over my life as I do over theirs. Adults have responsibilities to work, provide for their families, educate children, contribute to their communities, and even defend their country, responsibilities that the child down the street typically does not shoulder. This increased responsibility is why adults exercise power over children in many facets of life: as parents, teachers, workers, and much else. Politics, from this perspective, is no different. Voting is for adults because only adults can use its power responsibly.

In political philosophy, this idea is known as government paternalism. Government paternalism means that politics can be conducted without the consent of the governed if it either protects them from serious harm or provides them significant benefit. People have to wear seat belts whether they like it or not. They are prohibited from stealing and murder. They are forced to pay taxes because this funds larger social goods. Sometimes they are even required to serve in the military. In a democracy, these decisions are ultimately made by the people. But the people are still paternalistically required to follow the decisions made.[2]

Adult-only voting can be defended as an instance of government paternalism. Adults deserve the exclusive right to vote because this better protects children from harm and better provides for their benefit. Adult-run democracies have funded children's education, ensured children's vaccinations and health care, protected children from sexual abuse and marriage, removed children from violent homes, and limited children's rights to make self-harming medical, sexual, and other decisions. Adult political power over children exists for children's own good.

What is more, one can argue that adults are likely to comprehend children's interests more fully than the other way round. Adults have experienced childhood, but children have not experienced adulthood. Those controlling government need to be able to understand the interests of others. Even if children know what is best for themselves, they are not in a position to make decisions that are best for adults. My ten-year-old neighbor lacks the life experience to decide what would protect me from harm and advance my interests. They lack the perspective to exercise power over such things as tax rates, sending adults to war, higher education funding, women's protection from domestic violence, the legality of abortion, and much else. Children cannot responsibly exercise government paternalism over adults.

This critique of children's voting gets to the heart of the argument in this book. I have claimed that children should have the right to vote because this is the only way for them to hold power over the politicians who affect their lives. Children should have the power to pressure representatives to respond to children's interests. But the objection now being raised is that, while it may be fine for children to demand government accountability, it is not fine for children also to govern over adults. Children cannot know what accountability to adults really means. Voting would endow children with not only redress for their own concerns but also a shared rule over the concerns of everyone else. And most of those others are adults who carry much broader responsibilities in the world.

This critique is also a key challenge in another sense. I have suggested that children's voting rights are more like free speech rights, which children generally hold, than rights to such things as marriage and working, which they generally do not. But it can be argued that a key difference between free speech and voting is that the latter exercises a direct, rather than an indirect, power over others. Free speech is certainly powerful, but it does not itself determine law and policy. Protesting against new oil pipelines is different from actually electing anti-pipeline representatives. Even if one agrees that free speech should be universal, one could still argue that voting should be limited only to those capable of taking on such a responsibility on behalf of all. Children should have free speech but not the power to govern over adults.

One difficulty with these arguments is that they misunderstand how power in democracies actually functions.

In the first place, voting power is never direct but always indirect. It does not give anyone immediate power over anyone else. Rather, it aggregates power in the hands of a group of common representatives. You vote for the people you think will best use power over everyone. Even so-called direct democratic referenda themselves are overseen by representatives and enacted within the bounds of democratically established law. What is "direct" in a democracy is not the power held by citizens over each other, but the power held by citizens over representatives. Only in nondemocratic forms of government, like aristocracies and oligarchies, do the powerful hold direct power over particular citizens. Children's voting would give them direct power not over adults but over the political representatives whose job it is to represent them anyway.

This idea of indirect power has been central to democratic life since its inception. Ancient Athenian democracy forced ruling aristocrats to stop directly imposing their will on the citizens and, instead, start indirectly implementing the will of (at least some of) the citizens themselves. The medieval English parliament deliberately handed its own power to the people at large in order to limit the unchecked power of the king. The American and French Revolutions created systems of power in which politicians are forced to do the will of the people. A democratic representative is by definition someone whose power the people can take away.

Politicians are not empowered by voters to press the interests of any one special group over others. Rather, they are empowered to advance the greatest good of the people as a whole. According to the political theorist Michael Cummings,

> Listening to children does not spoil them, nor does it mean that children automatically get their way—just as a citizen's right to vote does not entitle him or her to carry the day politically. Rather, listening to children incorporates their voices into the dynamic creation of popular sovereignty that is a defining component of a democratic polity.[3]

Politicians are supposed to act on behalf of the people broadly rather that narrowly. They are even supposed to act on behalf of nonvoters, including not only children but also adults who don't care to vote, resident noncitizens, future generations, people impacted in other countries, animals, and even the natural environment. All affected by policy decisions are supposed to be taken into account. Democratic voting is not a means for one group to wield power over other groups. It is a means for indirectly sharing power among all.

Democracy still functions this way today. The fact that women can vote does not mean that women have direct power over men. It means that men no longer have direct power over women. Women and men now equally share in exercising power in common. Women's voting means that their concerns are made equally important in the eyes of their democratic representatives, whose jobs depend on satisfying adults of all genders instead of just one. Far from enabling women to rule over men, women's suffrage helps to bring about more just policies for all. It pressures policy-makers to consider both male and female perspectives when it comes to social security legislation, public health care, funding for education, protections against abuse and discrimination, equal pay laws, abortion rights, and so on. These gains serve all, not just women. The power women gained with suffrage was not to rule over men but to pressure representatives to rule more representatively. Since politicians were supposed to account for women's interests anyway, women's suffrage simply restructured the power dynamics in a way that would make this more likely to happen in reality.

Children's voting would have the same effect. It would provide children not a direct power over adults' lives but an indirect power to make their concerns equally heard. It would not empower the child down the street to tell me how to do my job or raise my family. Rather, it would make it more likely that work and families in general are governed in child-friendly ways. It would not enable children to send adults to war, only to weigh in on whether war is a good idea in the first place. It would not even force schools to respect children's rights to free speech, but instead force policy-makers to think harder about free speech rights themselves. Like women, the poor, and every other previously enfranchised group, children and youth would play a role in determining which representatives are likely to make the best decisions for the community as a whole.

The power to vote, in short, is not direct but indirect. Democracy is not a zero-sum competition. My gaining this power does not take it away from you. Nor does it put you under my thumb. Rather, voting is additive. It gives people the right to participate in collectively shared governance. It gives one a voice in the common political space. And it helps to ensure that marginalized groups are at least heard. Democracy pulls off this trick because it transfers power from a ruling elite to ruling representatives. Power is then exercised indirectly via the people's ruling agents. Children's voting would give them the same indirect power as other groups to pressure policy-makers, not to prioritize them over others, but to take into account the full range of the people's concerns.

In addition to being indirect, children's voting would not give them power over adult responsibilities they cannot understand. People with many responsibilities do not have more votes than people with only a few. Democracies are purposely agnostic about voters' levels of societal responsibility. The head of the Bank of England has the same number of votes as the janitor who sweeps its floors. The relevant experience needed for voting has nothing to do with responsibilities, importance in society, or status in the world. It has to do only and exactly with whether one is impacted by political decisions. Apart from necessary exceptions, everyone should get one vote regardless of how much responsibility they happen to have in the rest of their lives.

The idea that adults understand childhood but children do not understand adulthood assumes that childhood is universal and unchanging. But in reality, all childhoods are different. Even an adult's past childhood is different than a childhood now. Every person lives a distinct life under distinct circumstances. Everyone's experience of the world and politics is unique. The basic unit of a democracy is the person, pure and simple. It is a fiction for adults to assume that they already know about children's experiences simply because they were children once themselves. On the contrary, this may make adults more likely to oversimplify children's worlds. Or to think they grasp the full diversity of children's lives much more than they actually can.

If children do not understand everything about adulthood, neither do adults understand everything about childhood. Adults do not even understand each other's adulthoods. No voter comprehends another's life fully, let alone the lives of entire other groups. The rich do not know everything about being poor, men about women, Hindus about Muslims, or city dwellers about farmers. Doctors have different responsibilities than cooks, parents than grandparents, activists than politicians. Likewise, adults' lives are different in many ways from children's. This diversity of life experiences is precisely the strength of a democracy over other forms of government. Life differences are the meat in the democratic pie.

The mere fact that children may not understand adulthood, even if true, is wholly irrelevant. Men do not understand everything about the experiences of women, but that does not mean men should be banned from voting. A garment factory worker in the slums of Delhi may know very little about the lives of wealthy financiers in Mumbai, but this is utterly unimportant when it comes to their suffrage. Farmers in Ohio may not know much about theater directors in New York, or vice versa, but this does not cancel either group's right to vote. All that is important is whether one occupies the same political space.

The power that children and youth would gain by voting is, rather, something adults and politicians should welcome. Far from disempowering adults, it would empower them to act with greater understanding and responsibility. They would be able to make wiser voting choices based on expanded understandings of experiences they previously did not consider. Rather than having to guess about impacts of policies on children's lives, adults would gain vast new data sets of information about them. Better knowledge about childhoods would help adults vote in more informed ways. It would also better inform other adult responsibilities as parents and workers. Most importantly of all, politicians would be able to wield their vast powers with the knowledge that they are making broadly rather than narrowly responsible choices.

Children should have voting power, then, because it would pressure politicians to take children's experiences equally into account. As it currently stands, children can only influence political life through informal means like free speech and assembly. But as every other group in history has learned, such participation is never enough to actually change political dynamics. Real change depends on the formal power to enforce government accountability. The formal power to vote would not give children a direct power over adults but rather an indirect power to have their interests equally represented. The current adult-only system leaves a significant gap in the influence of the people over governance. Only a universal vote distributes power universally.

Another reason young people should not be denied the power to vote is that it is discriminatory. Discrimination is an abuse of power. It imposes a dominant group's perspective on a historically marginalized group to keep that group in its place. Banning children from voting, for no other reason than that they are young, uses adult power to discriminate against children's political interests.

The question of discrimination is central to the claims of many child suffragists. In the words of Robert Ludbrook, a lawyer and long-standing director of the National Children's and Youth Law Centre in Sydney, Australia: "Denial of political rights on the basis of an arbitrary age restriction is *prima facie* discriminatory. It should be for those who argue against lowering the voting age to justify their position."[4] Nondiscrimination has served as grounds for gaining voting rights for other groups. This includes minority suffrage campaigns in the United States using the Fourteenth Amendment's clause guaranteeing "equal protection" before the law. It includes first-wave feminist arguments against the abuse of political power by men. One could say, likewise, that it is unjustly discriminatory to be banned from voting simply because of one's age.

Discrimination denies power to groups that are victims of deep-seated historical bias. There is a difference between legitimate and illegitimate voter discrimination. It may be right to ban voting for, say, noncitizens (though this is debatable) on the grounds that they may not have the country's interests at heart. But racial voting discrimination— for example, through gerrymandering or voter suppression—violates a basic human right not to be treated differently for nonrelevant reasons. It takes advantage of historically engrained structures to advance the ends of those already in power. It persists because "whites are taught to think of their lives as morally neutral, normative, and average" and hence the standard against which other lives should be measured.[5] The discriminator uses their inherited power to enforce biases they consider normal.

Voter discrimination is a problem not only because it causes systemic harm but also because it is a significant harm in and of itself. Not having the vote without good reason is a violation of one's basic dignity as a human being. This is the felt experience of many children who would like to vote but cannot. Unless discrimination can be justified for clear and valid reasons, it reduces its target to a second-class citizen without an equal voice. Coloreds who were denied the vote under South African apartheid law had to live under the indignity of being treated thereby as lesser persons. Likewise, people under eighteen are daily told that their voices and concerns do not really count.

To understand children's political discrimination, consider history's most influential human rights document, the UN's 1948 Universal Declaration of Human Rights (UDHR). As previously noted, the UDHR has never been considered by its signatory nations as endorsing children's rights to vote. However, its own words suggest just the opposite. Articles 1 and 2 assert that "all human beings are born free and equal in dignity and rights ... [and] endowed with reason and conscience," and that "everyone is entitled to all the rights and freedoms set forth in this Declaration, without distinction of any kind." Article 7 then declares that "all are equal before the law and are entitled without any discrimination to equal protection of the law." And finally, as mentioned above, Article 21 on voting makes no reference at all to age: "Everyone has the right to take part in the government of his country, directly or through freely chosen representatives ... by universal and equal suffrage."

The logic of the UDHR is crystal clear. Since every human being is "born free and equal in dignity and rights," there can be no discrimination between persons when it comes to taking part in the governance of their country. Specifically, suffrage is a basic human right that must be universal and equal. The world's foundational human rights document strongly supports children's suffrage, at least in theory. And yet, the United Nations has never pressed for children's suffrage. And no country operating on the UDHR's principles of human rights has ever seriously considered ending voting age restrictions.

The best explanation for this disjuncture between the logic and the reality of the UDHR is that the third of human beings who are under eighteen are subject to an invisible discrimination that normalizes the idea that human rights are first of all adult rights. Adults accept without question their own adultist assumptions. They fail to see children as full political beings. If voting rights should not in fact be "universal" but only limited to adults, then signatories to the UDHR should have stated explicitly why. Such a large exception would have to be reasonably justified. Instead, there is a slippage within universal voting rights that is not warranted by the principles of the UDHR itself.

If voting is such a fundamental human right, then exceptions need to be convincingly explained if they are to rise above mere prejudice. The same kind of exceptions would need to be made as about, for example, rights to free speech. Free speech rights are universal and equal unless they cause significant harm to oneself or others, such as in hate speech, slander, libel, and online harassment. It is this kind of reasoning that is called for, both in the UDHR and in any democracy, to legitimately deny voting rights to children. It would have to be laid out clearly why children's voting would cause significant harm to people or societies. There would need to be an explanation for why a human right that is so basic to human dignity is nevertheless to be denied to a third of all humans.

Adult-only suffrage is discriminatory because it robs children of a power they should otherwise be provided as a human right. The exclusion of children is given no justification because it is based on assumptions and prejudices, not facts or reasoning. It is no accident that the UDHR and democratic governments fail to provide explanations for children's voting exclusion that can stand up to actual scrutiny. For no such explanation convincingly exists. As Bob Franklin puts it, "common sense" in this case "is no more than a thinly veiled justification which functions to protect and promote the interests and power of one social group against rival claimants—in this case, the power of adults over children."[6] Adult-only voting need not be defended in the political realm so long as adultist assumptions remain in force.

But the most important reason to give children equal voting power is that, otherwise, their political concerns will not receive equal or just consideration.

In every nation, children find themselves marginalized simply for being children. They lack not just political but many other kinds of influence in their societies. While most adults care deeply about the young, this is not the same thing as being forced to account for their distinctive perspectives in policy and law. Before Greta Thunberg, most adults did not contemplate young people's deep fears around their climate futures. Before Black Lives Matter, many adults remained blind to how systemically children are impacted by racism. Before youth marches for gun rights, US adults generally turned a blind eye to the climate of fear that exists in their schools. Children need the equal power to vote because otherwise their experiences are not equally heard in the public arena.

While many think young people are being taken care of just fine, in fact they face profound disadvantages simply on account of their age. While it is commonplace to recognize how other groups like women, racial minorities, and the poor are marginalized, children are not generally thought of as a socially oppressed group. Even the Convention on the Rights of the Child only mentions discrimination in terms of race, sex, disability, and so on, and not in terms being a child as such. But in reality, children's age often brings with it profound structural disadvantages.

Take for example economics. In most countries in the world—rich and poor, northern and southern, democratic and authoritarian—children are systematically poorer on average than adults. In France, a wealthy country with strong support systems, children zero to seventeen in 2019 had a poverty rate of 11 percent compared with 8 percent for adults eighteen to sixty-five and only 3 percent for adults over sixty-five. In Russia, a less wealthy country, poverty rates are 20 percent for children, 10 percent for adults, and 14 percent for the elderly. In South Africa, they are, respectively, 32, 24, and 20 percent. And globally, 20 percent of children under eighteen live in extreme poverty, compared to only 10 percent of adults. Almost anywhere you live, being a child is strongly correlated with poverty.[7]

Children are systematically poorer than adults largely because of choices made in the political sphere. It used to be the case in Global Northern countries that the poorest group in societies was the elderly; but over the twentieth century, policies were enacted that granted them social security and free health care. Why did the elderly receive more relief than children? One answer has to be that the elderly can vote—indeed are often a highly effective voting bloc—whereas children cannot. Without power over elected representatives, young people systematically lack power over economic policies. However generously adults might wish to fund and support children, the political headwinds blow in the opposite direction. There is little incentive for representatives to fight for children's economic security when so many other issues more directly impact their remaining in office.

A similar negative feedback loop pertains across almost every area of children's lives. Young people frequently enjoy less access to health care than adults and the elderly. In the United States, where most health insurance typically comes from jobs, per capita health expenditure for children up to eighteen is only half that for adults nineteen to sixty-five, and a mere fifth that for adults sixty-five and older (even though they too do not usually work). According to the Anti-Slavery Society, of the approximately eleven million people working in slavery-like conditions around the world, a disproportionate half of them are under eighteen. In 2017, of the 70.8 million people forcibly displaced by persecution, conflict, violence, or human rights violations, children under eighteen constituted around 50 percent. The list goes on and on.[8]

The reasons for children's disproportionate disempowerment are surely complex. But it does not help that they lack equal political power to redress their concerns. This lack of power places children and youth in what could be called a unique *triple bind*. Other marginalized groups are often thought of as facing a double bind, but for the young, there is an added layer of disempowerment because of their age.

The double bind confronting many groups has been well defined by feminists. Marginalized groups like women and racial minorities not only face systemic disadvantages, but they are also systemically denied a serious voice in redressing them. They are not only harmed, but their views on changing societies are assumed to be less worth hearing in the first place. Indeed, as feminists sometimes put it, women's and others' voices are constructed as childlike, as less worthy of public weight.

Children and youth obviously face this double bind just as much as do other groups. But their situation is also worse. Children too are harmed by their marginalized position and denied voices in addressing it. But in addition, they lack common underlying supports of power on which social movements can be built. Unlike women and minority adults, children and youth, in addition to not being able to vote, do not usually earn a living, belong to labor unions, hold positions at universities, run organizations, have access to political office, and much else. To a larger extent than anyone else, children cannot rely on larger organizational structures to support their efforts to empower themselves to redress social harms. On the contrary, their political inclusion typically depends on the ad hoc generosity of adults. It is no wonder, then, that political life frequently puts children's concerns on the back burner.

Children are not only (1) disadvantaged, and (2) marginalized from having a legitimate political voice, but also (3) removed from many of the basic organizational systems that are needed in gaining a voice in the first place.[9]

The right to vote would provide children one particular means for countering this triple bind that disempowers them so profoundly. It would remove some of this third layer of systemic ageist straightjacketing. As one commentator has put it, "by giving priority to a democracy in which each and every person shall have one vote, we begin to construct the conditions in which all citizens, children and adults alike, can claim their fair share of the primary goods of society."[10] Children's voting would force politicians to respond to children's lives, not just out of political generosity, and not even out of a simple sense of equality, but based on the necessity of including children deliberately in systems of power.

Overall, children's suffrage would not provide them too much power over adults but rather the equal power they are due. It would give children the same power that adults already exercise over each other, the power to hold governments accountable to their own lives. It would give them a basic power they are already supposed to have, except now not at the pleasure only of people who are not children themselves. And this power would even empower adults to better understand children's lives and so to make better informed voting choices. Representatives would find themselves equally pressured to account for all their actual constituents, not just the segment of them with formal political rights. And societies as a whole would be able to operate in less discriminatory ways. The power dynamics within democracies would change in such a way as to empower children's equal rather than lesser consideration.

The other objection to children's voting that has to do with power is that it might actually reduce rather than increase their power by exposing children to adult manipulation. If young people could vote, so the argument goes, they would find themselves beset by political campaigns, interest groups, advertisers, internet falsities, political brand merchants, and all kinds of other means for adults to exert undue political influence. Manipulation could also extend into the home as parents try to influence children with subtle messaging or not-so-subtle threats to vote certain ways by withdrawing allowances, privileges, or respect. And teachers, coaches, and organizational leaders might use their platforms to influence children's political minds. It is precisely because adults have more power in most areas of life that they would be able to bend children's voting behavior toward their own instead of children's best interests.

But this concern about manipulation does not hold up for various reasons.

The first reason is that political manipulation is already practiced by adults on adults without thereby necessitating the elimination of their vote. It is naïve to think that grownups are not susceptible to undue influence. In fact, voters are surprisingly easy to mislead. In the UK, for example, the Brexit vote to leave the European Union in 2016 was shown to have been influenced by a right-wing private company called Cambridge Analytica, founded by Donald Trump's campaign chairman Steven Bannon. This company mined data from fifty million Facebook users to target specific emotional appeals to different kinds of potential Brexit voters. Millions of UK citizens were influenced to vote for Brexit in part by a systematic campaign of targeted misinformation.

That same year in the United States, the presidential contest cost 2.4 billion dollars. On what was all this money spent? On advancing careful and reasoned arguments about alternative policy choices? Hardly. The billions were spent on rhetorical and emotional appeals. Much of it was smears, deceptions, and lies. Indeed, it turned out that millions of voters had been targeted by Russian agents, who were in part responsible for Donald Trump's surprising victory, by feeding voters misinformation about his opponent. Democratic campaigning in the United States is deliberately unrestricted. Within the limits of free speech, it can manipulate voters as much as it likes. Yet this does not mean that anyone should be disenfranchised.

In rural India, as in many poorer parts of the world, political parties routinely buy the votes of their most impoverished constituents. These constituents are desperate for resources. They make the not unreasonable calculation that they have little influence in political life, so they might as well take the money. The manipulation here is self-fulfilling. Politicians know that by ignoring the concerns of marginalized groups, those groups will not see much gain in voting, and so they will remain susceptible to having their votes bought. The powerful can then use the voting system for their own instead of the people's purposes. But even this level of manipulation does not mean that the poor adults involved should accordingly not have the right to vote.[11]

It is also not hard to imagine adults being manipulated within the home. After marriage, husbands and wives tend to vote more similarly than before. Young adults eighteen to twenty-five in the UK vote for the same party as their parents 89–92 percent of the time. Family also places voters into similar cultural, class, and tribal circumstances that themselves influence political ideas. The family you are born into impacts your politics your entire life and much more profoundly than you might like to admit. In wealthy countries throughout the twentieth century, middle-class voters had a strong tendency to vote for left-leaning candidates, working-class voters for right-leaning ones. Perhaps these are not exactly instances of undue influence. But they are certainly instances of influences that are powerful and largely unseen. But deep family ties and histories are not reasons to take away anyone's right to vote either.[12]

There are even undue influences that come into play at the ballot box. Studies show that if voting takes place in a church, people are more likely to vote conservatively; if it takes place in a school, they are more likely to vote liberally. Voting via post, instead of at a physical polling station, significantly increases the likelihood that adults forty-four and younger would vote for far-right candidates, and that adults forty-five and older would not.[13] The mere location of a voting box is hardly a helpful democratic influence.

In these and many other ways, adult voters are already being manipulated by one another or by circumstance, however deliberately or not. No one concludes that they should therefore be stripped of the right to vote. Why? Because no clear line exists between regular and undue influence, between ordinary democratic give-and-take and misleading political manipulation. Is an influence "undue" if it appeals to emotions and sentiment? If it creates brand loyalty to a political party? If it subtly reminds voters of class or ethnic affiliations? If it mines online data for targeted political marketing? If family members threaten to stop speaking to you? Where debate ends and manipulation begins is impossible to define clearly. And it is impossible to know who should get to define it in the first place anyway.

And even if manipulation could be measured, it would not correlate with age. Many adults would need to be barred from voting and many children would need to be included. It would be discriminatory to ban a whole class of persons just because, on average, people their age might be subject to greater undue influence. Perhaps adults with low

IQs are easily manipulable. This would not mean they should be denied suffrage on that account. As Bob Franklin observes regarding children, "to isolate one group within society and insist that they alone should display the mythical qualities of latterday Robinson Crusoes, or else be denied political rights, is unjust."[14] Manipulation offers no hard-and-fast criterion for disenfranchising anyone.

Nor are children uniquely manipulable because of their larger social dependence. Just because children may be dependent on adults in some ways does not mean they are dependent on adults politically. Voting independence is different from economic, emotional, or educational independence. It rests on nothing more than being able to decide how to vote for oneself. To the extent that any of us votes independently, it is because we interpret the various influences upon us in relation to our own particular ideas and values. Children vote independently of adult influence to the extent that they, just like adults, bring distinct life experiences to their voting decisions.

Voting without undue influence does not mean rising above partiality. Perhaps a good mathematician is someone who rises above ordinary ways of thinking about mathematics. Perhaps a good judge is someone who can apply the law especially equitably. Perhaps even a good dog-walker is someone who has greater-than-usual knowledge about dogs. But a good voter is not someone who is particularly expert in voting. A good voter is someone who uses the ballot box to express their own political thoughts and feelings. The only sense in which anyone needs to be impartial and independent enough to vote is that they need to be able to connect political choices to their own particular life.

Britain's *Guardian* newspaper decided to test the idea of children voting by asking six- to twelve-year-olds what policies would get their vote. Six-year-old Wilfie Tudor-Wills argued, for example, that "I think there should be less pollution, because it's bad for your lungs. If I could talk to [Prime Minister] Teresa May I'd tell her to get more people to have electric cars because they're better for the world." Seven-year-old Erica Gourley claimed, "We need to look after homeless people better.

We need to buy food for them and places for them to live." For nine-year-old Tom Ashworth, "climate change is the big issue politicians need to work on. ... We have to stop doing the things that cause climate change. It's really important right now." Eleven-year-old Petra Pekarik argues that "it doesn't make sense to me that Britain is putting up barriers [to immigrants]. I feel the opposite should be happening, and we should be taking barriers away."[15]

Are these children being manipulated or are they speaking independently? Are they being partial or impartial? It is, of course, impossible to say. The most one can suggest is that they do indeed appear to be expressing their own thoughts based on their own experiences. They do not sound, in this regard, particularly different from adults. Presumably there are a variety of political, cultural, and family influences at play in their ideas. But not in more pronounced ways than one would find with anyone else. On the contrary, these children are making policy proposals based on what is important to them.

The idea that children cannot think independently has deep historical roots. The same idea used to justify the disenfranchisement of women, minorities, and the poor. Women were thought to be dependent on men for political understanding. Minorities were thought lacking in democratic values. The poor were thought too stupid or wrapped up in immediate need. But time and again, each new group to gain the franchise has proven just the opposite: that people in general have their own political views and can assert them of their own accord. There is no reason to think that children are any different. As feminists have long insisted, "no persons, actions, or aspects of a person's life should be forced into privacy."[16] There is nothing specific about age that prevents one from having one's own political opinions.

The truth is that children and adults are all in different ways interdependent persons in society. In every area of their lives, everyone is both independent and dependent at once. No one stands wholly on their own two feet in politics or in any other arena of life. Rather, if children rely on parents for money, care, and learning, parents in turn rely on children for continuity, love, and meaning. Children and adults alike depend on larger social structures like clean water supplies, investment in roads, military protection, hospitals, legal rights, available work, and so much more. We depend on each other for moral respect, social relations, and structural inclusion. Sick and older adults rely on caregivers. Unemployed adults need economic protections. And everyone depends on just political policies. No one is purely independent. And no one is purely dependent either.

Children can vote without unusual manipulation because they bring their own independent perspectives to political life. They know what it is like to need an education. They understand why there should be parks, playgrounds, and opportunities for recreation. They have the most to lose from climate policy failures. They possess unique experiences of poverty and blight. They are impacted in their own ways by family violence and dysfunction. They know what it is like to have a parent sent off to war. They are immigrants, cultural ambassadors, and digital natives. They come to politics on their own particular and diverse terms.

In short, democracies do not bar people from voting just because they might be manipulated. Rather, they trust in the people's basic capacities to think and act for themselves. A well-functioning democracy does not ask people to trek alone to the Arctic. Rather, it asks them to build sustainable communities alongside one another. Children should be active participants in this interdependent endeavor. They are part of the political community just as much as anyone else. What really subjects children to undue political influence is *not* being able to vote. This gives adults undue power over them. The best way to reduce children's chances of political manipulation is to give them the vote.

Finally, it is important to look at both sides of the manipulation equation. The concern, after all, is that children might be manipulated by adults. To the extent that adults would indeed unduly influence the votes of children, the cure should surely lie not in the disenfranchisement of the victims but in the better regulation of the perpetrators. It is perverse to prevent children's political manipulation by banning them from the political sphere. You could just as absurdly disenfranchise minorities to prevent racial gerrymandering. As John Holt argues, "a society which had changed enough in its way of looking at young children to be willing to grant them the right to vote would be one in which few people would want or try to coerce a child's vote and in which most people would feel this was a very bad and wrong thing to do."[17] Manipulating voters ought to be deterred by censoring the manipulator, not banning the voter.

Democracies already contain numerous anti-manipulation devices. The secret vote, first developed in ancient Rome, ensures that when a vote is cast, the voter can make any choice they like without external influence. Democracies generally have laws against selling one's vote, precisely to avoid the undue influence of money. Many countries ban political advertising for similar reasons. US code law LII.18.594 imposes a fine or imprisonment on anyone who "intimidates, threatens, coerces, or attempts to intimidate, threaten, or coerce, any other person for the purpose of interfering with the right of such other person to vote or to vote as he may choose." Election observers are used worldwide to ensure fair campaigning, equal voting access, a free press, and nonintimidation by political parties.

To make elections nonmanipulative for children, governments might need to add laws—for example, preventing adults from entering voting booths, ensuring the possibility of mail-in ballots, providing child-friendly assistance with registration, and the like. It would probably help children too if governments reduced the role of money in campaigns, considering that children often have less money to spend on politics. They might more strictly regulate political advertising and internet disinformation. They might ban schools from influencing voting decisions. And they might educate parents about the line between debate and coercion.

But any such step is of a piece with voter protections already in place for adults. When women and other groups became enfranchised, new protections had to be instituted then too, such as against spousal manipulation and threats to cut off support. Any protection of voters against manipulation strengthens democracy for all. Reducing the role of money in campaigns benefits adults and the democratic process itself. In general, anti-manipulation policies make democracies safer, more inclusive, and more democratic.

Voting distributes power. If one group is tempted to manipulate another, the answer is to distribute more power to the victim, not to the perpetrator. Manipulators, by definition, already wield power. Those subject to manipulation already wield less. Voting exists to empower the powerless. If children felt they were being unduly influenced by adults, the best way to respond would be to protect children's voting rights more vigorously. Children are manipulated by adults in being denied the right to vote at all. They are subject to systemic adult control. Compared to not voting, simply being able to vote provides a degree of protection in itself. The answer to children's political manipulation is to give children the vote.

Questions about power take us to the heart of what voting is all about. Voting is not, at its core, an expression of political competence or knowledge, important though these may be. Rather, voting is most basically an expression of political power. It is how the people force policymakers to account for the people's actual lives.

It turns out, on close inspection, that voting would give children neither too much power nor too little. It would no more give children excessive influence over adults than it would give adults excessive influence over children. Rather, voting would provide children exactly the amount of power they should have: the power of one vote for one person. Truly universal suffrage would empower young people, at least in principle, to advance their otherwise frequently marginalized political concerns. These are the goals of voting for everyone. Children should be treated no differently in this regard.

Outcomes for Children

The true character of society is revealed in how it treats its children.
Nelson Mandela

Brothers Hakop and Hasmik Grigorian arrived with their family in Sweden at the ages of eight and nine as war refugees from Armenia. After having lived in Sweden for five years, now aged thirteen and fourteen, their applications for residence were rejected by the Swedish Migration Board, which decided they were to be deported back to Armenia. Under Sweden's asylum law, the boys had not legally resided in the country long enough. In response, as the childhood studies scholar Jonathan Josefsson documents, their schoolmates, teachers, and local community started a petition for them not to be deported and protested outside the Migration Board with signs like "We beg you, let them stay!" Sweden's largest morning newspaper, *Dagens Nyheter*, reported widely on the protests. It quoted a classmate: "We don't get it. Hakop and Hasmik are the nicest, kindest and best friends you could have." Their sister called the decision "naturally quite incomprehensible," pointing out that the brothers speak fluent Swedish, are fully integrated into Swedish society, and "all the family they have left in life live here in Sweden—in Armenia they have nothing."[1]

As the Grigorian brothers found out all too tragically, government laws and policies have real impacts on children's lives. Like much in government, Swedish asylum law is designed primarily with adults in mind. This is no surprise, as the representatives who make the laws are voted in and out of office only by adults. Adult voters and politicians did not account, for example, for the fact that young asylum-seekers are less likely to meet residence requirements because their age makes their time of residency generally shorter. Nor do they see clearly the problem in denying rights to young people who cannot represent their own cases in court. The brothers find themselves caught up in a system that is largely blind to their voices and interests. This blindness is due in no insignificant part to the fact that law and policy are designed with little input from children.

The question asked in this chapter is whether children's voting would lead to better or worse outcomes for children themselves. Even if young people are competent to vote, it could be argued that actually voting would hurt children's interests, rob them of their childhoods, and lead to other rights it would damage them to have. The next chapter considers outcomes for adults and societies at large. But here we ask: If laws have real and sometimes profound impacts on children, would those impacts be improved or worsened if children themselves had some say in choosing the politicians who make them?

My response is that voting rights would not only not harm children but, on the contrary, benefit them greatly. The simple reason is that governments would have to take children's interests much more centrally into account. Every other group in history to gain suffrage—the poor, minorities, women, and so on—has both immediately and in the long run ended up a great deal better off. A real voice in governance forces real political, social, and economic change. It pressures politicians to respond to that group's distinctive and otherwise ignored concerns.

Children's suffrage would have exactly the same effect. It would improve children's lives and positions across all areas of society. And it would do so not by making children just like adults but by giving a voice to what makes children distinct as children. Instead of children's lives becoming adultified, political life would become childified. Democracies would have to subject themselves to critiques, not only of feminism, anticlassism, anti-racism, and the like, but now also of childism, of the particular lived experiences of the young. Politicians would have to take children's long-ignored experiences, like those of the Grigorian brothers and their friends, into equal account. Dominant adult assumptions would be tested, and children would gain a systemic means for rising above their history of second-class citizenship.

The idea that children's voting would hurt them is based on longstanding assumptions about children's natural vulnerability. While on the whole voting is thought to be empowering, for children it is felt to be the opposite. Children are considered better off being protected by adults than being able to influence policy for themselves. The usual logic of voting gets inverted. For adults, the vote gives one's interests a political voice. For children, it is thought to take away one's special status as a protected class.

There are at least three sides to this objection to children's voting.

The first and most obvious way that voting might hurt children is that children might make voting decisions against their own interests. This argument has its roots in the Enlightenment. The founder of modern democratic rights theory, John Locke, asserted that children should have no rights at all, since as prerational beings their exercise of rights would only cause themselves harm. "The necessities of [a child's] life, the health of his body, and the information of his mind would require him to be directed by the will of others and not his own."[2] Rights themselves can belong only to independent and rational adults. Children's voting would allow them to force their immature and irrational desires on themselves and the body politic.

Today, this type of argument no longer holds sway when it comes to most rights besides the right to vote. There are even some rights that children have but adults generally do not, such as to a free education and a family. But the argument is still applied to rights like suffrage. Children obviously benefit greatly from rights against harm and violence, rights for education and social welfare, and even some participation rights such as to freedom of expression and assembly. But participation in actual political power is for many a step too far. Moral philosopher Geoffrey Scarre makes the usual case: "Most adults, because they have lived a long time, have this ability [to plan systematic policies of action and therefore to vote], but children, because their mental powers and experience are inadequate, do not."³ Children might vote for representatives who promise things that are not in children's actual interests: to shorten the school day, lower the driving age, remove parental controls from mass media, and so on. Children's relative lack of experience in the world means they do not understand as well as adults what their best interests really are.

A good illustration is compulsory education. Of course, there are many children around the world desperate for an education, some of whom even work long hours to make the money to pay the fees. But there are also many, perhaps in wealthier countries, who might be desperate to avoid it. Who wants to spend every day forced to sit still in a classroom? It is not beyond the realm of imagination that enough children would vote for politicians who promise to make education optional, at least past a lower age than now. These children might be joined by small government groups that do not wish to be taxed so much to pay for it. And perhaps even by parents who want to send their children out to work instead. In the end, the entire public school system could collapse and generations of children could grow up lacking the skills to sustain a thriving society and polity. Ironically, children's democratic voting could destroy the foundations of democracy itself.

Or, to take another example, children might use their vote to reduce the authority of parents. There are beneficial ways that parental authority can be curtailed, such as by preventing abuse, requiring the provision of nutrition and upkeep, and sharing responsibility after divorce. But what if children started demanding more? They might want the right to divorce their parents themselves (which some in fact have already tried), freedom of movement without parental constraint, abortion at any age without parental consent, prohibitions against parental monitoring of internet use, removal of parents' rights to see school report cards, and so on. The rights of parents over children are many. One could imagine their gradual erosion over time.

This brings us to a second objection. Some claim that the harm to children from voting would come from the act of voting itself. Voting would force children to grow up too quickly. It would rob them of their childhoods by placing too great a burden of responsibility on their shoulders. Young people should be focused instead on play, friends, school, and growing up, not the weighty cares of the world. As a result, children ought to be shielded from voting just as they are shielded from such things as sexuality and work. They should not have to make difficult political decisions about war, poverty, and prison reform or take on concerns about immigration, the climate emergency, or gender injustice. Politics can be too much even for adults. For children, the troubles of society should not interfere with the freedom to spend time growing up and finding one's footing in the world.

This second objection was first raised by the Enlightenment philosopher Jean-Jacques Rousseau, who argued that children should be preserved in a state of noble savage-like innocence. Rousseau believed this temporary child isolation from the world is necessary for a strong and functioning democracy. The young need time to develop what he called "self-love," meaning a secure and authentic understanding of their own thinking and values. If they are forced into public life too soon, children become pliant, unthinking, and corruptible. A fair and rational democracy depends on young people having sufficient time to grow up into democratic reason.

Another way to put this is to say that, by gaining the vote, children would lose their right to be treated as a special political class. The fact that children presently cannot directly influence politics means that adults bear a special responsibility toward them. Universal education, for example, is not something that children ever had to demand; it was given to them by adults because children need it as children. If children could vote, they might lose this privileged status. According to law professor Martin Guggenheim, "a caring society would insist on considering [children's] needs and interests" above their "rights" in order to "treat children as children."[4] If they could vote, young people would instead have to compete with adults on the rough political playing field. And they would likely lose, being less politically experienced and fewer in number.

A third and final objection is that children's voting would create a slippery slope into other rights that children should not have. If children had the right to vote, they might demand other rights that are properly reserved for adults. Why should they not also have rights, for example, to work, make major medical decisions, drive, engage in sex, marry, or serve in the military? Why would there be any special need for juvenile justice, children's hospitals, or rights to special family support? If voting is the foundational right of societies, then nothing in the special realm of children's rights would be off the table.

The legal scholar Katharine Silbaugh makes this claim using the example of juvenile justice. She argues that even lowering the voting age just to sixteen would remove any reason not to treat sixteen-year-olds with adult criminal responsibility. Indeed, even now in the United States, teens who commit serious crimes are sometimes sentenced as if they are adults. Silbaugh calls this process children's "adultification." She points to Greta Thunberg's statement at the 2019 UN Climate Action Summit at the age of sixteen: "I shouldn't be here. I should be back in school. ... You have stolen my dreams and my childhood with your empty words." Children themselves, she claims, wish to be allowed to keep their special status as children. They do not want to be tried as adults or forced into adult responsibilities. "16- to 18-year-olds are entitled to their childhoods, as Greta Thunberg contends, with our protection and support, not the burdens of adult hopes, adult expectations, and adult consequences." While children do have political capacities, the focus should be on their needs as children for protection and support.[5]

Another example is the right to have sex. If children are considered responsible enough to decide about foreign policy, the economy, and the size of government, then they would also by implication have to be considered responsible enough for the right to sex. If they are presumed competent to make laws about sex, they must also be presumed competent to have sex itself. Assuming that votes really count, a vote for a candidate who promises to wage war is much more consequential than a decision to have sex or even get married. The right to vote can have massive consequences for many, while the right to have sex only has consequences for oneself.

According to all three of these objections, even if you consider children competent and knowledgeable enough to vote, children's voting would still be a bad idea because it would lead to children being harmed. Children's voting would result in self-defeating choices, the loss of childhoods, and the gain of rights that should be preserved for adults. The whole point of voting would be defeated. Unlike for adults, the interests of children would not be strengthened but undermined. Societies establish ages of majority because they set up a web of special protections for children that guard them against adult dangers.

A closer look at these objections, however, reveals that they do not hold up. In essence, they have their logics backward. It is true that children have special needs and vulnerabilities. But so also do the elderly, the poor, women, minorities, and everyone else. The best way to protect special interests is not for special groups to be put under the democratic protection of other groups. It is for special groups to have the power to hold politicians accountable to their special concerns. Even if children as a group are more vulnerable than adults in certain respects—a generalization that itself can be put into question—the right to vote would not erase their special interests but elevate and empower them.

We can see this by examining each of the objections above in turn.

The easiest objection to deal with is the first one that children would vote against their own best interests. As we have seen, children are not in fact incompetent and irrational. Given the chance, they can take political life very seriously. They might vote against their own well-being, as also might adults. But the larger purpose of voting is not just to express your concerns. It is to force representatives to understand and respond to the people's lives. Children's voting would place children's experiences at the center rather than the periphery of democratic decisions. It would give children's interests the equal weight they deserve.

Failing to make good decisions is not in itself a reason to be barred from voting. As discussed in previous chapters, adults frequently make terrible political choices. The representatives they vote for are often charlatans, the policies they support regularly self-defeating, and the results frequently harmful both to themselves and to others. The right to vote includes the right to vote badly. It would be elitist and undemocratic to ban a group from voting simply because they might make poor voting choices. At the very least, if making poor choices has to be disqualifying, it should be applied to adults as well. As was said many years ago:

> It is adults who have chosen to pollute their environment with industrial, chemical and nuclear waste, fought wars, built concentration camps, segregated people because of the colour of their skin. ... Since we do not believe that adults should be denied rights [to vote] because they make mistakes, it both inconsistent and unjust to argue for the exclusion of children on this ground.[6]

It is also difficult to define what would count as a harmful voting decision in the first place. Voting itself is a means for measuring what a right decision should be. In a democracy, no one gets to say ahead of time which outcomes are to be preferred. Rather, the right outcomes are what voters have to decide. Banning children for this reason betrays a lack of confidence in the democratic process. Since children have never voted, nobody actually knows what choices they would make. Doubtless, their choices would be just as diversely idiotic as those of adults. Children's parliaments suggest that young people would in many cases vote more wisely than their elders. But in any case, whether children would hurt themselves or not through voting is not measurable with any kind of certainty.

But most importantly, it is certain that children's lives would vastly improve. Such has been the case for every new voting group in history. There are no strong reasons to think the situation would be different for children. On the contrary, children's voting would enable them to make their real experiences and concerns known and to pressure politicians to take them equally seriously. As Richard Farson puts it, at present "children are no one's constituency."[7] Voting would make children a real political constituency. Assuming democracy actually works, at least to some extent, being able to elect one's representatives puts one in a much stronger social position than not being able to.

The idea that children would make poor decisions for themselves is based on an old Enlightenment notion of democracy. On this view, rational individuals reach common rational conclusions. But we now know, and painful history has taught us, that there are many different definitions of "rationality" in the political sphere. Even the Nazis believed they were being rational. What democracy should really be about is accountability to the people's diverse grassroots experiences. People are all human, but they bring different perspectives to collective life. Democracy is not about rational gentlemen making wise decisions for societies. It is about including as many political voices and experiences as possible. This representational concept of democracy means that everyone affected needs to have an equal influence over their elected bodies.

An obvious example is the climate emergency. Children's demonstrations have made clear that this problem impacts children in more profound and long-lasting ways than adults. Children realize that they will live with its greatest consequences. They are more likely to suffer present and future economic, health, and other harms. Adults too, of course, face serious damage from human-made climate warming. But they have long and repeatedly failed to deal with the issue with anything like the needed urgency. This is because adults, however much they may care about children, are not actually forced to take children's interests centrally into account. If children could vote, adults would be much more likely to support—and politicians to enact—effective climate policies. We would be less likely to find ourselves in the terrible mess that adult voters have put us in.

What about education? Would children's voting undermine their schooling and development? Would children pressure politicians to reduce or eliminate it? No. Children are not stupid. They can see the value an education provides both for themselves and for their societies. The people who do not understand the value of an education are chiefly adults. It is adults who for decades have voted to slash education budgets, impose pointless testing regimes, and pay teachers inadequately. It is true that there may be just as many thoughtless children as there are thoughtless adults. It is true that some children would vote not to have to go to school. But children on the whole are more likely than adults to understand the consequences of poor choices around education policy. And they are more likely to be able to imagine meaningful solutions. They at least can help the rest of us see clearly what might and might not be productive ways forward. On the whole, voting children are likely to support politicians who promise to pay teachers well, provide sufficient educational resources, make schooling a meaningful experience, and invest in outcomes that will help children lead successful lives.

Then there is poverty. Children are the poorest age group in most countries. The political scientist Paul Peterson has shown that, in the United States, the poverty rate of children increased by 50 percent over the second half of the twentieth century, at the same time that the poverty rate of the elderly, especially with the onset of social security, declined by 300 percent. There are of course many reasons. But it is not a coincidence that, while children became the only group still lacking the vote, the elderly became much more politically organized. Peterson concludes that giving children the vote would have reduced their poverty levels as much as for the elderly if not more. Why? "Benefits to children would become a matter of right rather than a public benefaction."[8]

It stands to reason that when a group is enfranchised, that group also gains correspondingly improved government attention. Women's suffrage helped usher in massive increases in social spending on families, health care, social security, and education over the course of the twentieth century. These improvements helped both women and everyone else. When the poor got the vote, their share of government assistance and support rose through new laws around workplace anti-discrimination, union protections, and welfare policies. In the United States, African American enfranchisement helped bring about greater protections against racial discrimination and expanded government investments in minority education and health care.[9] Of course, there is still much to be done in all these cases. But does anyone truly believe these developments would have taken place if voting were still restricted only to wealthy white men?

Children's lives would even improve in terms of their understanding of politics. It is one thing to learn about politics in school, another to learn about it by practicing it in the world. Politics is always changing, and everyone involved is always learning. As laid out in a recent *Washington Post* op-ed:

> Giving young people the vote is the best civics lesson imaginable. When Takoma Park became the first city in America to lower the voting age to 16 just three years ago, 16- and 17-year-olds voted at twice the rate of the rest of the voting population. And studies show that the younger you are when cast your first vote, the more likely you are to make it a regular habit.[10]

Voting is itself an education, whether you are an adult or a child. It would benefit not only children's material lives but also their political growth.

Children's lives would improve with the vote because voting is about power. Politicians would finally be forced to take children's particular experiences as children into equal account. Rather than acting out of beneficence, or for the sake of children's futures as adults, political representatives would have to view children as full citizens in the here and now. Politicians are incentivized by those who can take away their jobs. It is helpful that children can already, in many places, exert pressure through free speech, campaigns, and demonstrations. But this does not give them the fundamental power of the ballot box. Those with the power to hire and fire politicians also have the power to ensure that their interests are properly heard.

Sixteen-year-old Vita Wallace already understood this in 1991. As she wrote in the US magazine *The Nation*:

> I am 16 now, still not old enough to vote. Like all children, then, the only way I can fight for children's rights is by using my freedom of speech to try to convince adults to fight with me. While I am grateful that I have the right to speak my mind, I believe that it is a grave injustice to deny young people the effective tool they could have to bring about change in democracy. For this reason, I suggest that the right of citizens under 18 to vote not be denied or abridged on account of age.[11]

It is a simple point but one generally lost on adults. Only the right to vote gives children equal power to bring about real change.

Children's suffrage, far from causing them harm, would instead place their interests at the center of the political map. Politicians would be able to understand children's experiences much better than they currently do and respond to them much more fairly. Climate change might finally be addressed. Juvenile justice might better serve juveniles. Immigrant children might be treated with genuine humanity. Schools might get proper funding. Poverty might be dealt with seriously. Health systems might be strengthened. The arts might receive greater support. Universities might be made more affordable. Wars might not be entered into so lightly. And children themselves might be treated with greater collective dignity.

Who knows what a more child-centered political calculus might produce? All that can be said for sure is that children would certainly find themselves a great deal better off.

The second concern that people often raise regarding outcomes for children is that voting might rob them of their childhoods. The very act itself could burden children with too much adult responsibility. On this view, voting is a bit like marriage. It involves obligations for which children are not yet fully ready. The freedoms involved are damaging to childhood as such. Young people should have full childhoods that enable them to focus on their own growth, play, and education instead of the weighty and difficult cares of the world.

To see why this view is problematic, imagine growing up as African American in the United States today. No matter your wealth or education, you will be confronted with systemic racism. You will have to be careful around police, work extra hard in school, deal with microaggressions in public, and face many other disadvantages in the world simply because of the color of your skin. And you will be part of a group that suffers disproportionate poverty, ill health, and imprisonment. Can anyone seriously say that such a child is protected from politics? Is it even possible for African American children not to be intimately familiar with the political realities around them every day? And is it really true that they do not have a valuable voice to bring to the table?

This is not an isolated example. Imagine being a child in Gaza City growing up under Israeli occupation (Figure 5). In South Africa as it untangles the legacy of apartheid. In Iceland as the snow caps disappear from the mountains. In Syria as the government bombs your neighborhood. Imagine being a child living in China who is the first in their family to attend university. Being a gay child in Argentina as it becomes the first Latin American country to legalize same-sex marriage. Being a Catholic child in Ireland as the country at long last confronts its problem with clergy pedophilia. Or a child in sub-Saharan Africa who now has enough food to eat.

The point is that children are already political beings. They always have been and always will be. It is a myth that children can be kept apart in a protected nonpolitical sphere. This myth may be useful for adults. It may make it easier for adults to set aside children's political concerns. But young people's lives are in reality just as bound up with politics as are those of adults. If anything, children experience the impacts of political life even more. Children are not only affected by government policies, but they also have opinions about them, see their consequences for themselves and others, and actively engage in political debate, protest, and organization. The idea that voting would destroy

Figure 5 Children protest on the occasion of World Children's Day, Gaza City, Palestine, November 2019. Credit: Ahmad Hasaballah/IMAGESLIVE/ZUMA Wire/Alamy Live News.

children's childhoods is based on a false and idealized conception of childhood. It imagines that childhood exists in a wholly private sphere. That is a state of utter vulnerability and innocence. But it is both deeply naive and highly self-serving for adults to proclaim that children need to be protected from political life. On the contrary, they need to be much better heard.

Still, is actual voting too much responsibility to place on children's shoulders?

It is hard to argue that this burden is life-consuming. Generally speaking, you have to make a half-hour trip to a ballot box once every few years. Of course, you also have to pay some attention to politics in between. You have to weigh each representative (or referendum option) against the alternatives. You have to be aware of political issues, have some sense of what you think about them, and imagine how different representatives might act if elected. But, as I have argued throughout this book, these capacities belong to almost anyone living in a political space. They are capacities that are already exercised by children in daily life. Politics is part of the air we breathe just living in a society. Voting is less of a burden, at any rate, than going to school, taking swimming lessons, or looking after your sister.

If political capacities already belong to children, then it is difficult to argue that exercising them constitutes a loss of childhood. If children are political beings, and if they want to use their right to vote, then it would be elitist of adults still to insist that it is too much for them to handle. *That* would be robbing children of their childhoods. It would deny children the right to their childhoods insofar as childhoods are political. It would deny children the right to act on their interests as children.

What is more, any child who wanted to vote would clearly be a child who themselves did not feel that voting overburdens them. On the contrary, voting would serve as a way to relieve the burden of not being heard. It could also potentially relieve other burdens on childhood that the political system might be able to fix. For any child capable of voting, being denied the right to do so is the greater harm.

Suffrage does not give one an obligation to vote, only a right to do so if one desires. It is true that in some countries voting is required by threat of a fine. If children voted, as is the case in Brazil for sixteen- to seventeen-year-olds, they could be exempted. Or there could be the option of voting for no candidate, as there generally is for adults. But in general, the right to vote is not something people are forced to use. Rather, it is something one opts into if one so desires. Worrying about the burden of voting is therefore like worrying about the burden of taking up golf. No one is forced to do it if they don't want to. Just like for adults, any child could simply decide that the responsibility of voting is too much for them. Or not think about it at all. It is a voluntary choice that you make if you want to, not a requirement forced on you against your will.

This is one reason why voting is not like marriage. While it is true that marriage also is a free choice to enter into, the consequences of marriage are not. Marriage legally binds you to another person, thereby tying your sexual, economic, health, and social fates. The personal consequences of voting, on the other hand, are virtually nil. Voting at, say, the age of eleven simply means making one's voice heard on the larger political stage and perhaps making a tiny difference in the electoral outcome. The consequence of marriage at this age could be sexual abuse or enslavement, economic ruin, and a lifetime of unhappiness. The choice to marry has such profound consequences for one's life that it is indeed a high burden. But the choice to vote is optional, harmless, and over in a few minutes.

Rather than being harmful to children, the act itself of voting would for the most part be of great personal benefit.

In the first place, it is beneficial in and of itself to be included as a respected member of one's political community. One harm to children from not being able to vote is that it teaches them (and others) that their experiences, views, and interests are of little value to society. Having the right to vote, in contrast, would signal to young people that their lives are equally esteemed in the political sphere. It would make it clear that their views are important, valued, and needed. This alone would be a benefit for children. It would endow them with greater social dignity.

What is more, children would on the whole become much more politically knowledgeable. As mentioned before, it is one thing to learn about government in schools, another to do so in order to cast a vote. Everyone including adults is engaged in a continuous political learning process as they absorb the news, examine candidates, and engage with diverse points of view. But at present this learning process for children is artificial and theoretical. People learn best not in abstraction but by doing. Children with the right to vote would on the whole become more informed citizens and more rounded people. As the political theorist Steven Lecce puts it: "Aside from encouraging various forms of democratic participation at home and in school, we should encourage children to take a more active interest in the values, processes and results of political decision-making. Lowering the voting age would be a good way of doing so." Or as a nine-year-old I know put it in a recent homework assignment: children "can learn more if they vote ... [I]f you are going to vote you learn about politics and follow those things."[12]

Finally, the act of voting is likely to benefit children in the rest of their lives too. Children who can vote are likely also to feel more confident exercising freedoms of speech and assembly beyond the ballot box itself. Children concerned about the climate emergency may feel more empowered to join demonstrations and to participate in organization. Children who are denied asylum might feel they have a right to protest. Less advantaged children may see themselves as deserving more. Children oppressed by sex slavery, labor exploitation, and violence might sense that, nevertheless, their lives and concerns are still valued by society at large. Children living in abusive or neglectful families would know that they remain important citizens in a larger sense. Indeed, children with great privileges would likewise have to see that, when it comes to democracy, other children are their equals. The vote gives you not only an immediate right to be heard but also a wider right to be counted as a valued member of your society.

In contrast, being excluded from the vote sends children the opposite message. It tells them that they should see themselves as secondary and powerless. If they cannot be entrusted to participate in shared political choices, neither should they understand themselves as having valued political voices, important political concerns, or distinct political experiences. Neither should they think themselves equally important members of their communities, empowered to stand up to harms and injustices, or respected actors in public life. Even within families, the message is that society values the dignity and well-being of your parents more than it does yours.

Finally, one could argue that telling people their voices do not count for the first eighteen years of their life undermines rather than enhances their capacities for democratic life in adulthood. It builds into democracy a level of authoritarianism. If you spend your formative years being told you are unfit to take part in politics, then you are ripe as an adult to gravitate toward domineering political leaders with simple and reassuring answers. You are less likely to think you can think for yourself. As the political scientist Michael Cummings puts it, "the civic disengagement and loss of social capital plaguing democracies today is rooted in the systematic silencing of people's political voice during their early years."[13] If you grow up disenfranchised, you are more easily exploited during times of social crisis, economic collapse, political fragmentation, or global instability. Every voter today was taught during the most formative years of their life that their political experiences and ideas do not count. No wonder so many do not feel politically empowered or engaged as adults. No wonder democracies are constantly lurching into apathy or authoritarianism.

The act of voting, then, is far from an undue burden that would rob children of their childhoods. On the contrary, it obeys the larger logic of democratic life. It would honor children as the political beings that they really are, provide them equal political consideration to everyone else, and empower them as political beings across their present and future lives. These are the reasons people have sought suffrage since the dawn of democracy. Democracies recognize that all the people's lives are political, not just those of the powerful few. The right to vote is the most basic way that political beings are ensured equal worth and dignity.

If children's voting would not lead to self-harm or undermine their childhoods, there is still the more complex objection that children's rights to vote might create a slippery slope that leads to other rights that would indeed be dangerous for children to have.

This third objection is that children's voting rights could lead to children's adultification. If children could vote, then why should they not also gain or demand other adult rights, such as to buy alcohol, drive, have sex, enjoy uncontrolled access to the internet, divorce their parents, work full time, join the military, run for office, and much else? Likewise, why should not societies start to treat children as adults by, for example, putting them on trial as adults, giving them adult sentences, requiring them to serve on juries, making them responsible for their own health care, demanding their economic self-sufficiency, and enlisting them in the draft? Since voting is such a fundamental right, it would seem to open the door to children gaining a wide range of other less fundamental rights and responsibilities that they are not yet ready to handle.

This objection rests, however, on a fundamental confusion between different kinds of rights. Rights to vote are general human rights. They should belong to anyone as a member of society unless there is an exceptional reason for them not to. Rights to marry, drive, be educated, be tried as a juvenile, and so on are not general rights but special or group rights. They are rights that belong specifically either to children as children or to adults as adults. Having general human rights does not in any way entail possessing the special rights of others. On the contrary, they empower persons to fight for the special rights they properly deserve.

Voting is a general, universal, or basic human right. This means that everyone should have it unless there is some good reason for them not to. Similar kinds of general rights include rights to life, liberty, protection from violence, basic health care, and fair trials, as well as freedoms of expression, conscience, religion, and assembly. Children in most democracies already have most of these general human rights because these in principle belong to everyone. Of course, there are always exceptions. Prisoners are denied rights to liberty. Soldiers give up a certain claim over rights of life. Bigots are denied rights to hate speech. Rights are complex and multisided and have to be balanced against one another. But human rights in general are "human" in that they can be abridged only for exceptional reasons.

Voting rights follow the same logic. Certain groups are denied voting rights not because voting rights belong only to special groups, but because, in their case, the universal rule admits of a valid exception. Noncitizens are denied voting rights because their sympathies are thought not to be necessarily clear. In some countries, felons cannot vote because they have violated the social trust. Sometimes people with severe mental illnesses are prevented from voting on the grounds that they lack even basic political understanding. Whether any of these exceptions are valid or not, the point is that voting is a basic human right that one has by default unless there is a good reason for an exception.

The kinds of rights that lie along our supposed slippery slope, however, are not general but special rights. They are rights reserved for children specifically as children or provided to adults specifically as adults. They are not universal human rights but particular rights based in this case on age. These special rights are either given or denied to children based on their own particular best interests as children. Rights to free education, families, and juvenile justice are provided only to children, and not to adults, because they are beneficial for children as children. Rights to work, marry, or have sex are generally reserved for adults because they harmful to children as children. The former are not general human rights but special to children. The latter are not general human rights from which children are excepted, but special to adults. In both cases, special rights for either children or adults are justified by the special interests of the particular group in question.

Every group with a general right to vote also has special rights as well. Voting rights and special rights are not mutually exclusive. Women in many societies have special rights to abortion, maternity leave, particular consideration in custody battles, intentional access to education and sports, and freedom from gender discrimination. These result from the particular needs and experiences of women as a group. Likewise, the elderly have special rights to government economic support and free health insurance. This is because the elderly specifically as elderly can no longer fully support themselves. Ethnic and racial minorities often have special rights to nondiscrimination and affirmative action. Members of the queer community sometimes have special rights to sexual nondiscrimination and use of identity bathrooms. Disabled persons have distinct rights to building access, employment safeguards, and freedom from exploitation. The poor in many societies have special rights to being provided a basic standard of living, free criminal defense, food stamps, tax breaks, unemployment insurance, and affordable housing. Many rights that exist in societies are special rights belonging to particular groups.

The reason it is possible to hold both voting and special rights at once is that they obey different rights logics. Voting rights are general or universal: you have them unless there are strong reasons for you not to. Special rights operate on the opposite basis: you do not have them unless there are strong reasons why you should. They are not universal but particular. They are responses to specific groups' special experiences. As the philosopher Nicholas Munn puts it, "political participation—of which voting is the prime example—is a human right, and protected as such. Driving is not. So the standard for justifying not letting someone vote is and should be higher than the standard of justification for not letting someone drive."[14]

Children gaining the right to vote would not rob them of children's special rights. Nor would it give them the special rights of adults. Special rights are given or denied to children solely on the basis of their particular experiences as children. Child voters would still be children. Just as women voters are still women and disabled voters are still disabled. Having a role in choosing elected representatives does not change in any way who you are as the member of a special group or the rights obtaining or not therein. It does not suddenly make you a generic human being. It does not eject you from special group status. Nor does it give you access to the special rights of other groups. All it does is to make it easier to gain the special rights you actually deserve by having an influence in larger political affairs.

Would children nevertheless start demanding rights they should not have? Would they gain enough power to overturn rights they might not like or insist on rights that should properly be reserved for adults? Could children organize to force an end to compulsory schooling, campaign to legalize youth sex, or eliminate the drinking age?

Why this is not the case is clear if children are recognized as at least minimally competent political actors. If children can use their own experiences to choose among voting options, as discussed in previous chapters, then they can sufficiently understand what voting choices will help or harm them as children. Of course, just as with adults, children will have a vast range of opinions. And, like adults, some of those opinions will be less than well-thought-out. But overall, children are no more likely than adults to vote for policies that will harm children as a group. Likewise, if children could vote, adults are not going to become any more blind than they already are to the needs of children as children. Special rights could be added or removed only by persuading the majority of the electorate of their validity. Or convincing court systems that they violate established law. Legalizing children's full-time employment, for example, would require convincing voters and politicians as a whole that this is a good idea.

A simple example is the right to drive. Driving requires physical capacities to handle powerful equipment as well as social capacities to take responsibility for the potential of inflicting great harm on others. If children gathered as a group to demand an end to age limits for driving, they would have to convince the majority of adults and politicians, as well as children, that this would not lead to significant harm. Their chance of succeeding would be vanishingly low. Only the most die-hard libertarian adults would even consider subjecting themselves to this kind of danger on the streets. No majority of representatives would risk their careers by unleashing transportation chaos. And a large enough percentage of children themselves is extremely unlikely not to realize that such a demand is unreasonable. It would not be in their own best interests either, either as drivers or as endangered pedestrians. Toddlers can see that toddlers in trucks spells trouble.

Or take sex and marriage. The right to have sex or marry comes at different ages in different societies, but it largely arrives at or close to adulthood. The reasons usually given are that sex and marriage require capacities for emotional maturity, responsibility for offspring, handling a potential abortion, avoiding sexual exploitation and disease, and, in the case of marriage, committing to a life-long social, economic, and legal institution. The burden of voting may be great, but it is not nearly as great as that of having sex or being married. There is no sensible reason why children having the right to vote would persuade either children or adults that they are therefore ready for sex and marriage. There would need to be a dramatic shift in cultural mores for the majority of children, adults, and legislators to start thinking that sex and marriage are not a special right for adults. On the contrary, with children voting, the potential harms of preadult sexuality and marriage are likely to become more visible, not less, especially for communities and individuals that currently do not see them.

What about compulsory schooling? It is understandable on the surface that children might organize to make schooling optional. They might find candidates who are happy to oblige them or form special interest groups that exert focused political pressure to advance the cause. But the democratic wager is that the most broadly sensible ideas will generally win the day. Large numbers of children are likely to recognize that they are much better off in school than working, that making school nonmandatory would vastly reduce its effectiveness, and that a good education is essential for their own futures, not to mention that of their larger societies. The overwhelming majority of adults and politicians are also likely to continue to believe that compulsory education is of value to them, that it is likewise of value for their own and other children, that their workplaces and the economy depend fundamentally on it, and that society overall needs it in order to function democratically and well. Indeed, this is why children in countries without strong education systems are fighting not to eliminate but to improve them. The majority of the electorate is not going to lose sight of the fact that compulsory education is a special right that children deserve. On the contrary, they are going to see more clearly why it is so important and why it needs significant societal investment.

Finally, consider juvenile justice. Would children gaining the right to vote mean that societies could end up burdening them with adult criminal responsibility? In the first place, it is difficult to see children and youth campaigning for such an outcome themselves. The vast majority of young people would surely be able to see that it would not be just or beneficial for them. And second, adults and legislators are unlikely to undergo a sudden change of mind either. If they did, it would not be because children could vote, but because adults would have forgotten why juvenile justice systems are in children's best interests. They would have to convince themselves that children and youth no longer deserve lighter sentences, rehabilitation, or second chances. They would have to convince themselves, in other words, that children are not children. It could happen and, to a certain extent in the United States, already has. But if it did, it would be the fault of bad ideas from adults, not of children gaining the right to vote. The opposite outcome is much more likely: that children's voting would help clarify to ill-informed adults why juvenile justice systems need to be strengthened and improved.

Overall, children's suffrage would neither logically nor in practice cost children their special rights as children. On the contrary, children's voting would tend to strengthen their special rights by enabling young people to hold politicians more accountable to their own particular and diverse life experiences. The idea that children would use the vote to gain self-harming rights is patronizing and undemocratic. Adults do not always vote in their own best interests either. But on the whole, children's voting would change the pressures on democratic representatives in such a way as to give children's special interests the special care and attention they deserve.

Far from creating a slippery slope into harmful adult rights, children's suffrage would build a staircase to significantly stronger children's rights. It would put children's rights at the center instead of the periphery of political discussion. There are at least three ways in which this improvement in children's special rights would come about.

First, democratic decisions that impact children's rights, which is virtually all of them, would be systematically better informed. Children in every society enjoy a large number of rights, but these have so far everywhere been designed with little to no input from actual children. Sometimes children are consulted, but they are almost never permitted to exercise influence. Removing age restrictions from the right to vote would immediately make it necessary for adults and politicians to respond to children's lives more equitably, concretely, and diversely. And it would empower children themselves to speak up for their rights, organize with other children, and hold representatives more accountable to their experiences.

Consider the case of public understanding about the climate emergency. It is only because of children's activism that children's rights in this matter are on the political radar. At the Fridays for Future rally that I mentioned at the start of this book, I was confronted with a sea of colorful handmade signs that made all too clear the diversity of children's rights at stake. One read: "Why get an education when nobody listens to the educated!!!" From an eight- to nine-year-old: "If you were smarter we'd be in school." "You'll die of old age. I'll die of climate change." From a teenager dressed as a dinosaur: "I'm sure the dinos thought they had time." From a 3-4-year-old in a stroller: "Don't burn my future!" A drawing of the Lorax with a raised middle finger: "The Lorax speaks for the trees and the trees say fuck you." And: "My outrage can't fit on this sign."

The climate emergency, despite what politicians say, is not just about adult rights to jobs and security. It is also about children's rights to an education, a healthy life, and a sustainable future. Not to mention future generations' rights to a habitable environment. There are general human rights at stake here such as to economic well-being and basic standards of health, but there are also special rights of children such as to viable futures and the continued availability of resources. All of this and more would be clearer in the minds of politicians if children and youth could vote.

Far from adultifying children, children's suffrage would childify politics. What I mean by this is not that politics would become dominated by children. What I mean is that it would be forced to include children's experiences and concerns. When women gained suffrage, they were not masculinized. Rather, politics itself was, at least to an extent, feminized. That is, women's special concerns carried more equal weight compared to men's. When minorities got the vote, they did not turn white. They instead had their special interests better represented. When the poor got the vote, they did not suddenly become rich. Rather, politics overall became more class-conscious. Neither would children stop being children. On the contrary, just as men have had to become more reflective about gender, whites about race, and the rich about class, so also adults would have to question their own adult-centrism and become more reflective about age. Democracies would be incentivized to deconstruct their own adultist biases and reconstruct themselves from childist points of view.

Instead of democracies becoming less informed, children's voting would give them new and previously suppressed insight and information. The epistemological playing field would expand to include knowledge from a wider base of the population. The democratic pie would grow. The premise of democracies is that political wisdom arises from the grassroots upward. At the moment, a third of the democratic field lies unplowed. Adults more or less guess at the meaning of policies for the corner set aside for children. They rely on their own adult-based experiences. But if children could vote, everyone would learn a great deal more about the realities of the people's shared existences. Both adults and children would be forced to consider children's perspectives in more complex, diverse, and sometimes surprising ways.

Even children themselves would learn more about children's rights. They would find new ways to understand both their own and other children's experiences in their society. They too would have to question their assumptions by more fully encountering multiple childhood perspectives. When women gained the vote, powerful white and wealthy women had to confront the ways in which their interests sidelined those of women of color and poorer classes. Just as for other groups, children would generate informational feedback loops in which their own views would be tested and expanded in dialogue with each other. They would become more aware of where other children disagree, both over broad political parties and over specific issues like climate change and education. In other words, they, like adults, would have to confront the fact that childhood is not a monolith. The resulting discourse among children would further enrich societies and their understandings of children's special rights.

Another reason children's suffrage would be a staircase to improved children's rights is that it would change the dynamics of core democratic processes.

Consider the issue of police brutality toward minorities in the United States and worldwide. The murder of the unarmed African American George Floyd by white police officers in Minneapolis set off weeks of Black Lives Matter protests around the globe. Large numbers of sometimes very young children participated in these protests, and sometimes there were protests specifically by and for children. My own family marched in a local protest organized by my daughter's elementary school that involved diverse members of the community aged zero on upwards. Why would the murder of an adult by adults be of concern to children? Because children of color are also deeply impacted by having to grow up under systemic white privilege. Racism is a matter of children's rights just as much as it is of adults'.

But the political calculus of an adult-only democracy is weighted against children's special concerns. It is weighted against the racial oppression of children being properly understood and accounted for. Currently, democracies have little concrete incentive to take young Black experiences especially seriously. And this skewed calculus harms racially oppressed adults as well. It leaves unaddressed the deep structures of violence that white children learn to perpetuate and Black children learn to fear. On a deeper level, the oppression of minorities relies on children's disenfranchisement itself. Racism historically equates minorities with children. Just as did sexism for women and classism for the poor. Disenfranchising children perpetuates the divide between "adults" and "children," which helps to feed the logic of systemic oppression itself, the logic of rightful rulers and rightless others.

If children could vote, these kinds of democratic distortions would be harder to maintain. Universal suffrage would defang the assumption that some of the people are real participants in democracies while others are not. It would undo the old binary opposition between adults who legitimately exercise power based on their superiority, and children who instead need to be protected and provided for. If children could vote, democracies would find it much more difficult to tolerate oppression overall. The right to dominate others would not be so easy to defend.

Children's rights in particular would become more central to the democratic process. They would no longer be treated as beneficial add-ons. The incentive structures of representatives would shift. At the moment, the main reason for politicians to promote children's rights is to please adults like parents and teachers who directly deal with children's lives. A further reason is to appear generous and compassionate. But these reasons fall short of political necessity. In the push and shove of democratic priorities, children's special rights stand at a systemic disadvantage. They fall through the cracks of scarce political attention. Ignoring children is not going to get you kicked out at the ballot box.

Take the right to education as one last example. In the UK, education policy is a notorious plaything of politicians, routinely revisited with each new administration. In the United States, schooling has gradually received less and less funding and more and more testing. In India, it is promised as a universal right even as teachers often fail to show up and poor students often cannot afford the fees. In these instances and elsewhere, education policy is a favorite trope of politicians but rarely makes real progress. Why? Because politicians know little about it and do not have much incentive to place it front and center. Politicians rarely step foot in classrooms or listen to the concerns of students or teachers. Their actual knowledge of education is often scant. Even though they wield enormous power over educational budgets, policies, curricula, and practices, they have little reason to exercise this power in ways responsible to children.

What if the children directly impacted by educational policies got the chance to weigh in on them as well? What if politicians felt as if their jobs in part depended on how well they responded to young people's educational concerns? What would happen is that politicians would not only gain a lot of important information about education, but they would also be compelled to act on it. They would have to give equal weight to the rights of an entire new swath of constituents. As a result, they would have to consider much more closely what happens in the classroom, the impacts of discrimination and exclusion, whether teachers are adequately supported, whether they undergo sufficient professional development, how funding priorities are made, what curricula are meaningful advances instead of just window dressing, the importance of free time and exercise, the value of education in music and the arts, and much else. Under the current pandemic, they would have to prioritize children being in schools over opening up bars. Overall, policies around children's education rights would have to be made in more responsive and responsible ways.

The idea that politicians would instead cave in to supposedly "childish" educational demands is clearly absurd. Not only do children have every reason to care about their own education a great deal, but they could actually help politicians better understand what special rights they really need. There are schools in the United States where students have to wear coats to class in winter because the heating no longer works. Children in these districts are likely to vote for representatives who recognize their right to a humane learning environment. And they will help adults see this problem too, compounding the pressure on lawmakers further. It is one thing to have your rights provided as a special benefit, another to be able to demand them as special rights through the ballot box.

Democratic processes would change in another way too. Children would bring to the table creative new ways of engaging in political discourse. When the poor gained the vote, they ushered in the electoral power of mass movements and labor unions. Minorities brought the influence of social justice and community organization. Women created new avenues of public protest and demonstration. Children have already introduced new forms of political engagement through school strikes for climate change, grassroots global mobilization, digitized organization, and even playfulness and humor. These are no more unique to children than labor organization or protest is unique to workers and women. They are ways of expanding political processes for all. With children's voting, democracies would discover new paths for effective and meaningful functioning.

Finally, a staircase to greater children's rights would build on the solid foundation of a new respect for children's equal political dignity. The current adult-only voting system makes children second-class citizens. It assumes that, on some level, children do not have the right to full democratic inclusion. The very fact of having the vote would instead pressure societies to recognize children as their own political beings. It would state loudly and clearly that young people are just as important as adults in policy and law. That their concerns are equally significant to the political space. Like many groups before them, children would take their rightful place among "we the people."

Dignity is the foundation stone of human rights. It is why people deserve equal rights and not to be marginalized or oppressed. Children's voting would reinforce children's dignity in many ways. It would lay a foundation of basic humanity that must be protected against violence and discrimination. It would include children as deserving fair provisions of resources instead of just generous handouts. And it would recognize children as whole people with rights to participate in shaping shared worlds. These are all expressions of children's rights to be treated with equal dignity. Children supposedly have these rights already. But without the vote, they ring hollow and lack force.

Put simply, the right to vote is the key to making children full political beings. It might not give them as much power or influence as adults. It would not solve all problems. But it would provide young people a platform for equal instead of secondary political consideration. Viewing others with equal humanity means treating them with equal respect. It means recognizing them for who they really are. It means attending closely to their distinct and concrete lived experiences. Voting rights would provide young people the political foundation of membership in the full human rights community.

Adults often think that children's special rights are taken care of just fine. Adults generally care about children, and this must also be the case in politics. But the reality is that merely caring about children is not the same as actually having to take their interests into account. Children's voting, far from undermining children's special rights, would greatly strengthen them. It would provide societies with more rather than less information about children's particular lives. It would incentivize adults and representatives to act with increased rather than decreased accountability. And it would endow children themselves with greater rather than lesser political dignity as children. These outcomes should not be surprising, given what always happens when new groups gain suffrage. Nor, however, should it be surprising that adults as a group are comfortable with how things currently stand.

When closely examined, the fear that children's voting would harm children is entirely unfounded. Quite the opposite is really the case. Children's voting would not lead to irrational political outcomes, but instead place children's real and diverse experiences at the center of political debate. It would not rob children of their childhoods, but instead make politicians accountable to the real complexities of children's lives. It would not destroy children's special rights, but instead strengthen and enrich them based on children's actual inputs. And it would not create a slippery slope into adultification, but instead build a staircase toward genuinely child-inclusive societies. What really harms children is *not* having the right to vote, since it reduces the young to second-class citizens lacking equal political concern and dignity.

Democracy actually does work. And so children's suffrage actually would improve their lives.

Outcomes for Societies

Recognition of the inherent dignity and of the equal and inalienable rights of all members of the human family is the foundation of freedom, justice and peace in the world.

United Nations' Universal Declaration of Human Rights

Black Lives Matter (BLM) is a global movement begun by activists Patrisse Cullors, Alicia Garza, and Opal Tometi in 2013 in the United States to combat racialized police brutality. It started as a hashtag in response to a jury's acquittal of 28-year-old George Zimmerman, a neighborhood watch coordinator who shot to death an unarmed African American youth, seventeen-year-old Trayvon Martin, on suspicion of trespassing, even though Martin was simply walking home from the store. BLM expanded spontaneously thereafter in response to further police killings of African Americans such as Michael Brown, Eric Garner, Breonna Taylor, and George Floyd, to name just a few. It also grew internationally to protest the mistreatment of Aboriginal Australians in Australia, police shootings of children in Brazil, the police killing of Mark Duggan in the UK, and so on around the world.

It might seem that BLM has little to do with children's voting. While Martin himself was only seventeen, the organizers and most of the victims of racialized police shootings have been adults. But, of course, the particular incidents being protested against, as well as the deeper racism behind them, are of central concern for children's lives. This is why so many children and youth have actively participated in the movement (Figure 6). It is also why children rose up previously against slavery, marched with Gandhi, battled to liberate Rwanda, fought in the

Mexican Revolution, organized against Jim Crow, and protested with Martin Luther King Jr. Racism impacts societies without regard to age.

Not only are children deeply affected by racism, but their perspectives on it are vitally important for anti-racism movements and for changing racial dynamics in societies at large. Children both experience and perpetuate white supremacy from birth, not only on the streets but also in the playground, at school, and via mass media. They confront racism as a structural part of their history. And they experience racism in their own struggles to grow up with dignity and strength. Children do not experience racism-lite, as if it were a lesser version of adult racism. Children therefore have much to contribute on racial issues. Their perspectives are not necessarily the same as adults', just as different adults experience racism differently too. Their perspectives are necessarily diverse and bring different critical concerns to the discussion. What is more, telling children their voices do not count on the subject only adds a further layer of oppression.

Figure 6 Nine-year-old participates in protests after the murder of George Floyd, Garden City, NY, June 2020. Photo by Steve Pfost/Newsday RM via Getty Images.

Just as for other groups, children lacking the right to vote is a problem not just for children but also for the larger societies around them. It robs societies of important angles of vision in collective debates. It reduces politicians' understandings of the full nature of social problems like racism and much else. And it distorts policy discussions around adult priorities. As a result, children's disenfranchisement harms not just children but also adults and whole political communities. It forces democracies to fly a third blind. The people fail to comprehend the perspectives of a large group of citizens. Politicians are not forced to take the full range of experiences into account. And children are denied important opportunities to make valued contributions. On the whole, the democratic space is severely limited.

These issues are especially apt in our times. Democracy today faces a rising global tide of authoritarianism. Children are particularly at risk as democratic governments slide under the control of reactionary minorities. It would be easy to conclude that this is not a time for advancing children's suffrage. Saving democracy for adults is a tall enough order. But throughout history, existential threats to democracy have been resolved by enfranchising new groups. Rising class warfare in the nineteenth century was deflated by enfranchising the poor, colonialist oppression by enfranchising minorities, the global crisis in the wake of the First World War by enfranchising women, and so on. Previously marginalized perspectives can help to realign democratic thinking in fresh new ways. Today, democratic authoritarianism builds on a sense that some are worthy of rule and others are not. Children's voting would go a long way toward proving that noxious assumption false.

Even though most believe that children's suffrage would harm adults and societies, in reality it would benefit them as much as it would benefit children. The most basic reason is that, as with prior exclusions, suppressing one group damages the democratic whole. Adultism harms not just children but also adults. It creates societies in which whole arenas of expertise are systematically suppressed. It leaves adults to blindly maintain their prejudices. And it fails to account for the fact that children's and adults' political lives are thoroughly intertwined. Although children's voting would be justified even if it only helped children, the fact is that a truly universal democracy would help adults and societies too.

Let us first take a look at the likely outcomes for individual adults. Later we'll consider the outcomes for social institutions and democratic systems.

One might fear that if children could directly influence policy, then policy would begin to undermine adults' interests. Children may not be able to understand the experiences of adults as well as adults can understand those of children. It is right for adults to hold more power than children in politics, on this view, just as in many other walks of life, because adults have experienced childhood, but the reverse is not the case. Children should not have a hand in deciding, for example, the rights of parents, how much adults pay in taxes, whether adults go to war, if same-sex marriage is to be legalized, and so on. Children's voting would create worse outcomes for adults because children lack sufficient understanding of adults' lives.

This view misunderstands how democracy works. For one thing, it imagines voting as a zero-sum game. In reality, however, voting is a collective enterprise that draws upon a diversity of voices to reach shared decisions. Democracies are built on the premise that no one person understands everything. People get to vote on representatives so that their different experiences might inform life in common. As a result, children's voting does not subtract understanding from the political sphere. Rather, it adds new kinds of understanding, this time from the perspective of the young. If adults' lives would be affected, it would be because more, not less, understanding is included in the collective decision-making process.

What is more, even without voting, children already have a right to influence adults' lives through politics. Indeed, in their political actions, children already advance adults' interests. For example, the Parkland, Florida, students who lobbied for stricter gun laws after a mass shooting in their school made an important and needed contribution to the national conversation about gun violence. Fridays for Future activists are helping adults understand better how to protect the planet. Neighborhood children's parliaments in India are improving local sanitation and safety for their entire communities. Voting is not the only, or even the most powerful, way to influence politics. But children already have rights to impact adults through political means.

But most importantly, it is simply false that adults understand children better than children understand adults. Children and adults certainly share much in common. And there are areas of adult life that children know little about. But no one can legitimately claim to fully understand the lives of an entirely other social group. There are areas of children's lives, too, that adults cannot as well understand—whether in school, growing up digital, experiencing poverty, fearing climate change, confronting racism, and much else. Having once been a child does not help. A childhood 20, 40, or 60 years ago is very different from a childhood today. A childhood in poverty is very different from a childhood in comfort. Any one adult can only understand the very particular childhoods around them and only to a certain extent. And they can also only understand particular adulthoods as well. Simply not experiencing adulthood is no reason to disqualify a child from having an important perspective to add.

The view that adults would lose out if children could vote is as a consequence undemocratic. Democracy rests on the idea that no one can fully stand in anyone else's shoes. The more voices are heard, the better the likely political outcome. Banning children because they cannot stand in the shoes of adults imposes a double standard. Adults do not have to prove they understand others' lives in order to vote; indeed, doing so is an impossibility. Why then should this be a requirement for children? The right to vote is not premised on the ability to anticipate the full range of outcomes for others unlike oneself. Rather, it is premised on precisely the opposite idea: that everyone's perspective is limited but still valuable.

Adult-only voting is in fact logically self-contradictory. It asserts that *all* adults should vote because they cannot stand in each other's shoes; but at the same time that *only* adults should vote because they can indeed stand in the shoes of others, namely children. The existing voting system assumes that no one can understand anyone else's experiences fully, but that adults can fully understand the experiences of children. The double standard is that while adults have the right to vote because they lack the perspectives of others, children are banned from voting for exactly the same reason.

The right to vote does not depend on being able to account for the impact of one's vote on others. Rather, it depends on being able to add one's perspective to the collective voting whole. The fact that children cannot know everything about adulthood is immaterial. The middle class cannot know everything about the working class, nor men about women, women about men, the rich about the poor, whites about Blacks, Blacks about Latinos, or any group however large or small about any other group. Humans are complex political beings who cannot understand others or even themselves. Adults should stop pretending they know everything about children. No one even knows very much about their neighbors down the street, let alone an entire third of their country's population. The right to vote simply does not rely on the ability to anticipate the consequences of one's choices for other sectors of society.

On the contrary, adding more voices only increases the likelihood of better democratic outcomes. Political philosophers Robert Goodin and Joanne Lau argue that children's voting would improve societies even if children could be considered less politically competent as a group. They suggest that children's voting is much like children cosigning contracts, something that in many countries they are legally permitted to do. In voting, "all the voters are 'co-signatories' with regard to an electoral outcome." All voters take on not a direct political responsibility but a co-responsibility for the outcomes enacted by politicians. "By adding more members to the voting pool, *even if the competence of the voters is lower than that of the existing voters*, the group will actually improve its overall performance, and the probability that the group will select the correct answer will approach certainty."[1] Overall outcomes improve with more voters because decisions are made with more diverse inputs. The more voters are involved, however broadminded they may be, the more their collective decisions approach impartiality.

I would argue that the competence of children is not lower but different. As is the competence of different societal groups in general. The point, however, remains the same. Children's voting would not harm the interests of adults because it does not exercise power over adults directly. Rather, it contributes to the collective co-decision-making process. It does not lower political understanding but instead raises it by adding otherwise neglected perspectives. It adds a further layer of political considerations and pressures to be taken into account by political representatives. Representatives are not thereby forced to abandon adults' interests. Rather, they are forced to balance adults' interests more fairly against those of children, something they are already supposed to be doing anyway.

Adults must finally exercise a measure of self-critique. The existing voting system provides adults significant advantages. Fears about children's impacts on adults' lives might really reflect fears that children would finally get a more equal due. It might represent a desire not to lose dominance. The elderly might no longer receive disproportionate shares of public spending compared to the young. Parents might be forced to account for children's concerns in custody battles. Adult workers might find themselves paying more taxes to support children's improved education. But this is how democracies work. Different groups' interests are supposed to be balanced. Adults as a group should have to share in this relativity of perspectives as well.

But more than this, not only would adults be no worse-off, in fact their lives would significantly improve.

Generally speaking, when new groups are enfranchised, it benefits others as well. Why? Because it expands the dataset on which collective decisions are made. And this improves collective decisions themselves.

This again is the logic of democracy. More voices lead to more highly informed policies. Even if some voices are ill-informed or even antidemocratic, a more diverse discussion leads to broader wisdom as a whole. A larger number of voters means a larger number of experiences and interests that representatives are pressured to take into account. And so it means more deeply and complexly informed policies for everyone.

Children's suffrage would provide adults and representatives more complex and realistic understandings of their society. Adults already live among children, but at present they have little incentive to understand how children's experiences might inform political policies. Were adulthood and childhood totally separate domains, as some seem to think, then children could safely (for adults) be ignored. But since people of all ages live intertwined with each other, ignoring children harms everyone. Insofar as children are badly off, so also are adults. Insofar as children remain unseen, adults are making decisions half-blind. As Lachlan Umbers puts it, children's enfranchisement would expand the "ongoing process of 'hypothesis testing' … [in which] democratic feedback mechanisms (deliberation, voting, and so on) provide data to be integrated into an assessment of policies."[2] The input provided by children's voting would necessarily force societies to test more diverse political hypotheses. This would help adults to make better choices not only for children but also for themselves.

Take the obvious example of teachers. Children's voting would improve teachers' lives by placing more pressure on governments to properly understand and support children's education. Governments would be more likely to provide adequate funding for schools. Legislators would have more reason to address educational problems like disability accommodations, gender inequities, meaningless curricula, over-policing, and cyber bullying. Should children's political power make a difference in any of these areas, it would be a gain for teachers, not a loss. Of course, ineffective teaching practices might also have to be rethought. Bad teachers might find themselves exposed. And teachers overall would likely need to become more responsive to children's needs. But teaching is supposed to be responsive to children. That is its whole point. Better informed education policies would help teachers better do their jobs. And this in turn would be better not only for children but also for parents, business leaders, and societies.

What about parents? One of the main complaints about children's voting is that it would give children too much power over parents in the home. What would really happen, however, is that children's voting would improve government policies around parenting and families. At the moment, legislators are only incentivized to consider family policy and law from the perspective of parents. If they also had to understand how families and parenting are experienced by children, any laws they enact touching on families would have more of the picture to work from. For instance, government support for families in poverty would be pressured to respond to the impacts of poverty not only on struggling adults but also on children's education, development, and life-long prospects. Governments are of course supposed to consider such factors, but they can also easily ignore them. Family leave policies might be understood less as parental entitlements than as children's rights. Domestic violence laws would need to treat child victims just as seriously as adult victims and make children's interests equally central in court hearings. Just as women's suffrage improved family policies overall, so also in new ways would children's suffrage. If parents' rights changed, it would only be to prevent harmful parenting and provide more support for parents in their difficult job of raising children.

Or consider the less obvious example of adult business owners. On the face of it, it does not seem that children's voting would make much of a difference to them. On the contrary, it might lead to more regulations and taxes. But a closer look makes it plain that business owners too would benefit, and in various ways. They would better understand children's public interests and concerns. They would be regulated in ways that respond to child consumers. They would have a better educated workforce to hire from. They would be able to pay teenagers better wages without losing competitiveness. They would be made more alert to racially and sexually discriminatory advertising to children. It might even turn out that children would demand more business opportunities themselves, in which case the market would benefit from increased innovation.[3]

Similar outcomes would result for medical professionals, lawyers, social workers, and adult professionals of all stripes. Anyone whose job has anything to do with children, however directly or indirectly, would find themselves living in a policy environment that better responds to children's actual lives, rather than adults' oversimplified guesses about them. Children's voting would help to unravel systemic ageism, just as other groups have unraveled systemic sexism, racism, ablism, classism, and much else. Any adult dealing at all with children and youth would benefit from living in a more child-friendly political culture overall.

The fact is that, on the whole, democracy works. By uniting diverse voices, it arrives at widely informed decisions. Policies are built on the broad foundation of the people's actual experiences. When democracies do make poor choices, it is often because whole groups have been ignored. Children's thinking is systematically excluded at everyone's peril. The real harm to adults comes from living in a distorted and unjust society. All societies are this way to some extent, of course. But children's suffrage would at least mitigate centuries of a deeply adultist bias that has narrowed societal choices dramatically.

Overall, the reason adults would be better off if children could vote is that political policies would have to better account for the children with whom adults actually share their lives. What effect will going to war have on the young? Is health policy disregarding children's particular needs? How is poverty uprooted early in life? What are children's real concerns about criminal justice? Why are the young so exercised about the climate emergency? Without these and millions of other pixels of democratic information, representatives are acting with blurred vision. They are seeing only two-thirds of the dots on the screen. It is time for them to make higher-resolution policies that are better for everyone.

Children's voting would have similar effects on social institutions. Social institutions like hospitals, schools, universities, religious organizations, business associations, and NGOs would find themselves both supported by and beholden to more child-responsive policies. Whether they deal with children directly or indirectly, social institutions would be governed by social climates that are more attentive to children's actual lives. They would need to consider the ways they are covertly or overtly perpetuating age discrimination. And they would have to respond better to young people's diversity of perspectives on public issues. Institutions of all kinds would be held more accountable to the populations they deal with.

Take for example hospitals. Are children's wards receiving equitable resources? Do pediatricians earn fair salaries? Are young children provided the particular attention and care they need? Are adolescent patients appropriate participants in decision-making? Do children have access to play spaces and nutritious food? Do parents have a bed to sleep in overnight? Are doctors, nurses, and other medical professionals trained in age-inclusive practices? Answers to these and myriad other questions make a significant difference in how well hospitals do their jobs. They change the effective running of hospitals as institutions. Hospitals should of course already be considering children's interests centrally. But they are more likely to do so if informed by a broader political context of child-friendly policies and laws.

Or consider religious institutions. Churches, synagogues, mosques, temples, and the like exhibit significant variation in how fully children are included. This variation is in part a function of religious beliefs. But the place of children in religious institutions is also an indirect function of children's places in society at large. When children are treated as second-class citizens in politics, it is more likely they will take back seats in religious institutions. It is more likely they will not be protected from clergy pedophilia, find themselves banned from services, receive only tokenistic pastoral support, and have their religious journeys taken less seriously. Apart from legal requirements against age discrimination and the like, children's voting would help religious institutions treat children with equal dignity, which would in turn improve religious institutions themselves.

Another example is NGOs. The local NGO Red Columbiana de Lugares de Memoria (Columbian Network of Places of Memory) is a grassroots group working for over twenty years on collective memory formation around the Columbian civil war.[4] Since children have been deeply impacted by the violence, both as soldiers and as members of war-torn communities, children's voting would help ensure their voices are heard in collective grassroots storytelling. Likewise, international NGOs such as the International Labor Organization (ILO) would feel greater pressure to respond to children's labor concerns in all their variations. The governments that fund the ILO would hold it to more child-inclusive account. Instead of seeking to ban children's labor altogether, for example, the ILO might be forced to consider the situation of children who actually want or need to work and to respond seriously to child labor unions fighting for children's worker rights.

Broadly speaking, social institutions are not isolated from their larger political contexts but rely on them for support and direction. When people come together to advance common goals, they do so as members of social systems. Women's and minorities' voting have both directly and indirectly helped social institutions to better account for multitudinous issues of gender and race. The same kind of benefit would accrue from voting by children. Children would become more visible members of societies at large. They would exert an indirect political pressure on social institutions to examine how they might marginalize children and to respond better to children's own particular and diverse lives.

Finally, what about outcomes for democratic systems as a whole?

As history shows, newly enfranchised groups do not leave democracies unchanged. They transform how democratic life is enacted and understood. Are children the great exception? Would young people's suffrage weaken democracy's foundations? Or would children gaining the right to vote would make democracies more just, healthy, and democratic?

In the first place, ageless voting would enable countries aspiring for strong democratic institutions to make themselves more genuinely inclusive. The word "universal" would no longer be a misnomer. It would no longer really mean only two-thirds of the citizens. The ideal of inclusiveness would not be based on unfounded assumptions about competence and knowledge. It would be based instead on the properly democratic ideal of the right to collaborate in one's own governance. Voting would become a right for all rather than a privilege for some. It would have to be guaranteed without conditions. Democracy would move closer to its own ideal of accountability to the *demos*.

A genuine embrace of voting universality would also encourage societies to reflect more carefully on other groups they currently leave out. Some democracies would need to ask themselves whether, for example, it is right to disenfranchise felons. The idea that very serious crimes remove one from the groundwork of democracy, either while in prison or thereafter, starts to look more like retribution than a genuine attempt to advance the interests of the people. Barring people who are mentally impaired would need more careful justification too. Even the exclusion of noncitizens might need to be rethought. The political scientist Claudio López-Guerra argues that the franchise criterion should be "residency" rather than "citizenship," since it is residency that comes with a genuine stake in a country's political outcomes.[5] These are examples of how the conversation might change about what it means for suffrage to be truly universal.

Children's voting is likely also to increase voter turnout and engagement among adults. It should hardly be surprising that democratic turnout is often low in democracies when the people have been told for the eighteen most formative years of their lives that their views do not count. In adult-only voting systems, the people are taught from birth to become passive and unengaged citizens. Being excluded from power for the first quarter of your life is likely to dimmish rather than enhance your sense of empowerment for the rest of your life. If, instead, the right to vote began whenever people desired the vote, then citizens would learn from an early age that their voices and concerns really matter to the democratic whole. They would grow up understanding that voting is powerful and important. As a consequence, they would be much more likely to vote throughout their lives.

If it is true that democracies are supposed to represent the people, then children's suffrage brings this ideal closer to reality. Unless it can be proven that children's voting would cause systemic democratic damage, the default position should be the enfranchisement of all regardless of age. In reality, what is most damaging to democracies at the moment is children's exclusion. With a huge part of the population barred from equal influence just because of their age, political life is distorted and the pressures on government weakened.

Not only would children's voting strengthen democracies, but it would also help reverse the contemporary slide of global democratic life into authoritarianism. This is because democratic authoritarianism is built on a logic of patriarchy, the dominance of those with historical power over those without it. Genuine democracy would be able to rebuild itself on the idea of accountability to those historically dominated and excluded. It would treat vulnerable and marginalized groups as needing to be welcomed.

After the fall of the Berlin Wall in 1989, it was generally felt that democracy would become the de facto global norm. In the words of political scientist Francis Fukuyama, we would witness "the end of history": "the end-point of mankind's ideological evolution and the universalization of Western liberal democracy as the final form of human government."[6] But this prognosis quickly turned out to be wrong. In fact, the current state of democracy is far from a happy one. Longstanding democracies like in the United States, the UK, and France contain growing authoritarian forces based on racial resentment and economic disparity. Newer democracies such as in Brazil, Indonesia, Turkey, and India are breaking down into sometimes violent populist factionalisms. Rising powers like China, Iran, and Russia are for the most part rejecting full democracy in favor of hierarchical oligarchy. And financial and corporate globalization means that even the strongest democracies are increasingly threatened by transnational authoritarian-like powers.

The Democracy Index of 2019 concludes that "the global march of democracy stalled in the 2000s and retreated in the second decade of the 21st century." Only twenty-two countries, representing a mere 5.7 percent of the world's population, can now be considered "full democracies," that is, democracies with free and fair elections, strong civil liberties, and responsive governance. A further fifty-four countries, involving 42.7 percent of the world's population, are "flawed democracies" that practice meaningful voting but contain systemic democratic deficiencies. Even adding these first two groups together, only a minority of the globe's countries and population live in actual democracies. The rest of the world, making up ninety-one countries and 51.6 percent of the global population, is either significantly or fully authoritarian. Their countries either systemically violate democratic norms or do not uphold them at all.[7]

The fact is that democracy has never followed a clear upward historical trajectory. The political historian David Runciman argues that periodic crises are built into the logic of democratic life. "The factors that make democracy work successfully over time—the flexibility, the variety, the responsiveness of democratic societies—are the same factors that cause democracies to go wrong."[8] Unlike autocracies, which survive by imposing a single iron will, democracies survive by placing their confidence in the people's collective ability to experiment and find new solutions. But this confidence can go too far, making democratic leaders passive and complacent in the face of existential threats, threats like today's climate emergency, populist uprisings, and economic inequalities. If large crises cause autocracies to collapse, they cause democracies to weaken and falter.

According to Runciman, the cure for democratic crises is often the enfranchisement of new groups. When democracies get stuck, broader voting rights breathe new life into them. "It happened [in America] in the 1860s, with the emancipation of slaves; in the early twentieth century, with the enfranchisement of women and the legal protection of labour; in the 1950s and 1960s, with the civil rights movement."⁹ Enfranchising new groups gives democracies more flexibility to work through existential crises. It is no accident that nonaristocrats first gained the right to vote during the collapse of medieval feudalism, the poor during the rising urban hardships of industrialization, and women after the breakdown of global order in the Great War. Why? Because old democratic norms reached their own points of exhaustion. Under severe crisis, autocracies have nowhere to go, but democracies are open to the potential of drawing upon previously untapped perspectives.

Authoritarian threats to democracy are in large part symptoms of their adult-only biases. Adultism places too much faith in supposedly rational and independent individuals. It assumes that racism, colonialism, sexism, and the like can be solved by supposedly impartial debate. It lacks the intergenerational timeline to handle longer-term global threats like climate change and market neoliberalism. And it reduces diverse groups and other nations to objects of competition. The association of democracy with individual independence was an improvement on the previous historical alternatives, but it has exhausted its advantages.

Children's suffrage injects the needed antidote. It does not solve all the world's democratic problems, but it provides the key to sufficiently radical change. This antidote is the full embrace of democracy as a space, not of rational independence, but of diverse interdependence. Democracy does not have to divide supposedly independent adult subjects from supposedly dependent child objects. It does not have to divide citizens between those occupying present democratic space and those still in predemocratic time. Instead, children's voting establishes democratic empowerment as a fundamental right for all, not just in their autonomy but in their complex interconnectedness. It grounds democracy not in supposedly impartial thought but in grassroots lived experience. The right to vote is then not just a right to asserting one's independent voice but a right to make a difference in shared decisions.

Authoritarian tendencies in democracies arise, in contrast, from powerful groups' beliefs that some of the people have more valid perspectives than others. Aryans are felt to have rights to rule over supposedly less advanced races. Whites are destined to supremacy over minorities. Men and masculinity are somehow more authoritative. The global rich are competitively entitled to dominate. Anyone with democratic power must have achieved it freely and independently by themselves. This adultistic approach sees no context for privilege. It recognizes no history of oppression. It ignores how those with power need those without. Authoritarian democracy is the logical outcome of an adult-centric valuation of individualism.

Likewise, an independence-grounded democracy tends to have trouble with longer-term thinking. It tends to remain focused on the immediate here and now. It has little incentive to consider impacts over a lifetime or on future generations. This is why democracies are largely paralyzed in the face of the climate emergency and not as effective as one would hope in uprooting long-term problems like racism and poverty. The idea of democratic independence favors short-term fixes. The people jostle for immediate competitive advantage. It is not their first order of business to strengthen networks of dependence and vulnerability. Or to uproot deep systems of oppression. Voting is about advancing the individual rather than creating sustainable communities.

Children's suffrage would cut off the oxygen of this kind of authoritarian thinking. It would help the people reimagine democracy as properly responsive to the people's lived experiences. Authoritarianism empowers might to control right. But democracy empowers right to control might. It aims to make itself accountable to the whole inter-reliant body of the people, not just those with power already. A democracy that fully included children would expose the cult of independence on which authoritarianism depends. It would expand power broadly among all affected rather than all considered important. In this way, child-inclusive democracies would seek to share power among everyone regardless of their ability to wield power autonomously. It would seek to be maximally responsive to the people as a whole.

Ultimately, although it is beyond the scope of this book, children's suffrage would demand revisions not only in democratic systems but also in democratic theory. It would mean rethinking the philosophical foundations on which democracy is based. I will only make a few small suggestions on this topic here. But it is clear that, just as feminism changed democracy's foundations in important ways, so also should childism, the effort to transform societies in response to children. There is a great diversity of theories of democracy, especially now that they are more responsive to historically marginalized perspectives of gender, race, class, and the Global South. But a systemic critique of democratic theory from the perspective of childism has yet to be made.[10]

A first step would be to examine why existing democratic theories assume an adult perspective in the first place. It would be to subject current ideas to childist critique. Let us take three prominent examples.

One theory of democracy is that it exists to defend and advance individual liberty. This is a relatively old theory of democratic liberalism, or what today could be called neoliberalism. From this perspective, democracy frees individuals from tyrannical political influence in order to pursue their own self-interest. A healthy competition among free persons is also the most efficient way to maximize the collective good. Voting, on this conception, is not about contributing to a common project but, on the contrary, liberating individuals to act for themselves without societal interference.[11]

This idea of democracy has many critics from a variety of progressive, feminist, postcolonialist, and other perspectives. From the point of view of childism, it turns out to be uniquely hostile. Neoliberals assume that political persons can act with complete independence. And that their doing so maximizes political rationality. It would be antidemocratic, on this view, to rely on the political collective for support. Children, however, insofar as they depend on governments for such things as education, health care, and economic well-being, are thereby lesser democratic persons. A democracy based on individual competition does not concern itself with dependency and need. These belong in the private sphere alone.

As a result, the neoliberal conception of democracy can hardly imagine children voting. It will draw a sharp line between independent adult voters and dependent child (and other kinds of) nonvoters. The core competence to vote is the ability to advance one's own interests in the public realm. If the poor, minorities, and women have over history gradually proven themselves autonomous enough to vote, children are much less likely to be able to follow suit. Indeed, it is all too likely that the young will lose out if exposed to a brute competition for power. What such a theory forgets is that people of any age are not just independent individuals. Adults as much as children rely on others, community supports, and social systems in every aspect of their lives. Freedom and dependency are not mutually exclusive. On the contrary, freedom is increased if you have been provided a good education, strong health care, and reliable societal supports. Human nature is interdependent, not independent.

Another theory of democracy gets us a little closer, but only a little. What I will call progressivism views democratic life as generating political agreement through impartial dialogue. Democracy is not a competition of private interests but a shared project of developing rational consensus. Voting means contributing your perspective to the larger public debate. Democracy therefore exists to bring a society's full diversity of voices into conversation with each other so as to make progress toward greater and more inclusive justice.[12]

A progressive view makes more space for children. Voters are supposed to consider the interests of others, not just themselves, and strive for an overall impartiality of outcome. Adults, then, are supposed to consider not only adult priorities but also those pertaining to the young. Politics aims to advance fundamental human rights that are in principle shared by all. Progressivism can support strong government programs that will provide children with much-needed educational and health resources as well as societal protections against violence and discrimination. Social supports such as these are necessary for well-functioning societies overall. Adult voters ought to consider children's needs in an equal way to their own.

The drawback for children, however, and the reason why progressivism too rarely contemplates children's voting, is that democracy so understood claims to base itself on impartial rationality. From this perspective, it is easy to ban from voting anyone supposedly unable to think and act with politically rational competence. Contributing to the progressive project means being skilled in critical discourse and having knowledge of a wide array of perspectives and potential outcomes. Children, on this logic, tend to be thought in need of a great deal of time and education before they can enter into the full democratic space. Indeed, the development of children is a crucial prerequisite for the progression of societies. On this model, it is difficult to see what a five-year-old could have to contribute. Adults with greater understanding of the world are more equipped, at least in theory, to advance the needed larger rational debate.

A third and more recently developed option in democratic theory gets us still closer. What I will call deconstructionism, again lumping various kinds of theory together, argues that democracies really exist to dismantle structures of oppression. They aim not for consensus but for dissensus, for undoing historical systems of power. The long democratic story is one of deconstructing or tearing away layer after layer of deep-rooted privilege. Democratic life is a site of struggle against hegemony. It fights against the all-seeing panopticon. Voting is a mechanism for speaking truth to power. It deconstructs or queers democracy via what can only appear as strange and unruly disruptions. It enables marginalized voices to assert their lived experiences of difference vis-à-vis historical norms. It empowers the poor, minorities, women, the colonized, and any other dispossessed group to challenge their political silencing.[13]

Children find more of a home in this theoretical perspective than in the other two options. The young too are a systemically marginalized group whose voices in politics have long been suppressed. And they are entirely capable of challenging oppressive political norms by marching, demonstrating, disrupting, and organizing against the powers that be. The deconstructive concept of democracy is also the basis for the idea used throughout this book that voting is a means to hold representatives accountable to the people's lived experiences. Voting is less about the expression of impartial reason and more about the demand for responsiveness to difference. It disrupts established norms by asserting grassroots experience. It empowers the people to hold representatives accountable to their otherwise marginalized voices.

However, it is no accident that major deconstructionist theorists of democracy rarely mention children either. They have been almost exclusively focused on empowering groups like women, racial minorities, queer and transgendered people, the poor, the disabled, subalterns, and the colonized. These, of course, often include children. But children themselves are almost never thematized as their own marginalized social group. If democracies are struggles for empowerment, then this is a curious lacuna. Children clearly hold less power than adults to give voice to their lived experiences in political life. Indeed, they generally have less power across the entire economic, social, and cultural board. Children would seem a prime demographic to include in concepts of deconstructive democracy.

The problem with deconstructionism, however, is that it assumes that the struggle against historical power must be enacted by the powerless themselves. Only the dispossessed can truly give expression to their experiences of normative difference. For others to help, however well intentioned, is to risk imposing their own alien hegemonic interpretations. White feminists should not claim to represent all feminists, or Black anti-racists Latinx anti-racists. But if such is the case, then infants, young children, and even older children and adolescents will remain marginalized even from the fight against marginalization. They will only participate properly if they lead their own struggle for themselves. It will be more important to protect their expressions of grassroots experience from the impositions of adults than for adults to provide them with any kind of substantive support.

The more complex reality, however, is that no group, child or adult, fights systemic injustice only by themselves or on their own behalf. Political persons and groups are, again, not independent but interdependent. Deconstructionism remains in the end adultist to the extent that it insists on oppressed groups being the only agents in their own demarginalization. It does not well account for the fact that speaking truth to power depends also on aid from others. Indeed, it depends on power itself providing a meaningful response. Children show that marginalized groups do not need social norms only to be dismantled. They require social norms also to be reconstructed in more mutually inclusive ways. In the case of children, the historically oppressive group is adults. It is therefore hard to imagine children's voting without, in addition, their adult dominators helping them to succeed. Children and adults are best empowered not simply on their own behalf but more complexly as members of interdependent networks. Political empowerment is not one-way.

If it is properly to include children, democracy needs a better theory. It can hardly be thought adequate if it makes a third of the people second-class citizens right from the very start. A lazy adultism has to be replaced with a critical childism that can imagine democratic life as accountable to all equally regardless of age. Just as people's conceptions of democracy have changed over history, now they need to change again. Otherwise, democracy threatens to buckle under the weight of its own intellectual incoherence. It is impossible in this chapter to develop a full new theory of democracy. But at least some initial suggestions can be made.[14]

In place of neoliberalism, progressivism, and deconstructionism, a new theory of democracy is needed that I would sum up under the concept of reconstructionism.[15] Reconstructionism combines deconstructionism with an additional demand for shared empowerment. Democracy on this view is a process of constantly recreating social norms in response to marginalized experiences. To reconstruct is constantly to expand or rebuild the space of politics to equally house all the people who live within it.

There have been feminist, Marxist, postcolonialist, and anti-racist philosophies of democracies. Now is time to develop a childist philosophy of democracy as well. What this means is that the deeply adultist biases of democratic theory need to be overcome by rethinking basic democratic norms and structures, so as to make them equally inclusive of children as children.[16] Even if I am a white male adult, I can still also be an anti-racist feminist childist. I can think outside the box of inherited history. I can think intersectionally from multiple points of view that include children's as well. A childist view of democracy would not compete with other views but at once learn from as well as enrich and deepen them.

Reconstructive democracy prioritizes the people's grassroots lived experiences of interdependence. It refuses to separate the people into one group whose differences are valued as expressions of independent experience and another group whose differences are coded as secondary expressions of dependence. Put differently, it refuses to separate democratic space from democratic time. There is no meaningful sense in which some people still need time before they can be fully admitted into democratic space. Rather, all persons of any age are equally impacted by the political sphere and equally able to contribute to it. All persons are dependent on their larger democratic society and, at the same time, are independently distinct contributors to it. The democratic space must be conceived of as vibrant, inclusive, and interwoven.

This different language of democracy asks us to imagine voting, in particular, in a new way. Voting exists, not to assert individual interests or experiences but to help reconstruct the shared democratic space. Just as individual concerns shift and grow over time, so also does the democratic space that people share in common as it responds to voters' diverse grassroots inputs. This common project is not the simple addition of all the people's independent voices. Rather, it is an always new recreation that embraces ever more expansive horizons over time. Just as each person has their own unique combination of influences upon them, so also is the body politic an ever-changing space of common life influenced by the diverse experiences of the people.

To say that democratic persons are not independent but deeply interdependent is to say that no one acts in a vacuum. We are happy to acknowledge this reality in virtually every other area of life. I need family members to have a household, coworkers to succeed at my job, friends and neighbors to lead a rich life, health workers to keep well, scientists to understand my world, innovators to make my life easier, writers and artists to make my life meaningful, and so on. It is highly unlikely that, once we step from the rest of our lives into the political sphere, we suddenly become completely independent individuals. We do not suddenly turn into Enlightenment gentleman free of all encumbrances. Even Enlightenment gentlemen depended on their wives, servants, laborers, children, and systems of privilege to enjoy their supposedly autonomous freedoms so freely.

Children's voting would mean that democracy is not only *of* the people and *by* the people but also, just as centrally, *for* the people. The people would have to be imagined as accountable not only to themselves but also, individually and collectively, to one another. Adults are accountable to children and children to adults. Most of all, representatives are accountable to the people. Despite what we have been taught to think, the people are deeply interdependent on one another for their justice and flourishing.

Democracies should reflect this more complex human reality. People in a democracy should be understood to act both *by* themselves and *for* one another. Voting is not a one-way but a two-way street. One of the consequences of children's voting would be to make this reality abundantly clear.

Reconstructionist theory would also imagine democracies to have a somewhat different aim or purpose. This aim would be for governments to expand rather than contract in their accountability to the people. At present, the aim of democracy is understood too narrowly. It can be theorized in different ways: as the maximization of people's interests, the advancement of human rights, or the deconstruction of oppression. But if it is equally to include children, the democratic aim should be understood instead as responsiveness to the people. The purpose of a democracy is to represent the people's diverse lives. This of course is an ideal. But ideals are important so that people and governments know what to shoot for.

Democracies should then base their decisions, if they are truly to enact rule by the people, on whatever responds to the widest possible diversity of the people's grassroots experiences. To this end, they should especially prioritize responsibility to experiences that have been historically marginalized. What they expand toward is not a predetermined fixed point but an open-ended representation of the people in their fullest possible plurality. A century ago, no democracy considered itself responsible for ending gender discrimination in the workplace. But women's different experiences of work were able to force governments to expand their senses of responsibility to the people. Collective life never accounts for everything. But it can continually reconstruct policy and law to make itself more accountable to the real diversity of the population's lives and concerns.

It might seem that existing ideas of democracy would not disagree. But, in fact, the neoliberal conception, for example, aims only to maximize the people's freedom to pursue their interests. As children show, this would actually make many in democracies less free as their interests are dominated by those of the powerful few. More importantly, it would make democracies less accountable to the people to the extent that people rely on shared government help. Likewise, progressivism seeks to make societies more equal and just, but only as equality and justice are defined by the prevailing political consensus. It does not well account for marginalized perspectives, such as those of children, that existing wisdom considers less than fully rational. And deconstructionism aims only to dismantle historical marginalization itself. This means it cannot imagine democracies as active spaces of political reconstruction, places in which the people create more expansive life in common. And so while it may be able to imagine undoing children's oppression, it cannot effectively help shape a more child-responsive democratic imagination.

A reconstructionist democracy imagines a different kind of political space. Simple though it may sound, democracy is the space of the people. Because the people provide ever new and unanticipated perspectives, so also should democracy aim to be a place of constant rebuilding. It is endlessly called upon to expand its own foundations. Democracy must seek to represent the lives of all the people as fully as it can. If it is equally to include children, it must create the conditions for the people's active responsiveness to each other. Democracy forges commonality on the basis of plurality. It houses the homeless, welcomes the stranger, makes room for always one more.

A childist perspective like this finally eliminates anyone's relegation to predemocratic time. It is the culmination of the centuries-long democratic project of turning the political time of aristocracy, lineage, and family into the political space of common geographic life. Democracy so understood does not imagine children to live in a separate time of prepolitical development. It does not project a future time of adult democratic reason. Instead, reconstructionist democracy insists that all the people, regardless of time in the world, can interdependently create a common political space together. There is no such thing as a time in life during which a person is not yet fit to help in the creation of shared democratic space.

Voting in particular is then understood not as a simple expression of interests but as a mechanism for holding governments accountable to the people. Voting empowers the people to live in common in response to their genuine diversity of concerns. It provides each and every person the opportunity to demand responses from government to their concrete and particular perspectives on the world. In other words, voting exists to constantly reconstruct the political terrain. It is there to expand and grow the shared imagination of societies.

Children not only can be included in voting so understood, but in fact they must. A democracy cannot make itself accountable to the people if it responds more fully and directly to some groups than others. It cannot claim to rule for the people if it does not permit all the people to bring their experiences equally to the table. It most especially needs to reconstruct itself through voices that have traditionally been suppressed. It needs to fertilize its own grassroots across the entire social field. It needs to seek out as diverse a range of pressures as possible on its collective decision-making.

If children cannot vote, a democratic government does not hold itself properly responsible to the people. It limits itself to the rule of some over others. It is, in fact, authoritarian. It decides ahead of time that some experiences are more important to respond to than others. Whether intentionally or not, it imposes the agenda of the powerful on the powerless, insisting that people of certain ages should systemically influence government more than people of other ages. And when one group can be assumed not to count, so also can other groups. Denying children the vote is ultimately a denial of the power of the people to forge a common life in response to each other.

There would, in the end, be various outcomes from children's voting beyond just for children themselves. And just as for children, these outcomes would not only not be harmful but instead would be systemically beneficial. Adults would live under policies that are better informed by the realities and diversities of the children with whom their lives are bound up. Social institutions would be able to pursue their goals in more child-inclusive and child-friendly ways. And democracies overall would make themselves more fully accountable to the people's diversity of grassroots experiences. Overall, children's voting would benefit societies because voting on the whole actually works.

The Proxy-Claim Vote

We can't save the world by playing by the rules, because the rules have
to be changed. Everything needs to change—and it has to start today.

Greta Thunberg

The infant mortality rate in Rwanda is far lower than in most countries
in sub-Saharan Africa. In 2020, Rwanda registered 29.7 infant deaths
(under one year of age) per 1,000 live births, compared, for example, to
69.8 in Nigeria, 56.1 in Uganda, and 49.6 in Ethiopia. This impressive
record is due chiefly to Rwanda's infant-responsive political policies.
Despite a lower per capita gross domestic product than in all the other
countries mentioned above, Rwanda has built a strong universal health
insurance system. It also has a mandatory minimum for the number
of women serving in parliament, which almost alone among nations
is at times majority female. What is more, the country responded to its
1994 genocide by taking aggressive steps to improve infants' health in
order to build a stronger future, such as through strengthened antenatal
care, women's education, early immunization, and the lowering of birth
rates.[1]

As this example shows, newborns are just as profoundly impacted
by democratic decisions as anyone else. Their very survival depends on
the right policies, as do their health, nutrition, housing, quality of care,
economic stability, environmental safety, future well-being, and much
else. But, of course, infants exercise very little, if any, direct political
influence. The only power they really hold is that used by adult voters
and politicians on their behalf. Representatives are theoretically just
as responsible to infants as they are to any other age group. But they

are not actually pressured in any formal way to respond to infants' particular lives (Figure 7).

Infants are the strongest test case for thinking about how children's voting rights might be carried out in practice. If there should be no age limit on the right to be included in the vote, and if ageless voting would benefit not only children but also adults and societies, and if, furthermore, child-inclusive voting would make democracies more democratic, then what would it mean to implement these ideals in reality? Can infants have a desire to vote? Can young children interpret ballots? Are older children and youth in a position to make their own decisions? Could adults vote on children's behalf? Would children deserve rights to run for office? These are just a few of the practical

Figure 7 Black-and-white card issued by the Brooklyn Woman Suffrage Party, 1900.

questions that might be raised. It is one thing to say that voting ought to be universal, another to see how it might work in actuality.

I argue in this chapter that the best way to realize the democratic ideal is by means of what I call a proxy-claim right to vote. A proxy-claim vote means that every person in a democracy is provided a *proxy* vote from birth to death that they can also *claim* to exercise for themselves at any point they desire. There would be no age, cognitive, knowledge, or any other irrelevant voting exclusion. Rather, each person in a democracy would have their right to vote exercised by a close proxy on their behalf unless they wish to claim their right to vote on behalf of themselves.

This proposal changes the structure of voting from the way it is practiced at present, or indeed has ever been practiced. Although there are a variety of democratic voting mechanisms at work around the world today, they all share one feature, namely inclusion by age. There are a certain number of years in a person's life when they are barred from voting; then at a certain age (say, 16, 18, or 20) they are automatically empowered to vote. Beforehand they are not represented formally at all. But then at a particular age they are simply given the right to vote whether they do anything to claim it or not. The current mechanism could be called a *granted* right to vote. It is granted by society at a general age at which the person is considered likely mature enough to hold it.

The proxy-claim right to vote operates on a different and more democratic logic.

The proxy side of the proxy-claim vote ensures the maximum possible accountability of representatives to the people. In the case of children, the proxy vote would belong to a parent or guardian. In the case of incompetent adults, it may belong to a guardian, next of kin, or power of attorney. Most populations would likely include around 10 percent children with proxies (those too young to claim their vote) and 10 percent adults with proxies (those who, for various reasons such as dementia, are incapable of claiming their vote). In whatever case, politicians would be made as responsive as possible to everyone in their constituency, regardless of political competence or any similar factor. Their use of power would be guided by the most expansive possible diversity of the people's grassroots experiences. A newborn infant may not be able to exercise the right to vote on their own behalf, but they would still be represented by a parent proxy. Likewise for an adult with severe dementia, profound mental illness, or even temporary disability or serious hospitalization. If competence is defined, as argued above, by the desire to vote, those unable to have or realize this desire should nevertheless factor into the pressures placed on the political system. The best way to do this is via a right to a voting proxy.

The claim side of the proxy-claim right to vote ensures the maximum possible empowerment of the people on their own terms. The claim vote replaces the proxy vote at any time a child or adult desires. It is not a function in any way of age. It could be instituted automatically at a culturally appropriate age such as twelve or fourteen if a political community so desired, though doing so would not strictly be necessary. The claim side of the vote simply places the right to influence political life in the hands of any person wishing to do so. By being able to claim their vote for themselves, whenever they desire, the people hold democratic representatives accountable to the most expansive possible diversity of their own particular lived experiences. The people are able to infuse policy-making with an inclusive understanding of their grassroots differences. Children in particular could demand accountability to their distinct and diverse concerns not as mini-adults but specifically as children. Any person with the minimum competence indicated by the desire to vote could claim their right to vote on their own behalf. The right to claim one's vote at any time puts into practice the basic idea that anyone should be able to vote if they want to.

The transition point between proxy and claim voting is the simple desire to claim the exercise of one's vote for oneself. As noted earlier, this desire proves three things: you know what it means to cast a ballot; you can compare your own and others' political views; and you can apply your lived experiences to concrete political choices. In a democracy, these are the only proper conditions that may be placed on the right to vote for yourself. They are the necessary and sufficient grounds for being competent to vote. Any additional demands on voters would be undemocratic. Nothing more is required for taking an active part in holding political representatives accountable.

It is not as strange as it might seem for voting practices to change. The proxy-claim vote might sound odd or radical, but so also would any of the other historical changes in voting at the time. When landowners gained suffrage, people had to prove their ability to vote by demonstrating that they met minimum property requirements, something no voter had previously had to do. When the poor and minorities gained enfranchisement, democracies had to eliminate those very same property requirements, along with poll taxes, literacy tests, and other discriminatory exclusions, and instead institute new kinds of proof of maturity and citizenship. When women won suffrage, nations created new laws to ensure balloting secrecy, prevent domestic coercion, and eliminate other forms of gender discrimination that could block women's ballot access. These changes improved voting practices for everyone, not just for the new groups in question. They were fiercely resisted by many, including within the very groups being enfranchised. But they won the day because they made voting more democratic. The same kind of shift will have to take place if voting rights are to be improved to now include children.

The proxy-claim idea learns from children that the people or *demos* in a democracy are not merely independent but deeply interdependent. The proxy side guarantees representation regardless of how dependent on others a person may or may not be. It does not reserve suffrage only for those presumed to be somehow politically autonomous. The claim side recognizes in everyone a degree of independence to act on their own behalf, a right to vote for themselves if they so desire. It acknowledges that each person brings to political life their own distinctive experiences and perspectives. The wall between dependent and independent persons is a false one. All children and adults are thoroughly interdependent. The proxy-claim right to vote is an interdependent right to vote that accounts for this more complex human reality.

Others in favor of children's voting have proposed various practical ways to make it happen. The idea of proxy-claim voting draws on some of these ideas. But in the end, other proposals retain vestiges of adult bias. Proxy-claim voting, however unusual it may seem, is in my view the most fully democratic possibility.

One proposal is to provide children a pure proxy vote, that is, an extra vote by a parent or guardian until they reach maturity. As we saw, a proxy vote on behalf of children has existed as an idea since at least the mid-nineteenth century and was even briefly enacted in early-twentieth-century Tunisia and Morocco (when fathers of four or more children were given one extra vote). Indeed, as we will see shortly, there already exist widespread proxy votes on behalf of adults. The overall rationale when it comes to children is that, even if children are not yet competent to vote for themselves, they still deserve equal political representation so that their interests directly influence political life. Proxy voting is usually imagined today as giving parents or guardians one extra vote for each of their prevoting children on the theory that, whatever form it takes, there should be one vote for each person.

This full proxy proposal is justified in various ways. The US demographer Paul Demeny—after whom proxy voting is sometimes called "Demeny voting"—proposed as far back as 1986 to "let custodial parents exercise the children's voting rights until they come of age." Demeny envisioned each of two parents having an extra half a vote for each child. The Italian economist Luigi Campiglio recently claimed that children's interests would be forced to the top of political agendas if "parents, who already represent their children's interests in everyday decisions, should naturally be entitled to represent them in the polling booth as well." Legal scholar Jane Rutherford argues that "just as members of Congress can vote on behalf of the populace, [parental or guardian] proxy-holders could vote on behalf of children." Similarly, the pediatric scholar Neena Modi, president of the Royal College of Paediatricians and Child Health, UK, claims that "trusting parents with a proxy vote while their children are very young might be another step towards a better future, and societally, represent a mark of growing maturity"; "society accepts that parents stand as proxies for their children in all other respects. Why not this one too?" And as another pediatric scholar, Lennart Köhler, has put it, "a family with five children should also have five extra votes to put on parties which show that they want to promote children's issues in society."[2]

My own proxy-claim proposal agrees with these suggestions, but only in part. My view is that a proxy vote is necessary for anyone who cannot vote directly on their own behalf. If you are not able to apply your own experience to voting choices, you deserve to be represented at the ballot box by an extra vote exercised by whoever is most likely to vote in your best interests. It is indeed necessary for democracies to enshrine one vote for each person. This undercuts the systematic marginalization of anyone not competent or able to vote. However, as I have argued, many if not most children are in fact sufficiently competent, knowledgeable, and independent to exercise their right to vote on their own behalf. Voting competence is not the same thing as age of maturity. No one with the desire to vote should have to give up that vote to their parent or guardian. Any such person is disenfranchised if they cannot vote on their own behalf.

Children and youth should be able to claim their own vote at any age they wish as a simple matter of democratic justice and effectiveness. Many children are intensely interested in politics and have important ideas to bring to the table. There is no uniform age at which this ability to apply oneself to political choices suddenly appears. Even if there were, it is certainly on the whole much lower than eighteen. Democracies and societies will function more inclusively and productively if anyone wanting the right to vote is able to exercise it instead of relying on others to do so on their behalf. That way, democratic leaders are subjected to the most diverse possible range of pressures from the people. They are forced to consider the most expansive possible pool of experiences. This pressure should come directly from children insofar as they are able and willing to exert it. While a pure proxy vote is therefore better than the current system of adult-only voting, it falls short of functioning as the most democratic way of ensuring children's political representation.

A second proposal that is often made is to lower the voting age to sixteen or perhaps even lower. Or to reduce it to sixteen as a stage on the way toward lowering it even further. As we saw, the voting age has already been reduced to sixteen in twenty-one countries and many cities and localities worldwide. Numerous other places have active movements to lower the voting age to sixteen, sometimes supported by major political platforms such as of the Labour Party in the UK.

There are many ways to justify this proposal. Psychologists Daniel Hart and Robert Atkins have demonstrated that, statistically speaking, sixteen-year-olds in the United States are "indistinguishable in their capacities to function as citizens to vote responsibly from the youngest adults." Sixteen-year-olds have measurably identical capacities as eighteen-year-olds in terms of civic knowledge, political skills, tolerance, and political interest. Legal scholar Joshua Douglas points in a different way to the benefits for voter turnout. With most sixteen-year-olds still living at home, they are more likely than eighteen-year-olds transitioning to adult life to "create a habit of voting and increase overall turnout in later years." Political philosophers Robert Goodin and Joanne Lau argue for lowering the voting age to fifteen on the theory that "enfranchising some less competent voters is no worry … so long as the electorate's competence averaging across all voters remains better-than-random." And the Vote at 16 campaign in the UK argues that sixteen-year-olds should have the vote because they can already give medical consent, pay taxes, consent to sex, join trade unions, direct companies, and much else of a similarly adult level of responsibility.[3]

A lowered voting age would, of course, be a step in the right direction. I would agree that sixteen-year-olds are clearly on average just as competent to vote as adults. Indeed, the empirical evidence is likely even stronger than it appears. Since adolescents have never actually had the opportunity to vote, their capacities are likely much better than they appear. If you had performed an empirical study of the voting competence of women in the nineteenth century, they too would likely have looked less capable of voting than they turned out to be in reality, once voting became for them an actual possibility. Were young people in fact able to vote, their voting skills and knowledge would certainly appear much higher than at present.

But the problem with a votes-at-sixteen approach is that it assumes that voting competence is best measured by one or another particular age of maturity. It retains the adult-centric view that suffrage requires adult-like competencies, simply moving back the age at which such competencies are thought to arise. But, as I have argued, adulthood is not the correct measure of voting competence in the first place. It leaves out large proportions of the electorate who would want to vote if they could and whom a democracy should want to include. And it lumps voters into age groups rather than actual voting abilities.

Furthermore, since many adults themselves are not particularly competent to vote, at least on the criteria proposed, a lowered voting age imposes a double standard. It makes demands of children that it does not make of adults. The idea of adult voting competence is in fact historically quite new, arising as it did in the early twentieth century to replace earlier criteria of gender, race, class, and wealth. The proper measure of voting competence is not maturity at all. It is desire. Limiting the vote by a predetermined age, whatever that age may be, prevents democracies from holding themselves properly accountable to the diverse experiences of the people.

The same logic applies even to proposals to lower the voting age much further, say even to as young as six.[4] The problem with any voting age is that it retains the notion of universal age capacities. More or less whatever age you propose, there will be some younger children who are ready to vote and some older ones who are not. The very concept of age as a marker of voting competence assumes that all children of each age are the same. It mistakes average and culturally specific ages of development for actual individual capacities. Everyone changes throughout their lifespan, but no one should be treated as if they are no more than the average of their age cohort. Otherwise, eighty-year-olds should probably be banned from voting too.

A proxy-claim vote, in contrast, ensures that anyone of any age can choose to vote if they are competent enough to do so. It treats voting rights as similar to free speech rights in that they are not legitimately tied to any age in particular. Rather, voting rights should belong to anyone with the desire to cast a ballot. It is this desire, and not the average capacities of one's age-mates, that should determine whether or not one can vote.

Finally, why not simply extend equal voting rights to all? Why not give children the same open right to vote that is currently granted to adults—the right simply to go and cast a ballot? Would this not be the fairer option?

This proposal was first made in the 1970s and remains popular today among scholars and activists advocating for children's political equality and liberation. It follows the model of women's and minorities' suffrage movements in their emphasis on voting as a fundamental human right of all individuals. The argument is that children deserve to be treated as political equals to adults. They too are impacted by policies and they too are capable democratic agents. Their exclusion from voting discriminates against their basic rights as participatory citizens.

An early proponent of this view was the psychologist Richard Farson, whose 1974 book *Birthrights: A Bill of Rights for Children* argues that, in addition to full freedoms of education, home environment, sex, work, and much else, "the liberation of children requires that they be given the right to vote." Otherwise, he claims, children's needs and perspectives will continue to take a back seat in public policy. The educator John Holt similarly argues in his 1975 *Escape from Childhood* for "the right to vote for people of any age." As he puts it, "to be in any way subject to the laws of a society without having any right or way to say what those laws should be is the most serious injustice." The journalism scholar Bob Franklin claimed in 1986 that, while some rights should belong only to adults, the right to vote is owed to children because it is fundamental to "the right to be a citizen." It would "give higher priority and emphasis to policies relating to youth affairs than at present."[5]

Similar proposals for full child voting are now also being made by political philosophers and scientists. Claudio López-Guerra argues at length in *Democracy and Disenfranchisement* that excluding minors cannot be justified because the "franchise capacity" for voting rests solely on the ability to value the act of voting itself. Like in my concept of the desire to vote, valuing the vote has no legitimate connection with any particular age. Michael Cummings presents extensive evidence to show in *Children's Voices in Politics* that "the alternative to seeking some magically 'correct' voting age is to allow every citizen to vote whenever in life the person develops public-policy preferences and wants them to count." Again, this proposal is very similar to my own. Children and youth, when asked, have much more complex and sophisticated political voices than generally supposed, indeed often more informed ones than adults.[6]

The cause of children's universal voting is now championed by numerous child and adult activists. As we have seen, youth-led groups like KRÄTZÄ, Foundation for the Rights of Future Generations, We Want the Vote, and National Youth Rights Association have been fighting for at least two decades for children's universal suffrage. Sixteen-year-old Vita Wallace argued in 1991 that "children be allowed to grow into their own right to vote at whatever rate suits them individually."[7] And young people have been joined in this movement by adult-led groups like the Freechild Institute, Amnesty International UK, the Association for Children's Suffrage, the Children's Rights International Network, Represent MA Children 2020, and the Children's Voting Colloquium. There is a diverse global movement, as we have seen, to provide children equal voting rights to adults.

I am largely in sympathy with this position. It is by far the most democratic alternative among the three most prominent options. Unlike a pure proxy vote or vote at sixteen, it recognizes that children have just as valid a claim to political agency as adults. And it insists that voting rights are not special rights but basic human rights that should belong by default to all. Children's suffrage is needed to reverse children's current second-class citizenship and make them full democratic people. Technically, as previously noted, the Universal Declaration of Human Rights enshrines this right to suffrage for all. Giving children equal voting rights would realize the ambitions of the larger human rights movement.

I do, however, have one hesitation. My hesitation is that universal voting of this kind is still, in a certain sense, grounded in the experiences of adulthood. It extends what adults already have to children as well. In the process, it thereby understands voting itself on existing adult terms. In my view, the change needs to be more fundamental. It needs to be as radical as when voting was extended to previously marginalized groups like the poor and women. That is, universal voting needs to learn from children what universal voting really means. It should not only fit children into adult practices but change practices overall so that children and adults are represented equally. This is the idea of childism, of responding to children's experiences by transforming historically adultist structures.

From this perspective, it is not enough only to declare children equal to adults. One must also expand the terms on which "equality" itself is defined. I believe that, even if current voting were universalized, it would soon become clear that it still marginalizes certain groups by age. Most obviously, it would disempower infants, who, even if given an open right to vote, are never actually going to use it. Infants cannot know what voting is. Younger children who might have some sense of what voting means are still likely to vote in much lower numbers than adults. And even older children might be less likely to take advantage of the opportunity to cast a ballot simply by virtue of having spent less time engaged in the political world. The result is that, if the different experiences of children are not taken into account, the youngest of children, at least, will find themselves even more politically disempowered than they are at present. They would end up in an even smaller disenfranchised minority, their political interests even less of a priority on the political stage. Age would end up making a massive difference in actual political influence. Younger children would be systematically dominated by even larger numbers of fellow citizens.

The universal voting solution is therefore not as universal as it first appears. It defines the "universal" in an adult-centric way. That is, it assumes that, to be universal, voting must be cast freely and independently. It is enough simply to remove any voting age restriction. Then all the people will enjoy equal access to political influence. But as in previous history, the very concept of "universal" needs to be put into question. When the founders of the United States declared that "all men are created equal," they appeared to be speaking universally but in fact defined this universality around wealthy, white, landowning gentlemen. When "universal" voting was extended to all men, it was assumed this also took care of women in men's households. The current concept of "universal voting" tends to presuppose that it can be limited to adults and still somehow also represent children. Likewise, merely extending this concept to all ages still presumes it includes the youngest of children when in reality it does not.

Proxy-claim voting imagines universal voting differently. It assumes that voters are not independent but rather interdependent. Rather than treating children like mini-adults, it unites children and adults along the same interdependent voting spectrum. The proxy side of proxy-claim voting recognizes the inherent political dependency of all. It allows for that dependency to include sometimes relying on others to vote on one's behalf. Some children and adults, for a variety of reasons, need others to make their right to vote an actuality. Political dependency takes many forms, from being new to the world to lacking political competence, suffering from severe dementia or mental illness, being incapacitated by illness, or even being at war or abroad. Truly universal voting would not gloss over such realities as mere exceptions. It would not punish people with insufficient autonomy. Rather, it would recognize that all persons have the right to influence democratic life however relatively dependent on others they may be.

There are, in fact, various kinds of proxy voting already practiced around the world. Indeed, the one group currently lacking any proxy representation is children. The UK permits proxy voting if a good reason is provided, such as being on vacation, being too ill, or having to work. In India, armed forces personnel can appoint a proxy to vote on their behalf while on duty. In Iraq, proxy voting is permissible for anyone who is illiterate. Canadian territories allow the assigning of a proxy if on polling day a voter will be absent from the country, away in the military, or working away as a fisherman or prospector. In the United States, as we saw, adults with severe cognitive impairments can have their ballots filled and mailed in by a surrogate. In Vietnam, proxy voting is technically illegal but tolerated by the government because it increases electoral turnout (by about 20 percent). That proxy voting exists for adults is a tacit recognition that people should be represented even if they depend on others to do so on their behalf.

Extending the vote to children should in the end mean responding to children, not just insofar as they are like adults, but also as children. Existing voting mechanisms were built for adults. Or, rather, they were built for a particular image of adults as wholly free and independent individuals. A proxy-claim vote, in contrast, rests on a more realistic and inclusive idea of the political person. It assumes that political beings are both independent from one another, in bringing their own diverse ideas and experiences to the political space, and at the very same time dependent on one another for responding to their concerns and sometimes speaking up on their behalf. Democracy is thereby imagined, not as a competition among the interests of individuals, but as a process of shared social responsiveness. If it is meant to respond to the people, democracy must also imagine the people themselves as responsive to one another.

There are various possible objections that can be made to the idea of proxy-claim voting. Over the years, I have encountered critiques of both theoretical and practical kinds. In the remainder of this chapter, I explain how I would respond to the main ones.

On the proxy side of the proxy-claim vote, the most common objection is that it undermines genuine voter equality. A parent may or may not vote in the actual interests of their child. She or he may not understand the world in the same way as their child experiences it. Indeed, a parent may fail to vote at all. The same problem would exist for proxies of noncompetent adults. Having someone vote on one's behalf leaves one open to one's vote's misuse or neglect. The whole concept of proxy voting creates a group of second-class citizens who are naturally not going to be taken as seriously by political representatives as those who can actually vote them out of office for themselves.

My response is that the wrong two things are being compared. The alternatives for an infant or any other noncompetent voter are not between having a proxy vote and voting for oneself. Rather, the only realistic alternative is between having a proxy vote and having no vote at all. This criticism of proxy voting does not acknowledge people's deep interdependence. It assumes that all voting must represent an individual's own independent views. But people's views are not divorced from their contexts and surroundings. Young children are overwhelmingly likely to vote as their parents suggest anyway. A parental proxy would rarely change what a young child would choose by themselves were they able to. But it is better to have a proxy vote than no vote at all, for then one's representatives are pressured to take one's particular experiences into account.

Furthermore, voting is already a proxy action in a sense. Adults do not vote directly for laws (except in certain kinds of referenda), but instead for representatives who act as their proxies when they vote for laws on the people's behalf. Even referenda are put to the people by legislators, not by the people themselves, and enacted not by the people but through legislative proxy processes. A proxy vote for young children and incompetent adults only adds one further proxy layer to an overall multilayered proxy system. What it adds is the possibility for noncompetent people to have their interests recognized up the political line. And it is more empowering than the alternative, which would be no direct political influence at all.

Second, the proxy side of a proxy-claim vote can seem unfair to adults who do not have children. I hear this concern frequently. A single parent with six young children would get seven votes, while an adult without any children would get only one vote. People might even start having more children to get more votes.

But this critique is easy to refute. It is based on the false assumption that children do not count as political beings. It asserts that children should have zero votes, not one. The reality, however, is that children are just as much political persons as adults. They are equally invested in and impacted by political decisions. Democratically speaking, they should count for exactly one vote each. The unit of voting is not the household but the person. A proxy vote is not an extra vote but an equal vote. It does not add a vote, but makes up for a vote that has been denied. A household with seven people in it should have seven votes. A household with one person only one.

Representation for all regardless of age is not only fairer but better for the whole of society, including for people without children. It forces democracies to function democratically. And, of course, it is patently ridiculous to suggest that a parent would go through all the trouble and expense of pregnancy, childbirth, and child-rearing just to get one extra vote! If such a person existed, they should be awarded a medal for outstanding political dedication. There may be a certain classism or even racism to this objection, insofar as the critic might have in the back of their mind larger families of specific kinds. Regardless, the objection is certainly adultist. It assumes that children should not count in the political sphere on their own terms.

A third issue is whom a proxy vote should be used by. For adults, the proxy vote could be provided to a next of kin or advanced designee. But for infants and children, it will generally be more complicated. What if there are two parents? What if the child is orphaned or in foster care? Or one parent has been declared unfit or is little involved? What if parents divorce or remarry? And if there are two parents raising a child, should each get half that child's vote or should it go, as some suggest, to the mother as the one most likely to consider the child's best interests? And should children themselves have any say in these matters?

The answers to these questions would depend, in part, on local and cultural contexts. But, overall, the guiding criterion should be whatever best represents each child's particular experiences. In the United States, there is a dangerous political precedent of assigning only a fraction of a vote to racial minorities, making it harder to imagine half a proxy vote per parent. It also does not seem right to give a blanket preference to mothers, since this discriminates against the world's many involved fathers. The best option, in my view, is for the parents in question themselves to decide. If they cannot decide, then the default would be half a vote each. I would give parents the right to assign the proxy vote in any of a number of possible ways: to one of them, split in half, alternating by election, and so on. Divorced parents could continue previous practices or renegotiate them as part of custody agreements. Children without parents would have a proxy vote assigned to their closest guardian. But, of course, these questions would also need to be worked out through legislation over time. And if children could vote, they could be worked out with inputs from the very people they most affect.

On the claim side of the proxy-claim vote, there is the objection, fourth, that a child claiming and exercising the vote could face special obstacles. Parents might seek to prolong their own proxy vote by keeping a child ignorant of their rights or delaying its takeover. They might impose undue influence once a child's vote has been claimed. They might prevent a child from claiming their vote unless they meet parentally superimposed extra standards. And for children themselves, there is the possibility that when claiming their vote, they could face undue hurdles. They might have to obtain proof of their address, hold government identification, or legitimate themselves in some other way that would tend to be more difficult for children than for adults.

The act of claiming one's vote should be as simple and straightforward as possible. There should be no literacy test. Proof of residence should not involve paid bills or other documents that only adults are likely to possess. In countries like my own where voters have to register, the process should involve only necessary information and be available through diverse formats such as in person, by mail, and online. The goal is not to erect barriers but to hear what children have to say. Politicians ought to enact whatever voting procedures give them the widest possible understanding of the wishes of the people.

As for undue parental stonewalling or influence, as already noted, no one is free of influence, but no one totally lacks agency either. Children ought to have the right to receive information and education about voting from multiple sources, including not only parents but also schools, mass media, and the government. Children live in public spaces from which they learn about politics in a diversity of ways. Within families, adults already influence children and each other. Their ability to claim their vote would not eliminate all influences. But it would empower children to have more rather than less independence in this regard. It would in addition gear political campaigning and debate toward children's lives. It would be up to political systems themselves—which again children would now be able to affect—to install the guardrails needed to enable children to claim and exercise their votes fairly.

Fifth, some worry about the potential manipulation of children's votes by schools. Children learn a great deal about their governments in the classroom. If children could vote, teachers and education leaders might be tempted to use their positions of power to slant children's preferences. Imagine an election coming up and a left-wing social studies teacher subtly denigrating right-wing views. Or a right-wing textbook company explaining the perspectives of big oil but not of climate protesters. Unlike adults, children and youth are forced to participate in educational settings that might impose undue political biases.

These are real concerns, but they underestimate the capacities of children to think for themselves. If a child has already claimed their right to vote, this means they already have the capacity to form their own political opinions. Such a child is already influenced from many directions: parents, siblings, friends, pop icons, the news, the internet, class, culture, and much else. Educators are but one part of this larger constellation. Still, teachers should not be permitted to use their power in the classroom to influence voter preferences, any more than they should be permitted to use this influence for their own personal gain or gratification in other ways. Adults are protected in the workplace from receiving undue political pressure from superiors. Likewise, teachers would need to be barred from using their power to educate for non-educational political ends.

Sixth, and more persuasively, some are concerned that children's ability to claim their own vote would increase inequality *between* children. It would tend to empower already privileged young people more than it might empower those who are poor, minorities, disabled, or otherwise already dispossessed. That is, having more voters in the voting pool would magnify existing political inequalities. Rather than causing governments to tackle child poverty, health care, and discrimination, children's rights to vote might give governments more reasons to privilege the already advantaged.

But this objection is oddly undemocratic. It is true that democracies tolerate social inequalities, but they do not tolerate them as much as nondemocracies. This is because, in general, democracy is an equalizing force. Both privileged and underprivileged children may very well vote at similar rates to their privileged and underprivileged parents. However, children are currently an underprivileged democratic group in their own right. Fears of enhancing inequalities of class and race cannot rule out solutions to inequalities of age. It would be paradoxical indeed to oppose solving one form of oppression because it does not also solve others.

But, in addition, children's gaining rights to vote would likely help to equalize rates of adult voting as well. One reason disempowered groups often vote in lower numbers is that political systems are perceived, rightly, to be less responsive to their concerns. If, however, all persons from childhood were empowered to vote, this would infuse a sense during voters' formative years that governments actually care what they think. Indeed, it would force governments to take them into greater account. Adults of all social classes as a result are likely to vote in higher numbers, which would help to close the overall voting gap. More voters with the habit of voting from an early age means greater influence for groups that would otherwise be left out in the cold. And in a broader sense, a democracy that is responsive to children is also more likely to be one that is responsive to the powerless and downtrodden.

There is a seventh and final objection of a different kind that needs more extensive consideration. This objection is that children's rights to vote could also entail children's rights to hold political office. The issue here is that child politicians would then wield power not only indirectly but also directly over adults. They might also effectively have to hold full-time jobs. The competencies they would need could surpass the minimum competencies needed just to vote. And the outcomes could be disastrous.

Some countries currently tie the age at which you can run for office to the age at which you can vote. For example, the age for both is eighteen in the UK, Sweden, Denmark, Spain, Turkey, South Africa, Australia, and New Zealand. Most countries, however, draw a distinction between the voting age and the age of candidacy. This distinction is permitted by UN international law, which states that "it may be reasonable to require a higher age for election or appointment to particular offices than for exercising the right to vote."[8] For example, the United States has a voting age of eighteen but sets minimum ages of office at twenty-five for the house, thirty for the senate, and thirty-five for the presidency. In Brazil, where the voting age is sixteen, the minimum age for representatives is thirty for governors and thirty-five for the president. In Greece it is twenty-five for any office. In India it is twenty-five for the lower house, thirty for the upper house, and thirty-five for the president and state governors. In Nigeria it is twenty-five for representatives and thirty-five for senators and the president.

In countries with different ages of voting and candidacy, large numbers of people can therefore vote for offices that they are too young actually to hold themselves. About a third of eligible voters in the United States are not old enough to serve as president (not to mention voters barred for not being born in the country). The justification is that the competencies needed to vote are not the same as those needed to legislate and govern. It is a similar logic as in other arenas of life, where all kinds of different age limits are set on sex, marriage, driving, renting a car, and drinking alcohol. If the right to vote were ageless like rights to free speech and assembly, the right to hold office could still be treated as an age-specific right. Holding office might be a special right requiring especially complex political capacities. Like rights to fly airplanes, practice medicine, or lead soldiers in war.

Children's voting does not in itself, then, necessitate that children also be able to run for office. It would be possible to argue that children are competent to vote but not yet competent enough to govern. This would follow the international norm. Holding office would be like teaching. Children are competent to have a say in how they are educated, but this does not mean they are competent to work as professional educators. For this, they need to gain the requisite skills and experience. The same is true for adults who can vote on policies governing social benefits for the elderly but do not have rights to those benefits themselves. Likewise, serving in government could reasonably be said to need different age limits than voting on who can serve.

That said, the argument made in this book suggests taking a look at the question from a somewhat different angle. From a childist point of view, the deeper question is not just whether children are competent to hold office, but rather whether their holding office would make democratic systems more accountable to children's particular lives. Are there certain capacities in office-holding adults that make them better at responding to children's interests than children would be themselves? Or would governments listen better to all the people if children could also share in governance?

Let us note, to begin with, that these are legislative matters that would benefit from direct voting inputs from children. Whether serving in government is harmful to children or not is a question that would be better answered by including children's perspectives as well. Whatever legislation might be crafted, and whatever legal challenges advanced, the process would be more richly informed if inclusive of children's ideas.

My view, though, is that governments would ideally make better decisions if people of any age had the right to serve in them. I say "ideally" because governments themselves would need to undergo significant reform in order to make this ideal a reality. Office-holding would have to be deprofessionalized or made part time so as not to interfere with school. This would return office-holding to something more like its volunteer state in early modern democracies. Retaining office would also need to be made less beholden to moneyed interests, since children on the whole have less access to financial resources. Of course, removing money from politics would also benefit most adults, indeed all but the wealthiest few. On the other hand, there is also an argument for legislators being full-time professionals who can devote their complete attention to the people's business. If so, there might need to be different kinds of representation available to all, some full time and some not.

In whatever form it might take, democracies would function more inclusively and justly if children and youth had the right to hold at least some political power. This would pressure governments to propose, craft, and institute more child-friendly policies. A democracy that allowed women the vote but not candidacy would be much worse for women. In the case of children, there is a built-in safety mechanism. To actually win office, a child would have to prove to a majority of both child and adult voters that they would be able to serve well and effectively. The basic mechanism for deciding who should hold office in a democracy is the vote itself. Children would only win if enough of the electorate considered them the best available candidate. Elections may not always result in competent leaders, and certainly plenty of adult office holders are ignorant, narrow-minded, and corrupt. But a politically astute youngster may be preferable to a corrupt oil baron. A youth leader of Fridays for Future is going to govern more justly and effectively than an adult neo-Nazi organizer. Greta Thunberg would be a smarter president than Donald Trump.

I admit that these are difficult questions that raise thorny issues. I do not have all the answers. And effective solutions will vary depending on diverse local contexts. The argument made in this book is only that children should have the right to vote. Since the right to vote does not automatically entail the right to run for office, my argument does not hinge on answering the latter question definitively. I simply suggest that the question is best decided on the basis of whatever political arrangement is more likely to hold representatives accountable to the full range of lived experiences of the people. In which case, the possibility for children to hold office is an important one to consider.

Overall, the proxy-claim right to vote is the most effective practical way to maximize democratic accountability. It holds democracies to their own democratic ideal. If the idea sounds strange, it is worth keeping in mind that every democratic innovation over the course of history also sounded strange at the time. The strength of democracies is that they can always change. Unlike autocracies, democracies bend with the strongest winds instead of resisting them and breaking. Democracy creates not only new legislation but also new procedures for legislating. It develops over time deeper ways to enfranchise the *demos*. It searches out the best available mechanisms for maximizing input and accountability.

No doubt further innovations will arise in the future. But at the moment, the greatest possible renovation of the franchise would lie in extending the vote to the vast group of disenfranchised people who are children. Imagine what democracy would mean if it truly welcomed the youngest among us. Imagine how we would think of political life if democracies truly searched out the grassroots concerns of us all. Imagine politics as not only passively but also actively responsive to the people. The most effective way to do that would be by means of a proxy-claim vote that enfranchises all regardless of age, dependency, experience, or any other factor irrelevant to political personhood.

We create political space by responding in common to one another's differences. Voters are already proxies for each other and claimants for themselves. They vote on behalf of both themselves and the others with whom their political spaces are shared. Proxy-claim voting recognizes this human reality of deep interdependence. It refuses to divide the people into independent actors and dependent objects and reaches down instead into the people's shared experiences of grassroots life. This is what democracy is all about. Responsiveness to one another as political beings.

Manifesto

[Man] has not ever permitted [woman] to exercise her inalienable right to the elective franchise. He has compelled her to submit to laws, in the formation of which she had no voice. ... Having deprived her of this first right as a citizen, the elective franchise, thereby leaving her without representation in the halls of legislation, he has oppressed her on all sides.

Declaration of Sentiments, 1848 Seneca Falls Convention, United States

I walked away from the Philadelphia Fridays for Future rally with something else. Not only were the climate strikers joined together in youthful solidarity. They were also claiming their power to change the climate justice conversation. I saw that this power is far stronger than mere voting. It goes beyond choosing among a given set of limited options. Instead, protest takes the political world into one's own hands in order to transform thinking. It is able to force marginalized experiences upon the common political space. Adults were not alone going to understand the climate danger, especially for the young. It took child and youth activism on the streets to clarify the real depths of humanity's shared climate emergency.

If children can act for climate and other kinds of justice, there is no reason they cannot vote. They are already, and have always been, engaged political actors. They have already marched for women's suffrage, protested against racism, desegregated schools, campaigned against nuclear weapons, changed disability policies, organized for gun regulation, fought in wars, demanded labor rights, spoken up for transgender equality, and a great deal much else. Indeed, they have played roles in every major political movement in history. There is no single age at which political agency suddenly springs into being. Nor is there any single age at which the people suddenly gain the capacity to vote.

As I have argued in this book, children's exclusion from voting is both unjust and counterproductive. Most children and youth are competent, knowledgeable, and independent enough to be able to hold representatives to account. And representatives will make better decisions for children, adults, and societies if they are pressured to respond equally to the diverse life experiences also of children. Just as in every advance in suffrage over history, children's voting would make democracies more fully, complexly, and effectively democratic.

There are many objections to children's voting rights, but none of them stands up to careful scrutiny. They are based on history, power, and bias instead of reflection, justice, and humanity. They represent a particular moment in democratic history that has run up against its inherent limitations. The future of democratic life needs to be imagined differently. It is time for a childist transformation that remakes democracy in the image of all instead of just some of the people.

To those who say that children lack voting competence, a careful consideration of what is required for responsible voting shows that most children in reality do not. Voting rights are more like rights to freedom of speech, conscience, and assembly than rights to driving, marriage, and employment. There is no good reason to limit them according to age. On the contrary, absent strong justifications otherwise, suffrage should be available to all who would like to exercise it. The competence to vote consists solely in being able to hold political views and apply them to the available political choices. This competence is precisely measured by a person's desire to vote. The desire to vote demonstrates one's capacity to pressure representatives to account for one's particular lived experiences. Any age criterion necessarily fails to match this competence and is therefore discriminatory. Anyone of any age who wants to vote should be able to do so.

Some believe that children lack sufficient political knowledge, that they cannot vote in sufficiently informed ways. But the relevant knowledge needed for voting is knowledge of one's own and others' grassroots lived political experiences. It is not information about formal democratic processes but rather bottom-up understanding of politics on the ground. The knowledge that holds representatives accountable to the people is knowledge of the people's diverse and different lives. Not only do children possess such knowledge, but their particular political knowledge is necessary for politicians to understand the people they are supposed to represent. Not only is age irrelevant to whether one has voting knowledge, but all ages need inclusion for knowledgeable democratic decisions. Without the direct and equal inputs of all the people, politicians cannot develop responsibly informed policies.

Similarly, it is unfair and unwise to deny children an equal share in political power. A healthy democracy distributes power across the people as a whole, secure in the knowledge that a greater diversity of influences leads to more just and effective policies. Children's voting would not give them special powers over adults. Rather, it would give them general powers to share equally in developing common democratic goals. It would help to reverse children's historical disempowerment. In addition, it would mitigate children's lesser power in other areas of life such as economics, culture, and society. Far from opening children up to undue adult manipulation, children's voting would empower them to assert their own perspectives as children. Suffrage would grant children the same power already enjoyed by adults, the power to hold governments accountable to the people's concerns.

To those who worry that children and youth would be harmed by their own right to vote, the evidence is overwhelming that, on the contrary, they would greatly benefit. The logic of democracy, witnessed time and again throughout history, is that it pressures governments to be more rather than less responsive to newly enfranchised groups. Rather than robbing children of their childhoods, children's voting would make childhoods an equal political concern. Rather than creating a slippery slope into unsuitable adult rights, it would build a staircase into more informed and meaningful special rights for children. The real harm to children comes from being denied a formal say in governance. Democracies benefit those who can hold them to account.

Nor would children's voting harm adults or societies. On the contrary, it would help them systemically and significantly. Voting is not a zero-sum game. Adults live in societies with children and so benefit from better understanding children's real and diverse societal experiences. Parents, teachers, doctors, lawyers, and any other adults who interact with children would stand to gain from more child-responsive legislation. Social institutions would be provided stronger conditions for child-inclusive work. Democracies themselves would become a great deal more richly informed. And they would better resist authoritarianism by rejecting the lure of raw power and instead embracing the people's deep-seated interdependence. Even democratic theory would be transformed under a new childist critique that combines rule *by* with rule *for* the people. All of these outcomes arise from the basic democratic truth that an expanded electorate expands the responsiveness of governments.

The result of these considerations is that all children should be given the right to vote. Suffrage cannot legitimately involve any restrictions of age. There are various ways of understanding how this goal could be accomplished. My own proposal is for a new kind of proxy-claim right to vote in which every person in a democracy is provided a proxy vote from birth to death that they can claim at any point they desire to exercise for themselves. Anyone incapable of voting, for any reason and at any age, should have their closest guardian invested with the right to vote on their behalf. And anyone capable of voting, as indicated strictly by their desire to vote, should have the right to vote on their own behalf. The proxy-claim vote is the best way to eliminate age discrimination and realize the democratic ideal of holding governments accountable to the people.

I am often asked if I think children's suffrage will ever be achieved. It is one thing to dream, another to see any real change. No one can predict the future, and there are many reasons for pessimism. The world does not necessarily improve. And those with power are not necessarily happy to share it. But I have some reasons for hope.

First, people tend to underestimate how quickly things can change. History shows dramatic transformations in voting rights in just the past 150 years. Only two lifetimes ago, suffrage belonged just to a few wealthy landowning white men in a handful of countries. Now it belongs to all adults in the majority of countries. This represents a shift from about 6 to 66 percent of democratic populations. On this trajectory, the remaining 34 percent should have the vote in about twenty years. At least if mathematics is any indication.

People tend to think their own situation is the final one. The past is clearer than the future. Even in most of our lifetimes, huge transitions have taken place. The Convention on the Rights of the Child is still only thirty-two years old. The modern internet barely existed thirty years ago and grew from 1 percent of telecommunicated information in 1993 to 97 percent by 2007. Fifteen years ago, the general public was largely unconcerned about the climate emergency; now it is front and center of the world's political agenda. Ten years ago, few would have thought same-sex marriage would be settled law in what so far is twenty-nine countries. The Black Lives Matter movement, while addressing a centuries-old issue, only took off in 2013 and is helping to lead a racial reckoning around the globe. It was only in 2015 that the last nation, Saudi Arabia, extended voting rights to women. And the 2020 coronavirus pandemic is fundamentally transforming economic, educational, and global governance systems before our eyes.

It would be rather strange if voting rights grew exponentially over history but then suddenly halted at the brick wall of age eighteen. This last barrier is already seeing cracks in the disparate countries where the voting age is now sixteen. The logic of democracy is powerful. Old norms tend to collapse under its pressure. The rising tide of pluralism tests longstanding biases until their foundations finally crumble. Democracy derives its power, in the end, not from the generosity of those above but from the imperceptible accumulation of desires and ambitions welling up from below. It renews itself through an endless grassroots transformation growing from the fundamental will of the people.

Second, not only is change possible, but it is increasingly necessary. Now is a ripe time for democratic innovation. Democracy as practiced so far is running up against its present limitations. It is in multisided crisis. Democratic governments are increasingly powerless to address the globalization of marketplaces and technologies. Democratic discourse lacks a radical enough edge to solve humanity's pressing challenges from the climate emergency to racism, sexism, migration, and poverty. Democracy is entering a new digital era in which differences are devolving into mutually incomprehensible silos instead of responding to each other as grounds for more expansive transformation. And democracy itself is under attack from a surging worldwide authoritarianism, and even outright autocracy, that imposes power on the disempowered instead of finding ways to share power in common.

These and other crises in democracy, some old and some new, suggest that existing democratic norms contain systemic weaknesses. There are doubtless many places to look, but the most obvious is the fact that a third of democratic populations lack any direct power in making their concerns heard. An influx of children and youth into voting systems presents arguably the best opportunity for democracy to renew itself again. It is time to strengthen and expand democracy's creaky Enlightenment foundations. The pillars of freedom and individualism need further support from those of interdependence and diversity. Suffrage for children would make clear that democracy is a political space of mutual responsiveness rather than individualistic competition.

Children's voting would not solve all the world's problems, but it would help democracies deal with them more justly and effectively. It would better inform representatives about the full range of human experiences instead of just preselected slices of it. It would pressure politicians to account for all the lives their policies really impact. And it would help both children and adults to better understand what it means to live diverse lives in common. Democracies would have to act in ways that are radically more responsive to the people.

Finally, however, what gives me the most hope for children's suffrage is the rising tide of political activism among children and youth themselves. This activism has been illustrated many times over in this book, whether in actual demands for the right to vote or in climate movements, gun rights organizations, children's parliaments, young people's labor unions, youth fighting in courts, children's voices in the media, Black Lives Matter protests, or any number of other political actions. Children have always been political, but this fact is rising ever more clearly to the surface of public consciousness.

Children and youth are, in effect, rejecting their confinement to a prepolitical time by forcing themselves into the common political space. They are challenging the assumption that they do not live in the political here and now. Every group that gains suffrage goes through the process of overcoming their marginalization into nonpolitical time. But every group does so in a distinct way according to the particular assumptions keeping them out. In the case of children, prepolitical temporality is thought to have been written into their bodies and brains, as if growth in biological years equates with growth in political capacity. But all children have to do is exercise political capacities to reveal why this equation is a false one.

Children are full human beings and fully democratic persons. To be human is to be part of the political sphere. The basis of any hope for children's suffrage lies in this. The real problem is not children's natures but existing democratic norms. Democracies at present do not imagine children as equal political beings. But, as I hope to have shown in this book, democracies can be imagined differently. They can be imagined as spaces of responsiveness to the people.

A Children's Suffrage Manifesto

Since democracy makes governments accountable to the people,

   The people deserving a say in the policies and laws impacting them,

   Each bringing to bear their particular differences of experience,

   Each exercising an equal claim to common representation;

And since democracies have long marginalized children and youth,

   Denying them the most basic forms of democratic participation,

   Reducing them to second class citizens across societies,

   And systematically suppressing their voices and concerns;

Democracies are called upon to acknowledge:

   That children and youth are full political persons;

   That their lives are owed equally meaningful responses;

   And that they bring to politics valuable and diverse contributions of their own;

And democracies need furthermore to recognize:

   That children's suffrage would benefit children's lives and situations;

   That it would improve as well the lives of adults and societies;

   And that it would render democracy itself more democratic;

So that democracies ought finally to affirm:

   That children be presumed competent to vote if they possess a desire to do so;

   That their knowledge is to be welcomed for more widely informed policies;

   And that nothing should abridge their power to vote without good reason;

As a result of which, democracies must adopt the following principles:

   The participation of all the people in the right to vote regardless of age;

   The provision of proxy voting for anyone unable to vote on their own behalf;

   And the protection of every person's right to claim their vote whenever they so desire.

Notes

Chapter 1

1 M. Olson, "Dictatorship, Democracy, and Development," *American Political Science Review* 87:3 (1993): 567–76.

2 Thorkild Jacobsen, "Primitive Democracy in Ancient Mesopotamia," *Journal of Near Eastern Studies* 2:3 (1943): 159–72; B. Isakhan, "Engaging 'Primitive Democracy,' Mideast Roots of Collective Governance," *Middle East Policy* 14:3 (2007): 97–117; Raychaudhuri Hemchandra, *Political History of Ancient India* (Calcutta: University of Calcutta, 1972).

3 Kurt A. Raaflaub, Josiah Ober, and Robert W. Wallace, *Origins of Democracy in Ancient Greece* (Berkeley: University of California Press, 2007).

4 Jørgen Møller, "Why Europe Avoided Hegemony: A Historical Perspective on the Balance of Power," *International Studies Quarterly* 58:4 (2014): 660–70; Gary W. Cox, "Political Institutions, Economic Liberty, and the Great Divergence," *Journal of Economic History* 77:3 (2017): 724–55; David Stasavage, "Representation and Consent: Why They Arose in Europe and Not Elsewhere," *Annual Review of Political Science* 19:1 (May 11, 2016): 145–62.

5 Adrian Jobson, *The First English Revolution: Simon de Montfort, Henry III and the Barons' War* (London: Bloomsbury, 2012).

6 Jürgen Habermas, *The Structural Transformation of the Public Sphere*, trans. T. Burger and F. Lawrence (Cambridge, MA: MIT Press, 1989 [1962]).

7 Sean Wilentz, *The Rise of American Democracy: Jefferson to Lincoln* (New York: W.W. Norton, 2005); Daniel Walker Howe, *What Hath God Wrought: The Transformation of America, 1815–1848* (New York: Oxford University Press, 2007); Chilton Williamson, *American Suffrage from Property to Democracy, 1760–1860* (Princeton, NJ: Princeton University Press, 1960); Donald Ratcliffe, "The Right to Vote and the Rise of Democracy, 1787–1828," *Journal of the Early Republic* 33 (2013): 219–54.

8   William Doyle, *The Oxford History of the French Revolution*
    (Oxford: Oxford University Press, 1989); Jack Censer and Lynn Hunt,
    Liberty, Equality, Fraternity: Exploring the French Revolution (University
    Park: Pennsylvania State University Press, 2001).

9   John Locke, "Two Treatises of Government," in *The Works of John Locke*,
    new edition, vol. 5 (London: W. Sharpe and Son, 1823).

10 Jack P. Greene, *Imperatives, Behaviors, and Identities: Essays in Early
    American Cultural History* (Charlottesville: University Press of Virginia,
    1992), 260.

11 "US 1920 Census," accessed January 2020 at https://www2.census.gov/
    library/publications/decennial/1920/volume-3/41084484v3ch01.pdf.

12 Mary Jo Buhle and Paul Buhle (eds.), *Concise History of Woman
    Suffrage: Selections from the Classic Work of Stanton, Anthony, Gage, and
    Harper* (Urbana: University of Illinois Press, 1978), 96; Elizabeth Cady
    Stanton et al., *The History of Women's Suffrage* (Salem, NH: Ayer, [1881]
    1985), vol. 3, 275; Representation of the People Bill of 1867, House of
    Commons Debates, May 20, 1867, 821.

13 Alexander Keyssar, *The Right to Vote: The Contested History of Democracy
    in the United States*, revised edition (New York: Basic Books, 2000), 141;
    Representation of the People Bill of 1867, 839; Sophia A. Wingerden,
    The Women's Suffrage Movement in Britain, 1866–1928 (New York: St.
    Martin's, 1999), 14.

14 Stanton et al., *The History of Women's Suffrage*, vol. 3, 697; Keyssar, *The
    Right to Vote*, 159; Millicent Garrett Fawcett, *Home and Politics: An
    Address Delivered at Toynbee Hall and Elsewhere* (London: Women's
    Printing Society, c. 1888), 3.

15 Stanton et al., *The History of Women's Suffrage*, vol. 3, 202; Keyssar, *The
    Right to Vote*, 155; Millicent Garrett Fawcett, *Women's Suffrage Journal*,
    April 1, 1870, 13; Women's Disabilities Bill, House of Commons Debates,
    April 30, 1873, 1238.

16 Stanton et al., *The History of Women's Suffrage*, 71; Wingerden, *The
    Women's Suffrage Movement in Britain, 1866–1928*, 73–85; Keyssar, *The
    Right to Vote*, 176.

17 National Youth Rights Association, accessed October 2020, at https://
    www.youthrights.org/; Jonathan Mitchell, "Teens Ask Court to Lower
    Voting Age to 16," *RNZ News*, August 24, 2020, accessed October

2020, at https://www.rnz.co.nz/news/national/424324/teens-ask-court-to-lower-voting-age-to-16; UK Labour Party, accessed October 2020, at https://labour.org.uk/latest/stories/time-votes-16/; European Youth Forum, "European Union Backs Right for 16 & 17 Year Olds to Vote," accessed October 2020, at https://www.youthforum.org/european-parliament-backs-right-16-17-year-olds-vote.

18 Paul Demeny, "Pronatalist Policies in Low-Fertility Countries: Patterns, Performance and Prospects," *Population and Development Review* 12:suppl. (1986): 335–58; Warren C. Sanderson, "A Near Electoral Majority of Pensioners," *Population and Development Review* 33:3 (2007): 543–54; Philippe Van Parijs, "The Disenfranchisement of the Elderly, and Other Attempts to Secure Intergenerational Justice," *Philosophy & Public Affairs* 27:4 (1998): 292–333 (309). This claim is based on Andre Toulemon, *Le Suffrage familial ou stffriage universel integral* (Paris: Librairie du Recueil Sirey, 1933); Jean-Yves Le Naour with Catherine Valenti, *La famille doit voter: Le suffrage familial contre le vote individuel* (Paris: Hachette Littératures, 2005); *Journal Officiel de la République Française* 233:25 (August 22, 1871) with supplément, accessed January 2020 at https://babel.hathitrust.org/cgi/pt?id=mdp.39015022 763927&view=1up&seq=1667; see also Jenny Gesley, "Family Voting as a Solution to Low Fertility? Experiences from France and Germany," *Global Law Guest Post*, April 19, 2018, accessed January 2020 at https://blogs.loc.gov/law/2018/04/family-voting-as-a-solution-to-low-fertility-experiences-from-france-and-germany/?fbclid=IwAR25FzSWs6w3twJv Md98eIHiT2i5QNlxEhxSmTIniU7aw43iFQks7LpqJK4; *Journal Officiel de la République Française, Débats Parlementaires, Chambre des Deputes*, December 6, 1923, 3957, accessed January 2020 at https://gallica.bnf. fr/ark:/12148/bpt6k62174312/f13.item; see also Stein Ringen, *Citizens, Families and Reform* (Oxford: Oxford University Press, 1997).

19 Philippe van Parijs, "The Disenfranchisement of the Elderly, and Other Attempts to Secure Intergenerational Justice," *Philosophy and Public Affairs* 27 (1999): 292–333; Harry De Quetteville, "Germany Plans to Give Vote to Babies," *Daily Telegraph*, July 9, 2008; K.R.Ä.T.Z.Ä. (die KinderRÄchTsZÄnker), www.kraetzae.de; Gesley, "Family Voting as a Solution to Low Fertility?"; see also a study by the German government on the pros and cons of this bill, "Fragen zum Wahlrecht von Geburt an"

(2017), accessed January 2020 at https://www.bundestag.de/resource/blo
b/531942/6669f3e29651882065938fc6a14fd779/wd-3-157-17-pdf-data.
pdf; Gesley, "Family Voting as a Solution to Low Fertility?"; National
Association of Large Families, accessed September 2020 at https://www.
famiglienumerose.org/appello-di-due-padri-per-il-voto-per-i-figli/; Leigh
Phillips, "Hungarian Mothers May Get Extra Votes for Their Children in
Elections," *The Guardian*, April 17, 2011, accessed January 2020 at https://
www.theguardian.com/world/2011/apr/17/hungary-mothers-get-extra-
votes?fbclid=IwAR1BARgMPkXK6eRQpXttDVnkePvwFYItsyaFrDmmq-
hTxMYm9Fo8J6qGZ-I; Ross Douthat, "Power to the Parents," *New York
Times*, March 3, 2018, accessed January 2020 at https://www.nytimes.
com/2018/03/03/opinion/sunday/parents-teenagers-voting.html?action=
click&pgtype=Homepage&clickSource=story-heading&module=opinion-
c-col-left-region&region=opinion-c-col-left-region&WT.nav=opinion-
c-col-left-region; R. W. Bennett, "Should Parents Be Given Extra Votes
on Account of Their Children: Toward a Conversational Understanding
of American Democracy," *Northwestern University Law Review* 94
(1999–2000), 503; R. Vaithianathan, R. Aoki, and Erwan Sbai, "Support
for Franchise Extension for Children: Evidence on Japanese Attitude to
Demeny Voting," Center for Intergenerational Studies Discussion Paper
610 (2013); Hanna Quintern, *Das Familienwahlrecht: Ein Beitrag zur
verfassungsrechtlichen Diskussion* (Münster: Lit Verlag, 2010); Sebastian
Müller-Franken, *Familienwahlrecht und Verfassung* (Tübingen: Mohr
Siebeck, 2013).

20 Stefanie Conrad, "Children as Active Citizens: Addressing
Discrimination against Children's Engagement in Political and Civil
Society Processes," *Plan International*, www.plan-international.org.uk;
Sara L. Austin, 'Children's Participation in Citizenship and Governance,'
in *A Handbook of Children and Young People's Participation*, ed. Barry
Percy-Smith and Nigel Thomas (New York: Routledge, 2010), 245–53;
Children's United Parliament of the World (2013), www.childrensstate.
net; Stephanie McCrummen, "'Children's Parliament' Sets High Bar
in Congo: Youthful Body in a Beacon of Justice," *Washington Post*,
August 11, 2007; Neighborhood Community Network (2013), www.
neighborhoodparliament.org; Jayashri Sarkar and Blanka Mendoza,
'Bolivia's Children's Parliament: Bringing Participation to the National

Stage,' *Children, Youth and Environments* 15:2 (2005): 227–44; Lalitha
Sridhar, "Bal Sansads: Members of Parliament at 11," *Infochange*, May
2004, accessed January 2020 at infochangeindia.org/20040508228/
Children/Features/Bal-Sansads-Members-of-Parliament-at-11.html;
Emma Williams, *Children's Participation and Policy Change in South Asia*
(London: Save the Children, Childhood Poverty Research and Policy
Center, 2004), accessed January 2020 at www.childhoodpoverty.org/
index.php/action=documentfeed/doctype=pdf/id=86.

21   Alan Turkie, "More than Crumbs from the Table: A Critique of Youth
Parliaments as Models of Representation for Marginalised Young
People," in *A Handbook of Children and Young People's Participation*,
ed. Barry Percy-Smith and Nigel Thomas (New York: Routledge, 2010),
262–69; Michael Wyness, "Regulating Participation: The Possibilities
and Limits of Children and Young People's Councils," *Journal of Social
Sciences* 9:special issue (2005): 7–18; Mary John, *Children's Rights and
Power: Charging Up for a New Century* (London: Jessica Kingsley,
2003), 235–39; Ahsa Bajpai, *Child Rights in India: Law, Policy, and
Practice* (New York: Oxford University Press, 2003), 469; Neighborhood
Community Network, "Neighborocracy," concept paper shared with
the author, January 2020; Sarkar and Mendoza, "Bolivia's Children's
Parliament; Manfred Liebel, "Protecting the Rights of Working Children
Instead of Banning Child Labour: Bolivia Tries a New Legislative
Approach," *International Journal of Children's Rights* 23 (2015): 529; Yves
Cabannes, "Children and Young People Build a Participatory Democracy
in Latin American Cities," *Children, Youth and Environments* 15:2
(2005): 185–210.

22   UNICEF, "Convention on the Rights of the Child," accessed September
2013, at http://www.unicef.org/crc/.

23   KRÄTZÄ, http://kraetzae.de/; Foundation for the Rights of Future
Generations, "Voting Age," accessed January 2020 at https://www.
intergenerationaljustice.org/topics/voting-age/; Wir Wollen Wällen ("We
Want the Vote"), accessed January 2020 at www.wir-wollen-waehlen.de.

24   National Youth Rights Association, "Voting Age," accessed January 2020
at https://www.youthrights.org/issues/voting-age/.

25   Katherine Walton, "Votes for Children: The Case for Universal Suffrage,"
Amnesty International UK, accessed January 2020 at https://www.amnesty.

org.uk/blogs/childrens-human-rights-network-blog/votes-children-case-universal-suffrage?fbclid=IwAR3c-bexlD8PZhdpQHJz4n6nINdTM_TBAFzc3p6tbziu2qk0mwN9W2LfCoU; Children's Voice Association, accessed January 2020 at https://www.childrensvoiceassociation.org/; Children's Rights International Network, "Right to Vote," accessed January 2020 at https://archive.crin.org/en/home/what-we-do/policy/minimum-ages/right-vote.html?fbclid=IwAR32RMNQBH4xenCg_egj4o FpNBpHiqR_0xDq4MvddOKgy8l8Bt7UbvFt81M.

26 Freechild Institute, "Youth + Social Change through Youth Voting," accessed January 2020 at https://freechild.org/youth-as-voters/?f bclid=IwAR1zByP6512nBFpzFNKOoYhLuOTk0p9mJ5ma3CT-QQS1FhNeHCAGwGRR8KQ; Association for Children's Suffrage, accessed January 2020 at http://web.archive.org/web/20070426231337/ http://www.brown.edu:80/Students/Association_for_Childrens_Suffrage/; Represent MA Children 2020, accessed January 2020 at https://www.facebook.com/representMAchildren2020; Children's Voting Colloquium (or Collaboration), https://www.childrenvoting.org/.

Chapter 2

1 See the documentary *Power to the Children* (Anna Kersting Filmproduktion, 2017), directed by Anna Kersting, http://www.powertothechildren-film.com.

2 David W. Archard, *Children, Family and the State* (Burlington, VT: Ashgate, 2003), 53.

3 Jason Brennan, "The Right to a Competent Electorate," *Philosophical Quarterly* 61:245 (2011): 700–24 (704); T. Christiano, *The Constitution of Equality: Democratic Authority and Its Limits* (Oxford: Oxford University Press, 2008); Immanuel Kant, *The Science of Right* (trans. W. Hastie) (Clifton, NJ: A. M. Kelley, 1974); see also John Rawls, *Political Liberalism* (New York: Columbia University Press, 1996), 245.

4 Monique Ernst and Martin P. Paulus, "Neurobiology of Decision Making: A Selective Review from a Neurocognitive and Clinical Perspective," *Biological Psychiatry* 58:8 (2005): 597–604; Valerie F. Reyna and Frank Farley, "Risk and Rationality in Adolescent

Decision Making: Implications for Theory, Practice, and Public Policy," *Psychological Science in the Public Interest* 7:1 (2006): 1–44; Laurence Steinberg and Elizabeth S. Scott, "Less Guilty by Reason of Adolescence: Developmental Immaturity, Diminished Responsibility, and the Juvenile Death Penalty," *American Psychologist* 58:12 (2003): 1009–18; S. B. Johnson, R. W. Blum, and J. N. Giedd, "Adolescent Maturity and the Brain: The Promise and Pitfalls of Neuroscience Research in Adolescent Health Policy," *Journal of Adolescent Health* 45:3 (2009): 216–21. M. Arain, M. Haque, L. Johal, P. Mathur, W. Nel, A. Rais, R. Sandhu, and S. Sharma, "Maturation of the Adolescent Brain," *Neuropsychiatric Disease and Treatment* 9 (2013): 449–61; S. J. Segalowitz and P. L. Davies, "Charting the Maturation of the Frontal Lobe: An Electrophysiological Strategy," *Brain and Cognition* 55:1 (2004): 116–33.

5 Jürgen Habermas, *Justification and Application: Remarks on Discourse Ethics* (trans. C. P. Cronin) (Cambridge, MA: MIT Press, 1993), 64; Benjamin R. Barber, "The Discourse of Civility," in *Citizen Competence and Democratic Institutions*, ed. Stephen L. Ekin and Karol E. Soltan (University Park: Pennsylvania State University, 1999), 39–47 (42–3).

6 Robert Ludbrook, "Should Children Have the Right to Vote?" National Children's and Youth Law Centre Discussion Paper, December 1995, 15.

7 American Bar Association Commission on Law and Aging, and the Penn Memory Center, "Assisting Cognitively Impaired Individuals with Voting: A Quick Guide," accessed October 2020, at https://www.americanbar.org/content/dam/aba/administrative/law_aging/2020-voting-guide.pdf.

8 Bob Franklin, "Children's Political Rights," in *The Rights of Children*, ed. B. Franklin (New York: Basil Blackwell, 1986), 24–53 (34); Francis Shrag, "Children and Democracy: Theory and Policy," *Politics, Philosophy and Economics* 3:3 (2004): 365–79 (371).

9 Lachlan Montgomery Umbers, "Enfranchising the Youth," *Critical Review of International Social and Political Philosophy* 1:24 (2018): 13; David Runciman, quoted in Matthew Weaver, "Lower the Voting Age to Six to Tackle Bias against Young, Says Academic," *The Guardian*, December 6, 2018, accessed July 2020, at https://www.theguardian.com/politics/2018/dec/06/give-six-year-olds-the-vote-says-cambridge-university-

academic?CMP=share_btn_tw&fbclid=IwAR1jVc7NxPPFv0s7ucwAZy1
Ujuw-PSKt-H-1cCSQM17ftfszsUtdMqgVg9U.

10 Commonwealth Electoral Act 1918, s93(8)a (Australia), accessed October
    2020, at https://www.legislation.gov.au/Details/C2016C01022.

11 "Here Are the Young Activists That Can Make the World a Better Place,"
    BookTrust, accessed March 2021 at https://www.booktrust.org.uk/news-
    and-features/features/2019/november/here-are-the-young-activists-
    that-can-make-the-world-a-better-place/; Darwen Aldridge Enterprise
    Studio, "Young People in Blackburn with Darwen Lead Food Poverty
    Day of Action," November 13, 2018, accessed March 2021 at http://www.
    daestudio.biz/post/young-people-in-blackburn-with-darwen-lead-food-
    poverty-day-of-action; Michael Cummings, *Children's Voices in Politics*
    (New York: Peter Lang, 2020), xiv; Zoe Beaty and Amelia Bowe, "9 Young
    Activists on How They Want to Change the World," *Refinery29*, October
    19, 2020, accessed March 2021 at https://www.refinery29.com/en-gb/
    dove-self-esteem-project-young-activists.

12 Eric Wiland, "Should Children Have the Right to Vote?" in *The
    Palgrave Handbook of Philosophy and Public Policy*, ed. David Boonin
    (London: Palgrave Macmillan, 2018), 215–60 (223); Stefan Olsson,
    "Children's Suffrage: A Critique of the Importance of Voters' Knowledge
    for the Well-Being of Democracy," *International Journal of Children's
    Rights* 16 (2008): 55–76 (56). For similar arguments, see also Ian Shapiro,
    Democratic Justice (New Haven, CT: Yale University Press, 1999); L.
    Cunningham, "A Question of Capacity: Towards a Comprehensive and
    Consistent Vision of Children and Their Status under Law," *UC Davis
    Journal of Juvenile Law and Policy* 10:2 (2006): 275–377; and Patricia
    M. Wald, "Making Sense out of the Rights of Youth, *Human Rights* 4:1
    (1974): 13–29.

13 Ludbrook, "Should Children Have the Right to Vote?," 4.

14 Nicholas Munn, "Capacity-Testing as a Means of Increasing Political
    Inclusion," *Democratization* 20 (2013): 1–19 (4).

15 Eric Wiland, "One Citizen, One Vote," Colorado University Boulder
    Center for Values and Social Policy blog What's Wrong?, August 12, 2015,
    accessed January 2020 at https://whatswrongcvsp.com/2015/08/12/one-
    citizen-one-vote/?fbclid=IwAR0gfWV-HHjFubbjALPMce7-90sJaIWT

NWWya7q9LxVbMv0dJzl1B8CKgis; see also Wiland, "Should Children Have the Right to Vote?," 222.

16   Vita Wallace, "Give Children the Vote," *The Nation*, October 14, 1991, 439–42 (339).

17   Umbers, "Enfranchising the Youth," 9–10.

18   Alison Gopnik, *The Philosophical Baby: What Children's Minds Tell Us about Truth, Love, and the Meaning of Life* (New York: Picador, 2010).

19   Jürgen Habermas, *Moral Consciousness and Communicative Action* (Cambridge, MA: MIT Press, 1990); Lawrence Kohlberg, *The Psychology of Moral Development: The Nature and Validity of Moral Stages* (New York: Harper & Row, 1984).

20   Claudio López-Guerra, *Democracy and Disenfranchisement: The Morality of Electoral Exclusions* (New York: Oxford University Press, 2014), 5.

Chapter 3

1   Jessica K. Taft, "'Adults Talk Too Much': Intergenerational Dialogue and Power in the Peruvian Movement of Working Children," *Childhood* 22:4 (2015): 460–73 (465). See also Isidro Maya Jariego, "'But We Want to Work': The Movement of Child Workers in Peru and the Actions for Reducing Child Labor," *American Journal of Community Psychology* 60 (2017): 430–38. Dena Aufseeser, "Control, Protection and Rights: A Critical Review of Peru's Begging Bill," *International Journal of Children's Rights* 22 (2014): 241–67.

2   Philip Cowley and David Denver, "Votes at 16? The Case Against," *Representation* 41:1 (2004): 57–62 (60); Tak Wing Chan and Matthew Clayton, "Should the Voting Age Be Lowered to Sixteen? Normative and Empirical Considerations," *Political Studies* 54 (2006): 533–58 (542); Robert A. Dahl, *Democracy and Its Critics* (New Haven, CT: Yale University Press, 1989), 126.

3   Matthew Yglesias, "The Case for Letting Children Vote," *Vox*, November 2015, accessed March 2020 at https://www.vox.com/2015/11/28/9770928/voting-rights-for-kids.

4 Jason Brennan, "The Right to a Competent Electorate," *Philosophical Quarterly* 61:245 (2011): 700–24 (701). See a critique of this idea in Ilya Somin, "Should We Let Children Vote? The Troubling Implications of Standard Reasons for Rejecting a Flawed Idea," *Reason*, December 7, 2018, accessed August 2020 at https://reason.com/2018/12/07/should-we-let-children-vote-the-troublin/?fbclid=IwAR0IeVMqPqX4zlwNu7l8CE WKl_eG17GDTj1QU2-DbrPtQfNYwxygzBy0wow#.

5 Annenberg Public Policy Center of the University of Pennsylvania, "Americans Are Poorly Informed about Basic Constitutional Provisions," September 12, 2017, accessed August 2020 at https://www. annenbergpublicpolicycenter.org/americans-are-poorly-informed-about-basic-constitutional-provisions/; Patrick Riccards, "National Survey Finds Just 1 in 3 Americans Would Pass Citizenship Test," Woodrow Wilson National Fellowship Foundation, October 3, 2018, accessed August 2020 at https://woodrow.org/news/national-survey-finds-just-1-in-3-americans-would-pass-citizenship-test/; Bryan Caplan, *The Myth of the Rational Voter: Why Democracies Choose Bad Policies* (Princeton, NJ: Princeton University Press, 2006), 95; Richard R. Lau and David P. Redlawsk, "Voting Correctly," *American Political Science Review* 91:3 (1997): 585–98.

6 Alison Gopnik, *The Philosophical Baby: What Children's Minds Tell Us about Truth, Love, and the Meaning of Life* (New York: Farrar, Straus, and Giroux, 2009), 5.

7 Richard Farson, *Birthrights: A Bill of Rights for Children* (New York: Macmillan, 1974), 179.

8 Stefan Olsson, "Children's Suffrage: A Critique of the Importance of Voters' Knowledge for the Well-Being of Democracy," *International Journal of Children's Rights* 16 (2008): 55–76 (74).

Chapter 4

1 Vera Eidelman and Sarah Hinger, "Some Schools Need a Lesson on Students' Free Speech Rights," *ACLU*, September 18, 2018, accessed April 2020, at https://www.aclu.org/blog/free-speech/student-speech-and-privacy/some-schools-need-lesson-students-free-speech-rights.

2   Gerald Dworkin, "Paternalism," *The Monist* 56 (1972): 64–84; and "Moral Paternalism," *Law and Philosophy* 24:3 (2005): 305–19.

3   Michael S. Cummings, *Children's Voices in Politics* (New York: Peter Lang, 2020), xiii.

4   Robert Ludbrook, "Should Children Have the Right to Vote?," National Children's and Youth Law Centre Discussion Paper, December 1995, 8.

5   Peggy McIntosh, "Unpacking the Invisible Knapsack: White Privilege and Male Privilege," in *Race, Class, and Gender: An Anthology*, ninth edition, ed. Margaret Andersen and Patricia Hill Collins (Belmont, CA: Cengage Learning, 2015), 74–8 (75).

6   Bob Franklin, "Children's Political Rights," in *The Rights of Children*, ed. B. Franklin (New York: Basil Blackwell, 1986), 24–53 (26).

7   Organization for Economic Cooperation, "Poverty Rate," accessed May 2020, at https://data.oecd.org/inequality/poverty-rate.htm#indicator-chart; Esteban Ortiz-Ospina, "Children and Poverty: Evidence from New World Bank Data," *Our World in Data*, February 22, 2017, accessed May 2020, at https://ourworldindata.org/children-and-poverty-results-from-new-data.

8   Centers for Medicare & Medicaid Services, "US Personal Health Care Spending by Age and Gender," accessed May 2020, at https://www.cms.gov/Research-Statistics-Data-and-Systems/Statistics-Trends-and-Reports/NationalHealthExpendData/Downloads/AgeandGenderHighlights.pdf; Anti-Slavery Society, "Does Slavery Still Exist?," accessed January 2014, at http://www.anti-slaverysociety.org/slavery.htm; UNHCR, "Global Trends: Forced Displacement 2018," June 2019, accessed May 2020 at https://www.unhcr.org/statistics/unhcrstats/ 5d08d7ee7/unhcr-global-trends-2018.html.

9   John Wall, "Theorizing Children's Global Citizenship: Reconstructionism and the Politics of Deep Interdependence," *Global Studies of Childhood* 9:1 (2019): 5–17.

10 Matt Gaughwin, quoted in "Should Children Be Allowed to Vote?," *Australian Politics*, April 18, 2001, accessed August 2020 at https://australianpolitics.com/2001/04/18/should-children-be-allowed-to-vote.html?fbclid=IwAR30zww1kJSrsnCxKaeTqFYqJ0trvnEHbFR_aH919_tuFUPa124PayodHX0.

11 Kwame N. Akosah, "Cracking the One-Way Mirror: How Computational Politics Harms Voter Privacy, and Proposed Regulatory Solutions,"

Fordham Intellectual Property, Media and Entertainment Law Journal 25:1007 (2015): 1012–15; Clarinda Still and Srinivas Dusi, "Vote Buying and 'Money-Politics' in Village Elections in South India," *Commonwealth and Comparative Politics* 58:1 (2020): 100–19.

12 Man-Yee Kan and Anthony Heath, "The Political Attitudes and Choices of Husbands and Wives," Centre for Research into Elections and Social Trends Working Paper 103 (2003): 1–40, accessed June 2013 at http://www.crest.ox.ac.uk/papers/p103.pdf; H. Elcock, "Young Voters 1988: Will They Break the Mold?," *Youth and Policy* 2:2 (1983): 30–4; C. Brooks, P. Nieuwbeerta, and J. Manza, "Cleavage-Based Voting Behavior in Cross-National Perspective: Evidence from Six Postwar Democracies," *Social Science Research* 35:1 (2006): 88–128.

13 A. M. Rutchick, "Deus Ex Machina: The Influence of Polling Place on Voting Behavior," *Political Psychology* 31:2 (2010): 209–25; S. Harrison and M. Bruter, *Mapping Extreme Right Ideology* (Hampshire: Palgrave, 2011).

14 Franklin, "Children's Political Rights," 36.

15 Joanna Moorhead, "Should We Give Children the Vote? We Ask Nine Kids What They Think," *The Guardian*, December 23, 2018, accessed October 2020, at https://www.theguardian.com/global/2018/dec/23/should-we-give-children-the-vote-voting-at-age-6-politics-interviews.

16 Iris Marion Young, *Justice and the Politics of Difference* (Princeton, NJ: Princeton University Press, 1990), 120.

17 John Holt, *Escape from Childhood* (New York: Penguin, 1975), 169.

Chapter 5

1 Jonathan Josefsson, " 'We Beg You, Let Them Stay!': Rights Claims of Asylum-Seeking Children as a Socio-Political Practice," *Childhood* 24:3 (2017): 316–32.

2 John Locke, "Two Treatises of Government," in *The Works of John Locke*, new edition, vol. V (London: W. Sharpe and Son, 1823), 130.

3 Geoffrey Scarre, "Children and Paternalism," *Philosophy* 55:211 (1980): 117–24 (123).

4 Martin Guggenheim, *What's Wrong with Children's Rights* (Cambridge, MA: Harvard University Press, 2005), 266.

5 Katharine Silbaugh, "Developmental Justice and the Voting Age," *Fordham Urban Law Journal* 47 (2020): 253–92 (257).

6 Bob Franklin, "Children's Political Rights," in *The Rights of Children*, ed. B. Franklin (New York: Basil Blackwell, 1986), 24–53 (33).

7 Richard Farson, *Birthrights: A Bill of Rights for Children* (New York: Macmillan, 1974), 177.

8 Paul Peterson, "An Immodest Proposal," *Daedalus* 121:4 (1992): 151–74.

9 Lachlan Montgomery Umbers, "Enfranchising the Youth," *Critical Review of International Social and Political Philosophy* (2018): 1–24; Toke S. Aidt and Bianca Dallal, "Female Voting Power: The Contribution of Women's Suffrage to the Growth of Social Spending in Western Europe (1869–1960)," *Public Choice* 134 (2008): 391–417; Tarik Abou-Chadi and Mattias Orlowski, "Political Institutions and the Distributional Consequences of Suffrage Extension," *Political Studies* 63 (2015): 55–72; Thomas A. Husted and Lawrence W. Kenny, "The Effect of the Expansion of the Voting Franchise on the Size of Government," *Journal of Political Economy* 105 (1997): 54–82.

10 Laurence Pevsner, "Let Children Vote. Even 13-Year-Olds," *Washington Post*, October 27, 2016.

11 Vita Wallace, "Give Children the Vote," *The Nation*, October 14, 1991, 439–42 (339).

12 Steven Lecce, "Should Democracy Grow Up? Children and Voting Rights," *Intergenerational Justice Review*, 9:4 (2009): 133–9 (137); name omitted, homework essay, March 2020.

13 Cummings, *Children's Voices in Politics*, 288.

14 Nick Munn, "Lowering New Zealand's Voting Age to 16 Would Be Good for Young People—and Good for Democracy," *The Conversation*, August 2020, accessed August 2020 at https://theconversation.com/lowering-new-zealands-voting-age-to-16-would-be-good-for-young-people-and-good-for-democracy-145008.

Chapter 6

1 Robert Goodin and Joanne Lau, "Enfranchising Incompetents: Suretyship and the Joint Authorship of Laws," *Ratio* 24:2 (2011): 154–66 (165), emphasis in original.

2 Lachlan Montgomery Umbers, "Enfranchising the Youth," *Critical Review of International Social and Political Philosophy* (2018): 1–24 (4).

3 Some of these economic arguments for children having a vote are made in Luigi Campiglio, "The Importance of Investing in Very Young People," in *Government, Governance, and Welfare Reform: Structural Changes and Subsidiarity in Italy and Britain*, ed. Alberto Brugnoli and Alessandro Colombo (Northampton, MA: Edward Elgar, 2012), 133–46.

4 Diana Carolina García Gómez, "Cultivating Hope: Children and Youth Participation in Collective Memory in Post-Accord Colombia," PhD dissertation, Department of Childhood Studies, Rutgers University Camden, 2021.

5 Claudio López-Guerra, *Democracy and Disenfranchisement: The Morality of Electoral Exclusions* (New York: Oxford University Press, 2014).

6 Francis Fukuyama, "The End of History?," *National Interest* 16 (1989): 3–18.

7 Economist Intelligence Unit, "Democracy Index 2019: A Year of Democratic Setbacks and Popular Protest," accessed October 2020, at https://www.eiu.com/topic/democracy-index.

8 David Runciman, *The Confidence Trap: A History of Democracy in Crisis from World War I to the Present*, revised edition (Princeton, NJ: Princeton University Press, 2018), xv.

9 David Runciman, *How Democracy Ends* (New York: Basic Books, 2018), 73.

10 I have examined these larger theoretical questions in more detail elsewhere: John Wall, "Can Democracy Represent Children? Toward a Politics of Difference," *Childhood: A Journal of Global Child Research* 19:1 (2012): 86–100; Wall, "Why Children and Youth Should Have the Right to Vote: An Argument for Proxy-Claim Suffrage," *Children, Youth and Environments*, 24:1 (2014): 108–23; Wall, "Democratizing Democracy: The Road from Women's to Children's Suffrage," *International Journal of Human Rights* (Special Issue) 18:6 (2014): 646–59;

and Wall, *Children's Rights: Today's Global Challenge* (Lanham, MD: Rowman & Littlefield, 2016). The concept of childism is developed in John Wall, *Ethics in Light of Childhood* (Lanham, MD: Georgetown University Press, 2010); and Wall, "From Childhood Studies to Childism: Reconstructing the Scholarly and Social Imaginations," *Children's Geographies* (Special Issue) 17:6 (2019): 1–15.

11 See, for example, Joseph A. Schumpeter, *Capitalism, Socialism and Democracy*, third edition (New York: Harper & Row, [1942] 1950); Friedrich A. Hayek, *The Constitution of Liberty* (Chicago: University of Chicago Press, 1960); and Milton Friedman, *Capitalism and Freedom* (Chicago: University of Chicago Press, 1962).

12 John Rawls, *A Theory of Justice* (Cambridge, MA: Belknap Press, 1971); Jürgen Habermas, *Moral Consciousness and Communicative Action* (Cambridge, MA: MIT Press, 1991); Seyla Benhabib, *The Rights of Others: Aliens, Residents, and Citizens* (New York: Cambridge University Press, 2004).

13 Judith Butler, *Bodies That Matter: On the Discursive Limits of "Sex"* (New York: Routledge, 1993); Hannah Dyer, *The Queer Aesthetics of Childhood: Asymmetries of Innocence and the Cultural Politics of Child Development* (New Brunswick, NJ: Rutgers University Press, 2019); Ernesto Laclau and Chantal Mouffe, *Hegemony and Socialist Strategy: Towards a Radical Democratic Politics*, 2nd edition (New York: Verso, 2001); Iris Marion Young, *Inclusion and Democracy* (New York: Oxford University Press, 2000).

14 The following shares much with ideas from Néstor García Canclini, *Imagined Globalization* (trans. G. Yúdice) (Durham, NC: Duke University Press, 2014); Sara Marzagora, "The Humanism of Reconstruction: African Intellectuals, Decolonial Critical Theory and the Opposition to the "Posts" (Postmodernism, Poststructuralism, Postcolonialism)," *Journal of African Cultural Studies* 28:2 (2016): 161–78; and Nadia Urbinati, *Representative Democracy: Principles and Genealogy* (Chicago: University of Chicago Press, 2006).

15 For a detailed development of this idea, see John Wall, "Theorizing Children's Global Citizenship: Reconstructionism and the Politics of Deep Interdependence," *Global Studies of Childhood* 9:1 (2019): 5–17.

16 Wall, "From Childhood Studies to Childism," 1–15, 11–12. See also similar uses of the idea of childism in Tanu Biswas, *Little Things Matter Much: Childist Ideas for a Pedagogy of Philosophy in an Overheated World* (Munich: Büro Himmelgrün, 2020); Kathleen Gallagher Elkins, "Biblical Studies and Childhood Studies: A Fertile, Interdisciplinary Space for Feminists," *Journal of Feminist Studies in Religion* 29:2 (2013): 146–53; Olof Franck, "Highlighting Ethics, Subjectivity and Democratic Participation in Sustainability Education: Challenges and Contributions," in *Ethical Literacies and Education for Sustainable Development: Young People, Subjectivity and Democratic Participation*, ed. Olof Franck and Christina Osbeck (New York: Palgrave Macmillan, 2017), 1–17; Kristine Garroway, "2 *Kings* 6:24–30: A Case of Unintentional Elimination," *Journal of Biblical Literature* 137:1 (2018): 53–70; Gregory Mannion, "Children's Participation in Changing School Grounds and Public Play Areas in Scotland," PhD dissertation, University of Stirling, Scotland, 1999; Shelly Newstead, "De-constructing and Reconstructing the Unorthodox Recipe of Playwork," doctoral thesis, Institute of Education, University College London, 2016; Kate Ott, "Taking Children's Moral Lives Seriously: Creativity as Ethical Response Offline and Online," *Religions* 10 (2019): 525–37; Julie Faith Parker, *Valuable and Vulnerable: Children in the Hebrew Bible, Especially the Elisha Cycle* (Providence, RI: Brown Judaic Studies, 2017); Julie Faith Parker, "Children in the Hebrew Bible and Childist Interpretation," *Currents in Biblical Research* 17:2 (2019): 130–57; Jeanette Sundhall, "A Political Space for Children? The Age Order and Children's Right to Participation," *Social Inclusion* 5:3 (2017): 164–71; Sarah Wadsworth, "The Year of the Child: Children's Literature, Childhood Studies, and the Turn to Childism," *American Literary History* 27:2 (2015): 331–41; John Wall, "Childhood Studies, Hermeneutics, and Theological Ethics," *Journal of Religion* 86:4 (2006): 523–48; John Wall, "Human Rights in Light of Childhood," *International Journal of Children's Rights* 16:4 (2008): 523–43; John Wall, *Ethics in Light of Childhood* (Washington, DC: Georgetown University Press, 2010); and Ohad Zehavi, "Becoming-Woman, Becoming-Child: A Joint Political Programme," in *Feminism and the Politics of Childhood*, ed. Rachel Rosen and Katherine Twamley (London: UCL Press, 2016), 241–56.

Chapter 7

1 World Population Review, "Infant Mortality Rate by Country 2020," accessed July 2020, at https://worldpopulationreview.com/country-rankings/infant-mortality-rate-by-country; R. Hong, M. Ayad, S. Rutstein, and R.L. Ran, "Childhood Mortality in Rwanda: Levels, Trends, and Differentials," *DHS Further Analysis Report* 66 (2009): 1–33.

2 Paul Demeny, "Pronatalist Policies in Low-Fertility Countries: Patterns, Performance and Prospects," *Population and Development Review*, 12:suppl. (1986): 335–58; Luigi Campiglio, "Children's Right to Vote: The Missing Link in Modern Democracies," *Sociological Studies of Children and Youth* 12 (2009): 221–47 (222); *Prima le donno e i bambini. Chi rappresenta i minorenni? (First, the Women and Children: Why It Is Indispensable to Give Political Weight to the Under-Age Ones)* (Bologna: Il Mulino, 2005); Jane Rutherford, "One Child, One Vote: Proxies for Parents," *Minnesota Law Review* 82 (1998): 1463–525, 1495–6 (1502); Neena Modi, "Votes for a Better Future," *Archives of Disease in Childhood* 105:1 (2020): 13–14 (14); "A Radical Proposal: To Promote Children's Wellbeing Give Them the Vote," *BMJ* 361 (2018): k1862; Neena Modi quoted in Sarah Soseley, "Top Paediatrician Says It's Time to Give Parents Extra Votes for Their Children," *The Guardian*, January 23, 2019; Lennart Köhler, "Rösträtt för barn" ("Voting Rights for Children"), *Dagens Medicin (Daily Medicine)*, November 12, 2008; Manuel Carballo, "Extra Votes for Parents?," *Boston Globe*, December 17, 1981, 35; Miles Corak, "Citizenship as a Privilege or as a Right: Should Children be Given the Vote?," https://www.youtube.com/watch?v=anYFFlOtZKo.

3 Daniel Hart and Robert Atkins, "American Sixteen- and Seventeen-Year-Olds Are Ready to Vote," *Annals of the American Academy of Political and Social Science* 633 (2011): 201–22; see also Daniel Hart and James Youniss, *Renewing Democracy in Young America* (New York: Oxford University Press, 2018); Joshua A. Douglas, "In Defense of Lowering the Voting Age," *University of Pennsylvania Law Review Online* 165 (2017): 63–72 (64); Robert E. Goodin and Joanne C. Lau, "Enfranchising Incompetents: Suretyship and the Join Authorship of Laws," *Ratio* 24 (2011): 154–66 (154); Votes at 16, "The Case for Votes at 16," accessed July 2020, at http://www.votesat16.org/about/; Markus Wagner, David

Johann, and Sylvia Kritzinger, "Voting at 16: Turnout and the Quality of Vote Choice," *Electoral Studies* 31:2 (2012): 372–83; Greg Hurst, "Ministers Contemplate Lowering the Voting Age to 16," *The Times*, February 14, 2003; Alex Folkes, "The Case for Votes at 16," *Representation* 41:1 (2004): 52–6.

4   Matthew Weaver, "Lower Voting Age to Six to Tackle Bias against Young, Says Academic," *The Guardian*, December 6, 2018.

5   Richard Farson, *Birthrights: A Bill of Rights for Children* (New York: Macmillan, 1974), 175; John Holt, *Escape from Childhood* (New York: Penguin, 1975); Bob Franklin, "Children's Political Rights," in *The Rights of Children*, ed. B. Franklin (New York: Basil Blackwell, 1986), 24–53 (24, 46).

6   Claudio López-Guerra, *Democracy and Disenfranchisement: The Morality of Electoral Exclusions* (New York: Oxford University Press, 2014), 3; see also Matthew Yglesias, "The Case for Letting Children Vote," *Vox*, November 28, 2015, accessed at https://www.vox.com/2015/11/28/9770928/voting-rights-for-kids; Cummings, *Children's Voices in Politics*, 401.

7   Vita Wallace, "Give Children the Vote," *The Nation*, October 14, 1991, 439–42 (440).

8   United Nations Human Rights Committee, "General Comment No. 25: The Right to Participate in Public Affairs, Voting Rights and the Right of Equal Access to Public Service (Art. 25)," Article 4, December 7, 1996, accessed August 2020 at https://www.equalrightstrust.org/ertdocumentbank/general%20comment%2025.pdf.

References

Abou-Chadi, Tarik, and Mattias Orlowski, "Political Institutions and the Distributional Consequences of Suffrage Extension," *Political Studies* 63 (2015): 55–72.

Aidt, Toke S., and Bianca Dallal, "Female Voting Power: The Contribution of Women's Suffrage to the Growth of Social Spending in Western Europe (1869–1960)," *Public Choice* 134 (2008): 391–417.

Akosah, Kwame N., "Note, Cracking the One-Way Mirror: How Computational Politics Harms Voter Privacy, and Proposed Regulatory Solutions," *Fordham Intellectual Property, Media & Entertainment Law Journal* 25:1007 (2015): 1012–15.

American Bar Association Commission on Law and Aging, and the Penn Memory Center, "Assisting Cognitively Impaired Individuals with Voting: A Quick Guide," accessed October 2020, at https://www.americanbar.org/content/dam/aba/administrative/law_aging/2020-voting-guide.pdf.

Annenberg Public Policy Center of the University of Pennsylvania, "Americans Are Poorly Informed about Basic Constitutional Provisions," September 12, 2017, accessed August 2020 at https://www.annenbergpublicpolicycenter.org/americans-are-poorly-informed-about-basic-constitutional-provisions/.

Anti-Slavery Society, "Does Slavery Still Exist?," accessed January 2014, at http://www.anti-slaverysociety.org/slavery.htm.

Arain, M., M. Haque, L. Johal, P. Mathur, W. Nel, A. Rais, R. Sandhu, and S. Sharma, "Maturation of the Adolescent Brain," *Neuropsychiatric Disease and Treatment* 9 (2013): 449–61.

Archard, David W., *Children, Family and the State* (Burlington, VT: Ashgate, 2003).

Association for Children's Suffrage, accessed January 2020 at http://web.archive.org/web/20070426231337/http://www.brown.edu:80/Students/Association_for_Childrens_Suffrage/.

Aufseeser, Dena, "Control, Protection and Rights: A Critical Review of Peru's Begging Bill," *International Journal of Children's Rights* 22 (2014): 241–67.

Austin, Sara L., "Children's Participation in Citizenship and Governance," in *A Handbook of Children and Young People's Participation*, ed. Barry Percy-Smith and Nigel Thomas (New York: Routledge, 2010), 245–53.

Bajpai, Ahsa, *Child Rights in India: Law, Policy, and Practice* (New York: Oxford University Press, 2003).

Barber, Benjamin R., "The Discourse of Civility," in *Citizen Competence and Democratic Institutions*, ed. Stephen L. Ekin and Karol E. Soltan (University Park: Pennsylvania State University, 1999), 39–47.

Beaty, Zoe, and Amelia Bowe, "9 Young Activists on How They Want to Change the World," Refinery29, October 19, 2020, accessed March 2021 at https://www.refinery29.com/en-gb/dove-self-esteem-project-young-activists.

Benhabib, Seyla, *The Rights of Others: Aliens, Residents, and Citizens* (New York: Cambridge University Press, 2004).

Bennett, R. W., "Should Parents Be Given Extra Votes on Account of Their Children: Toward a Conversational Understanding of American Democracy," *Northwestern University Law Review* 94 (1999–2000): 503.

Biswas, Tanu, *Little Things Matter Much: Childist Ideas for a Pedagogy of Philosophy in an Overheated World* (Munich: Büro Himmelgrün, 2020).

BookTrust, "Here Are the Young Activists That Can Make the World a Better Place," accessed March 2021 at https://www.booktrust.org.uk/news-and-features/features/2019/november/here-are-the-young-activists-that-can-make-the-world-a-better-place/.

Brennan, Jason, "The Right to a Competent Electorate," *Philosophical Quarterly* 61:245 (2011): 700–24.

Brooks, C., P. Nieuwbeerta, and J. Manza , "Cleavage-Based Voting Behavior in Cross-National Perspective: Evidence from Six Postwar Democracies," *Social Science Research* 35 (2006): 88–128.

Buhle, Mary Jo, and Paul Buhle (eds.), *Concise History of Woman Suffrage: Selections from the Classic Work of Stanton, Anthony, Gage, and Harper* (Urbana: University of Illinois Press, 1978).

Butler, Judith, *Bodies That Matter: On the Discursive Limits of "Sex"* (New York: Routledge, 1993).

Cabannes, Yves, "Children and Young People Build a Participatory Democracy in Latin American Cities," *Children, Youth and Environments* 15:2 (2005): 185–210.

Campiglio, Luigi, "Children's Right to Vote: The Missing Link in Modern Democracies," *Sociological Studies of Children and Youth* 12 (2009): 221–47 (222).

Campiglio, Luigi, "The Importance of Investing in Very Young People," in *Government, Governance, and Welfare Reform: Structural Changes and Subsidiarity in Italy and Britain*, ed. Alberto Brugnoli and Alessandro Colombo (Northampton, MA: Edward Elgar, 2012), pp. 133–46.

Campiglio, Luigi, *Prima le donno e i bambini. Chi rappresenta i minorenni? (First, the Women and Children: Why It Is Indispensable to Give Political Weight to the Under-Age Ones)* (Bologna: Il Mulino, 2005).

Canclini, Néstor García, *Imagined Globalization* (trans. G. Yúdice) (Durham, NC: Duke University Press, 2014).

Caplan, Bryan, *The Myth of the Rational Voter: Why Democracies Choose Bad Policies* (Princeton, NJ: Princeton University Press, 2006), 95.

Carballo, Manuel, "Extra Votes for Parents?," *Boston Globe*, December 17, 1981.

Censer, Jack, and Lynn Hunt, *Liberty, Equality, Fraternity: Exploring the French Revolution* (University Park: Pennsylvania State University Press, 2001).

Centers for Medicare & Medicaid Services, "US Personal Health Care Spending by Age and Gender," accessed May 2020, at https://www.cms.gov/Research-Statistics-Data-and-Systems/Statistics-Trends-and-Reports/NationalHealthExpendData/Downloads/AgeandGenderHighlights.pdf.

Chan, Tak Wing, and Matthew Clayton, "Should the Voting Age Be Lowered to Sixteen? Normative and Empirical Considerations," *Political Studies* 54 (2006): 533–58.

Children's Rights International Network (CRIN), "Right to Vote," accessed January 2020 at https://archive.crin.org/en/home/what-we-do/policy/minimum-ages/right-vote.html?fbclid=IwAR32RMNQBH4xenCg_egj4oF pNBpHiqR_0xDq4MvddOKgy8l8Bt7UbvFt81M.

Children's United Parliament of the World (2013), www.childrensstate.net.

Children's Voice Association, accessed January 2020 at https://www.childrensvoiceassociation.org/.

Children's Voting Colloquium, https://www.childrenvoting.org/.

Christiano, T., *The Constitution of Equality: Democratic Authority and Its Limits* (Oxford: Oxford University Press, 2008).

Commonwealth Electoral Act 1918, s93(8)a (Australia), accessed October
   2020, at https://www.legislation.gov.au/Details/C2016C01022.

Conrad, Stefanie, "Children as Active Citizens: Addressing Discrimination
   against Children's Engagement in Political and Civil Society Processes,"
   Plan International, 2009, www.plan-international.org.uk.

Corak, Miles, "Citizenship as a Privilege or as a Right: Should Children be
   Given the Vote?," https://www.youtube.com/watch?v=anYFFlOtZKo.

Cowley, Philip, and David Denver, "Votes at 16? The Case Against,"
   Representation 41:1 (2004): 57–62 (60).

Cox, Gary W., "Political Institutions, Economic Liberty, and the Great
   Divergence," *Journal of Economic History* 77:3 (2017): 724–55.

Cummings, Michael S., *Children's Voices in Politics* (New York: Peter
   Lang, 2020).

Cunningham, L., "A Question of Capacity: Towards a Comprehensive and
   Consistent Vision of Children and Their Status under Law," *UC Davis
   Journal of Juvenile Law and Policy* 10:2 (2006): 275–377.

Dahl, Robert A., *Democracy and Its Critics* (New Haven, CT: Yale University
   Press, 1989).

Darwen Aldridge Enterprise Studio, "Young People in Blackburn with
   Darwen Lead Food Poverty Day of Action," November 13, 2018, accessed
   March 2021 at http://www.daestudio.biz/post/young-people-in-blackburn-
   with-darwen-lead-food-poverty-day-of-action.

Demeny, Paul, "Pronatalist Policies in Low-Fertility Countries: Patterns,
   Performance and Prospects," *Population and Development Review* 12:suppl.
   (1986): 335–58.

Douglas, Joshua A., "In Defense of Lowering the Voting Age," *University of
   Pennsylvania Law Review Online* 165 (2017): 63–72.

Douthat, Ross, "Power to the Parents," *New York Times*, March 3, 2018,
   accessed January 2020 at https://www.nytimes.com/2018/03/03/opinion/
   sunday/parents-teenagers-voting.html?action=click&pgtype=Homepage&
   clickSource=story-heading&module=opinion-c-col-left-region&region=
   opinion-c-col-left-region&WT.nav=opinion-c-col-left-region.

Doyle, William, *The Oxford History of the French Revolution* (Oxford: Oxford
   University Press, 1989).

Dworkin, Gerald, "Moral Paternalism," *Law and Philosophy* 24:3 (2005):
   305–19.

Dworkin, Gerald, "Paternalism," *The Monist* 56 (1972): 64–84.

Dyer, Hannah, *The Queer Aesthetics of Childhood: Asymmetries of Innocence and the Cultural Politics of Child Development* (New Brunswick, NJ: Rutgers University Press, 2019).

Economist Intelligence Unit, "Democracy Index 2019: A Year of Democratic Setbacks and Popular Protest," accessed October 2020, at https://www.eiu.com/topic/democracy-index.

Eidelman, Vera, and Sarah Hinger, "Some Schools Need a Lesson on Students' Free Speech Rights," ACLU, September 18, 2018, accessed April 2020, at https://www.aclu.org/blog/free-speech/student-speech-and-privacy/some-schools-need-lesson-students-free-speech-rights.

Elcock, H., "Young Voters 1988: Will They Break the Mold?," *Youth and Policy* 2:2 (1983).

Elkins, Kathleen Gallagher, "Biblical Studies and Childhood Studies: A Fertile, Interdisciplinary Space for Feminists," *Journal of Feminist Studies in Religion* 29:2 (2013): 146–53.

Ernst, Monique, and Martin P. Paulus, "Neurobiology of Decision Making: A Selective Review from a Neurocognitive and Clinical Perspective," *Biological Psychiatry* 58:8 (2005): 597–604.

European Youth Forum, "European Union Backs Right for 16 & 17 Year Olds to Vote," accessed October 2020, at https://www.youthforum.org/european-parliament-backs-right-16-17-year-olds-vote.

Farson, Richard, *Birthrights: A Bill of Rights for Children* (New York: Macmillan, 1974).

Fawcett, Millicent Garrett, "Home and Politics: An Address Delivered at Toynbee Hall and Elsewhere," c. 1888.

Folkes, Alex, "The Case for Votes at 16," *Representation* 41:1 (2004): 52–6.

Foundation for the Rights of Future Generations, "Voting Age," accessed January 2020 at https://www.intergenerationaljustice.org/topics/voting-age/.

Franck, Olof, "Highlighting Ethics, Subjectivity and Democratic Participation in Sustainability Education: Challenges and Contributions," in *Ethical Literacies and Education for Sustainable Development: Young People, Subjectivity and Democratic Participation*, ed. Olof Franck and Christina Osbeck (New York: Palgrave Macmillan, 2017), 1–17.

Franklin, Bob, "Children's Political Rights," in *The Rights of Children*, ed. B. Franklin (New York: Basil Blackwell, 1986), 24–53.

Freechild Institute, "Youth + Social Change through Youth Voting," accessed January 2020 at https://freechild.org/youth-as-voters/?fbclid=IwAR1zByP6 512nBFpzFNKOoYhLuOTk0p9mJ5ma3CT-QQS1FhNeHCAGwGRR8KQ.

Friedman, Milton, *Capitalism and Freedom* (Chicago: University of Chicago Press, 1962).

Fukuyama, Francis, "The End of History?," *National Interest* 16 (1989): 3–18.

Garcia, Diana Carolina, "Cultivating Hope: A Visual Ethnography on the Production and Consumption of Collective Memory by Colombian Youth," PhD dissertation, Rutgers University, 2021.

Garroway, Kristine, "2 *Kings* 6:24–30: A Case of Unintentional Elimination," *Journal of Biblical Literature* 137:1 (2018): 53–70.

Gaughwin, Matt, quoted in "Should Children Be Allowed to Vote?," *Australian Politics*, April 18, 2001, accessed August 2020 at https://australianpolitics. com/2001/04/18/should-children-be-allowed-to-vote.html?fbclid=IwAR3 0zww1kJSrsnCxKaeTqFYqJ0trvnEHbFR_aH919_tuFUPa124PayodHX0.

German Government, "Fragen zum Wahlrecht von Geburt an," 2017, accessed January 2020 at https://www.bundestag.de/resource/blob/531942/6669f3e2 9651882065938fc6a14fd779/wd-3-157-17-pdf-data.pdf.

Gesley, Jenny, "Family Voting as a Solution to Low Fertility? Experiences from France and Germany," *Global Law Guest Post*, April 19, 2018, accessed January 2020 at https://blogs.loc.gov/law/2018/04/family-voting-as-a-solution-to-low-fertility-experiences-from-france-and-germany/?fbclid =IwAR25FzSWs6w3twJvMd98eIHiT2i5QNlxEhxSmTIniU7aw43iFQk s7LpqJK4.

Goodin, Robert, and Joanne Lau, "Enfranchising Incompetents: Suretyship and the Joint Authorship of Laws," *Ratio* 24:2 (2011): 154–66.

Gopnik, Alison, *The Philosophical Baby: What Children's Minds Tell Us about Truth, Love, and the Meaning of Life* (New York: Picador, 2010).

Greene, Jack P., *Imperatives, Behaviors, and Identities: Essays in Early American Cultural History* (Charlottesville: University Press of Virginia, 1992).

Guggenheim, Martin, *What's Wrong with Children's Rights* (Cambridge, MA: Harvard University Press, 2005).

Habermas, Jürgen, *Justification and Application: Remarks on Discourse Ethics* (trans. C. P. Cronin) (Cambridge, MA: MIT Press, 1993).

Habermas, Jürgen, *Moral Consciousness and Communicative Action* (Cambridge, MA: MIT Press, 1990).

Habermas, Jürgen, *The Structural Transformation of the Public Sphere* (trans. T. Burger and F. Lawrence) (Cambridge: MIT Press, [1962] 1989).

Harrison, S., and M. Bruter, Mapping Extreme Right Ideology (Basingstoke: Palgrave Macmillan, 2011).

Harry, De Quetteville, "Germany Plans to Give Vote to Babies," *Daily Telegraph*, July 9, 2008.

Hart, Daniel, and Robert Atkins, "American Sixteen- and Seventeen-Year-Olds Are Ready to Vote," *Annals of the American Academy of Political and Social Science* 633 (2011): 201–22.

Hart, Daniel, and James Youniss, *Renewing Democracy in Young America* (New York: Oxford University Press, 2018).

Hayek, Friedrich A., *The Constitution of Liberty* (Chicago: University of Chicago Press, 1960).

Hemchandra, Raychaudhuri, *Political History of Ancient India* (Calcutta: University of Calcutta, 1972).

Holt, John, *Escape from Childhood* (New York: Penguin, 1975).

Hong, R. M. Ayad, S. Rutstein, and R. L. Ran, "Childhood Mortality in Rwanda: Levels, Trends, and Differentials," *DHS Further Analysis Report* 66 (2009): 1–33.

Howe, Daniel Walker, *What Hath God Wrought: The Transformation of America, 1815–1848* (New York: Oxford University Press, 2007).

Hurst, Greg, "Ministers Contemplate Lowering the Voting Age to 16," *The Times*, February 14, 2003.

Husted, Thomas A., and Lawrence W. Kenny, "The Effect of the Expansion of the Voting Franchise on the Size of Government," *Journal of Political Economy* 105 (1997): 54–82.

Isakhan, B., "Engaging 'Primitive Democracy,' Mideast Roots of Collective Governance," *Middle East Policy* 14:3 (2007): 97–117.

Jacobsen, Thorkild, "Primitive Democracy in Ancient Mesopotamia," *Journal of Near Eastern Studies* 2:3 (1943): 159–72.

Jariego, Isidro Maya, "'But We Want to Work': The Movement of Child Workers in Peru and the Actions for Reducing Child Labor," *American Journal of Community Psychology* 60 (2017): 430–8.

Jobson, Adrian, *The First English Revolution: Simon de Montfort, Henry II and the Barons' War* (London: Bloomsbury, 2012).

John, Mary, *Children's Rights and Power: Charging Up for a New Century* (London: Jessica Kingsley, 2003), 235–9.

Johnson, S. B., R. W. Blum, and J. N. Giedd, "Adolescent Maturity and the Brain: The Promise and Pitfalls of Neuroscience Research in Adolescent Health Policy," *Journal of Adolescent Health* 45:3 (2009): 216–21.

Josefsson, Jonathan, "'We Beg You, Let Them Stay!': Rights Claims of Asylum-Seeking Children as a Socio-Political Practice," *Childhood* 24:3 (2017): 316–32.

Journal Officiel de la République Française, 233:25, August 22, 1871, with supplement, accessed January 2020 at https://babel.hathitrust.org/cgi/pt?id =mdp.39015022763927&view=1up&seq=1667.

Journal Officiel de la République Française, Débats Parliamentaires, Chambre des Deputes, December 6, 1923, 3957, accessed January 2020 at https:// gallica.bnf.fr/ark:/12148/bpt6k62174312/f13.item.

Kan, Man-Yee, and Anthony Heath, "The Political Attitudes and Choices of Husbands and Wives," *Centre for Research into Elections and Social Trends Working Paper 103* (2003): 1–40, accessed June 2013 at http://www.crest. ox.ac.uk/papers/p103.pdf.

Kant, Immanuel, *The Science of Right* (trans. W. Hastie) (Clifton, NJ: A. M. Kelley, 1974).

Kersting, Anna, *Power to the Children* (documentary) (Anna Kersting Filmproduktion, 2017), http://www.powertothechildren-film.com.

Keyssar, Alexander, *The Right to Vote: The Contested History of Democracy in the United States*, revised edition (New York: Basic Books, 2000).

Kohlberg, Lawrence, *The Psychology of Moral Development: The Nature and Validity of Moral Stages* (New York: Harper & Row, 1984).

Köhler, Lennart, "Rösträtt för barn" ("Voting Rights for Children"), *Dagens Medicin* (*Daily Medicine*), November 12, 2008.

KRÄTZÄ (die KinderRÄchTsZÄnker), www.kraetzae.de.

Laclau, Ernesto, and Chantal Mouffe, *Hegemony and Socialist Strategy: Towards a Radical Democratic Politics*, 2nd edition (New York: Verso, 2001).

Lau, Richard R., and David P. Redlawsk, "Voting Correctly," *American Political Science Review* 91:3 (1997): 585–98.

Le Naour, Jean-Yves with Catherine Valenti, *La famille doit voter: Le suffrage familial contre le vote individuel* (Paris: Hachette Littératures, 2005).

Liebel, Manfred, "Protecting the Rights of Working Children instead of Banning Child Labour: Bolivia Tries a New Legislative Approach," *International Journal of Children's Rights* 23 (2015): 529.

Locke, John, "Two Treatises of Government," in *The Works of John Locke*, new edition, vol. V (London: W. Sharpe, 1823).

López-Guerra, Claudio, *Democracy and Disenfranchisement: The Morality of Electoral Exclusions* (New York: Oxford University Press, 2014).

Ludbrook, Robert, "Should Children Have the Right to Vote?" *National Children's and Youth Law Centre Discussion Paper*, University of New South Wales, December 1995.

Mannion, Gregory, "Children's Participation in Changing School Grounds and Public Play Areas in Scotland," PhD dissertation, University of Stirling, Scotland, 1999.

Marzagora, Sara, "The Humanism of Reconstruction: African Intellectuals, Decolonial Critical Theory and the Opposition to the 'Posts' (Postmodernism, Poststructuralism, Postcolonialism)," *Journal of African Cultural Studies* 28:2 (2016): 161–78.

McCrummen, Stephanie, "'Children's Parliament' Sets High Bar in Congo: Youthful Body in a Beacon of Justice," *Washington Post*, August 11, 2007.

McIntosh, Peggy, "Unpacking the Invisible Knapsack: White Privilege and Male Privilege," in *Race, Class, and Gender: An Anthology*, 9th edition, ed. Margaret Andersen and Patricia Hill Collins (Belmont, CA: Cengage Learning, 2015), 74–8.

Mitchell, Jonathan, "Teens Ask Court to Lower Voting Age to 16," *RNZ News*, August 24, 2020, accessed October 2020, at https://www.rnz.co.nz/news/national/424324/teens-ask-court-to-lower-voting-age-to-16.

Modi, Neena, "A Radical Proposal: To Promote Children's Wellbeing Give Them the Vote," *BMJ* 361 (2018): k1862.

Modi, Neena, quoted in Sarah Soseley, "Top Paediatrician Says It's Time to Give Parents Extra Votes for their Children," *The Guardian*, January 23, 2019.

Modi, Neena, "Votes for a Better Future," *Archives of Disease in Childhood* 105:1 (2020): 13–14 (14).

Møller, Jørgen, "Why Europe Avoided Hegemony: A Historical Perspective on the Balance of Power," *International Studies Quarterly* 58:4 (2014): 660–70.

Moorhead, Joanna, "Should We Give Children the Vote? We Ask Nine Kids What They Think," *The Guardian*, December 23, 2018, accessed October 2020, at https://www.theguardian.com/global/2018/dec/23/should-we-give-children-the-vote-voting-at-age-6-politics-interviews.

Müller-Franken, Sebastian, *Familienwahlrecht und Verfassung* (Tübingen: Mohr Siebeck, 2013).

Munn, Nicholas, "Capacity-Testing as a Means of Increasing Political Inclusion," *Democratization* 20 (2013): 1–19.

Munn, Nicholas, "Lowering New Zealand's Voting Age to 16 Would Be Good for Young People—and Good for Democracy," *The Conversation*, August 25, 2020, accessed August 2020 at https://theconversation.com/lowering-new-zealands-voting-age-to-16-would-be-good-for-young-people-and-good-for-democracy-145008.

National Youth Rights Association, "Voting Age," accessed January 2020 at https://www.youthrights.org/issues/voting-age/.

Neighborhood Community Network (2013), www.neighborhoodparliament.org.

Neighborhood Community Network, "Neighborocracy," concept paper shared with the author, January 2020.

Newstead, Shelly, "De-constructing and Reconstructing the Unorthodox Recipe of Playwork," doctoral thesis, Institute of Education, University College London, 2016.

Olson, M., "Dictatorship, Democracy, and Development," *American Political Science Review* 87 (1993): 3.

Olsson, Stefan, "Children's Suffrage: A Critique of the Importance of Voters' Knowledge for the Well-Being of Democracy," *International Journal of Children's Rights* 16 (2008): 55–76.

Organization for Economic Cooperation, "Poverty Rate," accessed May 2020, at https://data.oecd.org/inequality/poverty-rate.htm#indicator-chart.

Ortiz-Ospina, Esteban, "Children and Poverty: Evidence from New World Bank Data," *Our World in Data*, February 22, 2017, accessed May 2020, at https://ourworldindata.org/children-and-poverty-results-from-new-data.

Ott, Kate, "Taking Children's Moral Lives Seriously: Creativity as Ethical Response Offline and Online," *Religions* 10 (2019): 525–37.

Parijs, Philippe van, "The Disenfranchisement of the Elderly, and Other Attempts to Secure Intergenerational Justice," *Philosophy and Public Affairs* 27 (1999): 292–333.

Parker, Julie Faith, "Children in the Hebrew Bible and Childist Interpretation," *Currents in Biblical Research* 17:2 (2019): 130–57.

Parker, Julie Faith, *Valuable and Vulnerable: Children in the Hebrew Bible, Especially the Elisha Cycle* (Providence, RI: Brown Judaic Studies, 2017).

Peterson, Paul (1992), "An Immodest Proposal," *Daedalus* 121:4 (1992): 151–74.

Pevsner, Laurence, "Let Children Vote. Even 13-Year-Olds," *Washington Post*, October 27, 2016.

Phillips, Leigh, "Hungarian Mothers May Get Extra Votes for Their Children in Elections," *The Guardian*, April 17, 2011, accessed January 2020 at https://www.theguardian.com/world/2011/apr/17/hungary-mothers-get-extra-votes?fbclid=IwAR1BARgMPkXK6eRQpXttDVnkePvwFYItsyaFrD mmq-hTxMYm9Fo8J6qGZ-I.

Quintern, Hanna, *Das Familienwahlrecht: Ein Beitrag zur verfassungsrechtlichen Diskussion* (Münster: Lit Verlag, 2010).

Raaflaub, Kurt A., Josiah Ober, and Robert W. Wallace, *Origins of Democracy in Ancient Greece* (Berkeley: University of California Press, 2007).

Ratcliffe, Donald, "The Right to Vote and the Rise of Democracy, 1787–1828," *Journal of the Early Republic* 33 (2013): 219–54.

Rawls, John, *Political Liberalism* (New York: Columbia University Press, 1996).

Rawls, John, *A Theory of Justice* (Cambridge, MA: Belknap Press, 1971).

Represent MA Children (2020), accessed January 2020 at https://www.facebook.com/representMAchildren2020.

Representation of the People Bill of 1867, House of Commons Debates, May 20, 1867.

Reyna, Valerie F., and Frank Farley, "Risk and Rationality in Adolescent Decision Making: Implications for Theory, Practice, and Public Policy," *Psychological Science in the Public Interest* 7:1 (2006): 1–44.

Riccards, Patrick, "National Survey Finds Just 1 in 3 Americans Would Pass Citizenship Test," *Woodrow Wilson National Fellowship Foundation*, October 3, 2018, accessed August 2020 at https://woodrow.org/news/national-survey-finds-just-1-in-3-americans-would-pass-citizenship-test/.

Ringen, Stein, *Citizens, Families and Reform* (Oxford: Oxford University Press, 1997).

Runciman, David, *The Confidence Trap: A History of Democracy in Crisis from World War I to the Present*, revised edition (Princeton, NJ: Princeton University Press, 2018).

Runciman, David, quoted in Matthew Weaver, "Lower the Voting Age to Six to Tackle Bias against Young, Says Academic," *The Guardian*, December 6, 2018, accessed July 2020, at https://www.theguardian.com/politics/2018/

dec/06/give-six-year-olds-the-vote-says-cambridge-university-academic?CMP=share_btn_tw&fbclid=IwAR1jVc7NxPPFv0s7ucwAZy1U juw-PSKt-H-1cCSQM17ftfszsUtdMqgVg9U.

Rutchick, Abraham M., "Deus Ex Machina: The Influence of Polling Place on Voting Behavior," *Political Psychology* 31 (2010): 209–25.

Rutherford, Jane, "One Child, One Vote: Proxies for Parents," *Minnesota Law Review* 82 (1998): 1463–525, 1495–6 (1502).

Sanderson, Warren C., "A Near Electoral Majority of Pensioners," *Population and Development Review* 33:3 (2007): 543–54.

Sarkar, Jayashri, and Blanka Mendoza, "Bolivia's Children's Parliament: Bringing Participation to the National Stage," *Children, Youth and Environments* 15:2 (2005): 227–44.

Scarre, Geoffrey, "Children and Paternalism," *Philosophy* 55:211 (1980): 117–24.

Schumpeter, Joseph A., *Capitalism, Socialism and Democracy*, 3rd edition (New York: Harper & Row, [1942] 1950).

Segalowitz, S. J. and P. L. Davies, "Charting the Maturation of the Frontal Lobe: An Electrophysiological Strategy," *Brain and Cognition* 55:1 (2004): 116–33.

Shapiro, Ian, *Democratic Justice* (New Haven, CT: Yale University Press, 1999).

Shrag, Francis, "Children and Democracy: Theory and Policy," *Politics, Philosophy and Economics* 3:3 (2004): 365–79.

Silbaugh, Katharine, "Developmental Justice and the Voting Age," *Fordham Urban Law Journal* 47 (2020): 253–92.

Somin, Ilya, "Should We Let Children Vote? The Troubling Implications of Standard Reasons for Rejecting a Flawed Idea," *Reason*, December 7, 2018, accessed August 2020 at https://reason.com/2018/12/07/should-we-let-children-vote-the-troublin/?fbclid=IwAR0IeVMqPqX4zlwNu7l8CE WKl_eG17GDTj1QU2-DbrPtQfNYwxygzBy0wow#.

Sridhar, Lalitha, "Bal Sansads: Members of Parliament at 11," *Infochange*, May 2004, accessed January 2020 at infochangeindia.org/20040508228/ Children/Features/Bal-Sansads-Members-of-Parliament-at-11.html.

Stanton, Elizabeth Cady, Susan B. Anthony, Matilda Joslyn Gage, and Ida Husted, *The History of Women's Suffrage*, volume 3 (Salem, NH: Harper, [1881] 1985), 275.

Stasavage, David, "Representation and Consent: Why They Arose in Europe and Not Elsewhere," *Annual Review of Political Science* 19:1 (2016): 145–62.

Steinberg, Laurence, and Elizabeth S. Scott, "Less Guilty by Reason of Adolescence: Developmental Immaturity, Diminished Responsibility, and the Juvenile Death Penalty," *American Psychologist* 58:12 (2003): 1009–18.

Still, Clarinda, and Srinivas Dusi, "Vote Buying and 'Money-Politics' in Village Elections in South India," *Commonwealth and Comparative Politics* 58:1 (2020): 100–19.

Sundhall, Jeanette, "A Political Space for Children? The Age Order and Children's Right to Participation," *Social Inclusion* 5:3 (2017): 164–71.

Taft, Jessica K., " 'Adults Talk Too Much': Intergenerational Dialogue and Power in the Peruvian Movement of Working Children," *Childhood* 22:4 (2015): 460–73.

Toulemon, Andre, *Le Suffrage familial ou stffriage universel integral* (Paris: Librairie du Recueil Sirey, 1933).

Turkie, Alan, "More Than Crumbs from the Table: A Critique of Youth Parliaments as Models of Representation for Marginalised Young People," in *A Handbook of Children and Young People's Participation*, ed. Barry Percy-Smith and Nigel Patrick Thomas (New York: Routledge, 2010), 262–9.

UK Labour Party, accessed October 2020, at https://labour.org.uk/latest/stories/time-votes-16/

Umbers, Lachlan Montgomery, "Enfranchising the Youth," *Critical Review of International Social and Political Philosophy* 23:6 (2018): 1–24.

UNHCR, "Global Trends: Forced Displacement 2018," June 2019, accessed May 2020 at https://www.unhcr.org/statistics/unhcrstats/ 5d08d7ee7/unhcr-global-trends-2018.html.

UNICEF, "Convention on the Rights of the Child," accessed September 2013, at http://www.unicef.org/crc/.

United Nations Human Rights Committee, "General Comment No. 25: The Right to Participate in Public Affairs, Voting Rights and the Right of Equal Access to Public Service (Art. 25)," article 4, December 7, 1996, accessed August 2020 at https://www.equalrightstrust.org/ertdocumentbank/general%20comment%2025.pdf.

Urbinati, Nadia, *Representative Democracy: Principles and Genealogy* (Chicago: University of Chicago Press, 2006).

US 1920 Census, accessed January 2020 at https://www2.census.gov/library/publications/decennial/1920/volume-3/41084484v3ch01.pdf.

Vaithianathan, R., R. Aoki, and Erwan Sbai, "Support for Franchise Extension for Children: Evidence on Japanese Attitude to Demeny Voting," *CIS DP* 610 (2013): 1–14.

Van Parijs, Philippe, "The Disenfranchisement of the Elderly, and Other Attempts to Secrure Intergenerational Justice," *Philosophy & Public Affairs* 27:4 (1998): 292–333.

Votes at 16, "The Case for Votes at 16," accessed July 2020, at http://www.votesat16.org/about/.

Wadsworth, Sarah, "The Year of the Child: Children's Literature, Childhood Studies, and the Turn to Childism," *American Literary History* 27:2 (2015): 331–41.

Wagner, Markus, David Johann, and Sylvia Kritzinger, "Voting at 16: Turnout and the Quality of Vote Choice," *Electoral Studies* 31:2 (2012): 372–83.

Wald, Patricia M., "Making Sense Out of the Rights of Youth, *Human Rights* 4:1 (1974): 13–29.

Wall, John, "Can Democracy Represent Children? Toward a Politics of Difference," *Childhood: A Journal of Global Child Research* 19:1 (2012): 86–100.

Wall, John, "Childhood Studies, Hermeneutics, and Theological Ethics," *Journal of Religion* 86:4 (2006): 523–48.

Wall, John, *Children's Rights: Today's Global Challenge* (Lanham, MD: Rowman & Littlefield, 2016).

Wall, John, "Democratizing Democracy: The Road from Women's to Children's Suffrage," *International Journal of Human Rights*, special issue, ed. Sonja Grover 18:6 (2014): 646–59.

Wall, John, *Ethics in Light of Childhood* (Lanham, MD: Georgetown University Press, 2010).

Wall, John, "From Childhood Studies to Childism: Reconstructing the Scholarly and Social Imaginations," *Children's Geographies*, special issue, ed. Hanne Warming 17:6 (2019): 1–15.

Wall, John, "Human Rights in Light of Childhood," *International Journal of Children's Rights* 16:4 (2008): 523–43.

Wall, John, "Theorizing Children's Global Citizenship: Reconstructionism and the Politics of Deep Interdependence," *Global Studies of Childhood* 9:1 (2019): 5–17.

Wall, John, "Why Children and Youth Should Have the Right to Vote: An Argument for Proxy-Claim Suffrage," *Children, Youth and Environments*, 24:1 (2014): 108–23.

Wallace, Vita, "Give Children the Vote," *The Nation*, October 14, 1991, 439–42.

Walton, Katherine, "Votes for Children: The Case for Universal Suffrage," *Amnesty International UK*, accessed January 2020 at https://www.amnesty. org.uk/blogs/childrens-human-rights-network-blog/votes-children-case-universal-suffrage?fbclid=IwAR3c-bexlD8PZhdpQHJz4n6nINdTM_TBA Fzc3p6tbziu2qk0mwN9W2LfCoU.

Weaver, Matthew, "Lower Voting Age to Six to Tackle Bias against Young, Says Academic," *The Guardian*, December 6, 2018.

Wiland, Eric, "One Citizen, One Vote," *What's Wrong?*, Colorado University Boulder Center for Values and Social Policy blog, August 12, 2015, accessed January 2020 at https://whatswrongcvsp.com/2015/08/12/one-citizen-one-vote/?fbclid=IwAR0gfWV-HHjFubbjALPMce7-90sJaIWTNW Wya7q9LxVbMv0dJzl1B8CKgis.

Wiland, Eric, "Should Children Have the Right to Vote?," in *The Palgrave Handbook of Philosophy and Public Policy*, ed. David Boonin (New York: Palgrave Macmillan, 2018), 215–60.

Wilentz, Sean, *The Rise of American Democracy: Jefferson to Lincoln* (New York: W.W. Norton, 2005).

Williams, Emma, *Children's Participation and Policy Change in South Asia* (London: Save the Children, Childhood Poverty Research and Policy Center, 2004), accessed January 2020 at www.childhoodpoverty.org/index. php/action=documentfeed/doctype=pdf/id=86.

Williamson, Chilton, *American Suffrage from Property to Democracy, 1760–1860* (Princeton, NJ: Princeton University Press, 1960).

Wingerden, Sophia A., *The Women's Suffrage Movement in Britain, 1866–1928* (New York: St. Martin's Press, 1999).

Wir Wollen Wällen (We Want the Vote), accessed January 2020 at www.wir-wollen-waehlen.de.

Women's Disabilities Bill, House of Commons Debates, April 30, 1873, 1238.

World Population Review, "Infant Mortality Rate by Country 2020," accessed July 2020, at https://worldpopulationreview.com/country-rankings/ infant-mortality-rate-by-country.

Wyness, Michael, "Regulating Participation: The Possibilities and Limits of Children and Young People's Councils," *Journal of Social Sciences* 9, special issue (2005): 7–18.

Yglesias, Matthew, "The Case for Letting Children Vote," *Vox*, November 2015, accessed at https://www.vox.com/2015/11/28/9770928/voting-rights-for-kids.

Young, Iris Marion, *Inclusion and Democracy* (New York: Oxford University Press, 2000).

Young, Iris Marion, *Justice and the Politics of Difference* (Princeton, NJ: Princeton University Press, 1990).

Zehavi, Ohad, "Becoming-Woman, Becoming-Child: A Joint Political Programme," in *Feminism and the Politics of Childhood*, ed. Rachel Rosen and Katherine Twamley (London: UCL Press, 2016), 241–56.

Index

prejudice 41, 97, 144 (*see also* bias)
Pressley, Ayanna 30
privacy 21–8, 36–7, 46, 49, 53, 105, 122, 159 (*see also* family; school)
privilege
  social 101, 113, 125, 135, 157, 164, 187
  voting 19, 153, 160
progressivism 158, 159–60, 162, 165 (*see also* liberalism)
property
  children as 21, 37
  voting and 18, 20, 22–4, 38, 40, 56, 173
protection
  adults' 89, 92, 95, 96, 105–6, 107, 119, 127
  children's 57, 113–15, 121–2, 108, 114–15, 160, 200
proxy voting 31–2, 35, 174–5, 182 (*see also* Demeny voting)
proxy-claim voting 8–9, 169–92, 196, 200
psychology 59, 76, 176, 178
public space (*see* space, public)
Puerto Rico 73

Qatar 25
queer 70, 73, 76, 128, 160, 161

race (*see also* anti-racism; racism)
  as lens 5–7, 53, 63, 74, 76, 134, 152, 157, 158, 177
  as exclusion 22–3, 27, 43, 46–7, 81, 98, 187
racism (*see also* race; anti-racism)
  as lens 5, 51, 61, 80, 87, 135
  as exclusion 2, 47, 78, 82, 98, 141–3, 145, 184, 193, 198
  as systemic 121, 150, 156–7
reconstructionism 7–8, 162, 164–7
referenda 90, 122, 183
religion 58, 73, 93, 121, 127, 150, 151
Represent MA Children 6, 35, 179

Represent PA Children 35
representation
  children's 8, 18, 32, 35, 56, 67, 81, 88–92, 99, 109, 115–17, 132–9, 148, 150, 169–76, 194–8, 200
  democratic 41, 48, 50, 52, 60–2, 83, 147–8, 161, 164
responsibility
  adults' 88–9, 90, 94, 120, 146
  children's 28, 38, 41–2, 68, 87, 92–3, 113–14, 120–3, 127, 130–1, 146, 176
  legislators' 82, 165, 199
rights
  adults' 4, 12, 28, 29, 59, 86, 113–15, 127–9
  children's (*see* rights, children's)
  democratic 13–14, 18–20, 23, 36–8, 95, 101, 111, 136–7
  gay 61, 121
  human 33, 96–7, 99, 127–9, 133, 138–9, 141, 159, 165, 179–80
  men's 14, 17, 21–2, 29
  minorities' 61, 73, 156
  transgender 35, 76, 161, 193
  women's 24–6, 29, 156, 197
  universal (*see* rights, human)
rights, children's
  disabilities 128
  driving 41, 114, 126–9
  education 111, 112, 137
  emancipation 9
  environmental 11, 133
  family 114, 144, 149, 185
  freedom of expression 40, 85, 90, 92, 97, 111, 127–9, 178, 189, 194
  gun 98, 199
  health 9, 89, 114
  internet 126, 197
  judicial 110, 114, 127
  labor 2, 56, 66, 90, 126–9, 152, 193
  marriage 9, 41, 56, 90, 114, 127–9
  nondiscrimination 32, 135, 138, 187

Turkey 11, 24, 28, 154, 188
turnout 153, 176, 182
tyranny 72, 158

Uganda 169
Umbers, Lachlan 45, 148
UNESCO 32
United Arab Emirates 24
United Kingdom (UK) (*see also*
    England; Scotland; Wales)
    children 2, 46
    organizations 6, 31, 34, 35,
        141, 179
    policies 22, 104–5, 136
    voting 24–8, 31, 68, 72, 101–2, 154,
        174–6, 182, 188
United Nations (UN) 4, 11, 33,
    86, 96, 114, 141, 188 (*see also*
    Convention on the Rights of
    the Child (CRC); Universal
    Declaration of Human Rights
    (UDHR))
United States (US) (*see also* North
    America)
    children 1, 46, 71–2, 118, 121, 132,
        137, 176
    Constitution 19
    Declaration of Independence 20
    organizations 6, 27, 30, 34–5, 135,
        141, 193
    policies 11, 47, 99, 114, 136
    Revolution 4, 20, 91
    voting 19, 23, 24–8, 30, 44, 49,
        50, 95, 102, 119, 141, 181, 182,
        185, 188–9
    Voting Rights Act 23
Universal Declaration of Human
    Rights (UDHR) 33, 34, 96–7,
    141, 180

Vietnam 182
violence
    domestic 39, 80, 89, 106, 149
    gun 46, 145

social 21, 99, 111, 125, 127, 135,
    138, 152, 159
voice (*see also* freedom of expression;
    women, voices of)
    democratic 52, 58, 81, 110–11, 117,
        121, 159–63, 167, 200
    political 1, 39, 65, 142, 179, 199
    voting 4, 87, 91–2, 96–100, 124–6,
        144–53, 156
Vote at 16 (UK group) 176
votes at sixteen 6, 28, 30–1, 34, 68,
    70, 75, 114, 123, 176–7, 188, 197
voting (*see also* proxy voting; proxy-
    claim voting)
    children's 6–10, 30–8, 47, 55, 60–3,
        78–9, 81–3, 87–90, 95–7, 100–1,
        110–11, 131–2, 136, 143–5,
        153–62, 167, 179–80, 183–8,
        193–200
    men's 4, 12, 17, 20–4, 29, 197
    minorities' 5, 12, 29, 95, 110, 119,
        173, 178
    women's 3, 5, 12, 24–9, 31, 38, 66,
        91–2, 110, 118, 133, 149, 170,
        173, 178, 193
    universal 3, 8, 33, 96, 108, 153, 179
vulnerability 18, 111, 115, 122,
    154, 157

Wales 30, 46 (*see also* United
    Kingdom)
Wallace, Vita 58, 120, 179
war
    children and 58, 106, 109, 152,
        189, 193
    civil 17, 23, 152
    First World War 27, 31, 156
    history of 16–18, 23, 27–8, 31,
        143, 156
    Second World War 31
    voting on 42, 55, 89, 92, 113–14,
        116, 120, 144, 150, 181
We Want the Vote 34, 179
West 23, 154